HOW MANY IS TOO MANY?

how many is too many?

THE PROGRESSIVE ARGUMENT FOR REDUCING IMMIGRATION INTO THE UNITED STATES

philip cafaro

THE UNIVERSITY OF CHICAGO PRESS

Chicago and London

Philip Cafaro is professor of philosophy and an affiliated
faculty member in the School of Global Environmental
Sustainability at Colorado State University. He is the
author of *Thoreau's Living Ethics*.

The University of Chicago Press, Chicago 60637
The University of Chicago Press, Ltd., London
© 2015 by The University of Chicago.
All rights reserved. Published 2015.
Printed in the United States of America

24 23 22 21 20 19 18 17 16 15   1 2 3 4 5

ISBN-13: 978-0-226-19065-5 (cloth)
ISBN-13: 978-0-226-19762-3 (e-book)
DOI: 10.7208/chicago/9780226197623.001.0001

Library of Congress Cataloging-in-Publication Data
Cafaro, Philip, 1962– author.
    How many is too many? : the progressive argument for reducing
immigration into the United States / Philip Cafaro.
        pages ; cm
    Includes bibliographical references and index.
    ISBN 978-0-226-19065-5 (cloth : alk. paper) — ISBN 978-0-226-
19762-3 (e-book) 1. United States—Emigration and immigration.
2. United States—Emigration and immigration—Social aspects.
3. United States—Population—Environmental aspects. 4. United
States—Emigration and immigration—Economic aspects.
5. United States—Emigration and immigration—Government
policy. I. Title.
    JV6465.C34 2015
    325.73—dc23
                                                    2014016936

♾ This paper meets the requirements of ANSI/NISO Z39.48–1992
(Permanence of Paper).

CONTENTS

one

GOOD PEOPLE, HARD CHOICES,
AND AN INESCAPABLE QUESTION

How many immigrants should we allow into the United States annually, and who gets to come?

The question is easy to state but hard to answer, for thoughtful individuals and for our nation as a whole. It is a complex question, touching on issues of race and class, morals and money, power and political allegiance. It is an important question, since our answer will help determine what kind of country our children and grandchildren inherit. It is a contentious question: answer it wrongly and you may hear some choice personal epithets directed your way, depending on who you are talking to. It is also an endlessly recurring question, since conditions will change, and an immigration policy that made sense in one era may no longer work in another. Any answer we give must be open to revision.

This book explores the immigration question in light of current realities and defends one provisional answer to it. By exploring the question from a variety of angles and making my own political beliefs explicit, I hope that it will help readers come to their own well-informed conclusions. Our answers may differ, but as fellow citizens we need to keep talking to one another and try to come up with immigration policies that further the common good.

Why are immigration debates frequently so angry? People on one side often seem to assume it is just because people on the other are stupid, or immoral. I disagree. Immigration is contentious because vital interests are at stake and no one set of policies can fully accommodate all of them. Consider two stories from among the hundreds I've heard while researching this book.

*

It is lunchtime on a sunny October day and I'm talking to Javier, an electrician's assistant, at a home construction site in Longmont, Colorado, near Denver.[1] He is short and solidly built; his words are soft-spoken but clear. Although he apologizes for his English, it is quite good. At any rate much better than my Spanish.

Javier studied to be an electrician in Mexico, but could not find work there after school. "You have to pay to work," he explains: pay corrupt officials up to two years' wages up front just to start a job. "Too much corruption," he says, a refrain I find repeated often by Mexican immigrants. They feel that a poor man cannot get ahead there, can hardly get started.

So in 1989 Javier came to the United States, undocumented, working various jobs in food preparation and construction. He has lived in Colorado for nine years and now has a wife (also here illegally) and two girls, ages seven and three. "I like USA, you have a better life here," he says. Of course he misses his family back in Mexico. But to his father's entreaties to come home, he explains that he needs to consider his own family now. Javier told me that he's not looking to get rich, he just wants a decent life for himself and his girls. Who could blame him?

Ironically one of the things Javier likes most about the United States is that we have rules that are fairly enforced. Unlike in Mexico, a poor man does not live at the whim of corrupt officials. When I suggest that Mexico might need more people like him to stay and fight "corruption," he just laughs. "No, go to jail," he says, or worse. Like the dozens of other Mexican and Central American immigrants I have interviewed for this book, Javier does not seem to think that such corruption could ever change in the land of his birth.[2]

Do immigrants take jobs away from Americans? I ask. "American people no want to work in the fields," he responds, or as dishwashers in restaurants. Still, he continues, "the problem is cheap labor." Too many immigrants coming into construction lowers wages for everyone—including other immigrants like himself.

"The American people say, all Mexicans the same," Javier says. He does not want to be lumped together with "all Mexicans," or labeled a problem, but judged for who he is as an individual. "I don't like it when my people abandon cars, or steal." If immigrants commit crimes, he thinks they should go to jail, or be deported. But "that no me." While many immigrants work under the table for cash, he is proud of the fact that he pays his taxes. Proud, too, that he gives a good day's work for his daily pay (a fact confirmed by his coworkers).

Javier's boss, Andy, thinks that immigration levels are too high and that too many people flout the law and work illegally.[3] He was disappointed, he says, to find out several years ago that Javier was in the country illegally. Still he likes and respects Javier and worries about his family. He is trying to help him get legal residency.

With the government showing new initiative in immigration enforcement—including a well-publicized raid at a nearby meat-packing plant that caught hundreds of illegal workers—there is a lot of worry among undocumented immigrants. "Everyone scared now," Javier says. He and his wife used to go to restaurants or stores without a second thought; now they are sometimes afraid to go out. "It's hard," he says. But: "I understand. If the people say, 'All the people here, go back to Mexico,' I understand."

Javier's answer to one of my standard questions—"How might changes in immigration policy affect you?"—is obvious. Tighter enforcement could break up his family and destroy the life he has created here in America. An amnesty would give him a chance to regularize his life. "Sometimes," he says, "I dream in my heart, 'If you no want to give me paper for residence, or whatever, just give me permit for work.'"

*

It's a few months later and I'm back in Longmont, eating a 6:30 breakfast at a café out by the Interstate with Tom Kenney.[4] Fit and alert, Tom looks to be in his mid-forties. Born and raised in Denver, he has been spraying custom finishes on drywall for twenty-five years and has had his own company since 1989. "At one point we had twelve people running three trucks," he says. Now his business is just him and his wife. "Things have changed," he says.

Although it has cooled off considerably, residential and commercial construction was booming when I interviewed Tom. The main "thing that's changed" is the number of immigrants in construction. When Tom got into it twenty-five years ago, construction used almost all native-born workers. Today estimates of the number of immigrant workers in northern Colorado range from 50% to 70% of the total construction workforce. Some trades, like pouring concrete and framing, use immigrant labor almost exclusively. Come in with an "all-white" crew of framers, another small contractor tells me, and people do a double-take.

Tom is an independent contractor, bidding on individual jobs. But, he says, "guys are coming in with bids that are impossible." After all his time in the business, "no way they can be as efficient in time and materials as me." The difference has to be in the cost of labor. "They're not paying the taxes and insurance that I am," he says. Insurance, workmen's compensation, and taxes add about 40% to the cost of legally employed workers. When you add the lower wages that immigrants are often willing to take, there is plenty of opportunity for competing contractors to underbid Tom and still make a tidy profit. He no longer bids on the big new construction projects and jobs in individual, custom-built houses are becoming harder to find.

"I've gone in to spray a house and there's a guy sleeping in the bathtub, with a microwave set up in the kitchen. I'm thinking, 'You moved into this house for two weeks to hang and paint it, you're gonna get cash from somebody, and he's gonna pick you up and drive you to the next one.'" He seems more upset at the contractor than at the undocumented worker who labors for him.

In this way, some trades in construction are turning into the equivalent of migrant labor in agriculture. Workers do not have insurance or workmen's compensation, so if they are hurt or worn out on the job, they are simply discarded and replaced. Workers are used up, while the builders and contractors higher up the food chain keep more of the profits for themselves. "The quality of life [for construction workers] has changed drastically," says Tom. "I don't want to live like that. I want to go home and live with my family."

Do immigrants perform jobs Americans don't want to do? I ask. The answer is no. "My job is undesirable," Tom replies. "It's dirty, it's messy, it's dusty. I learned right away that because of that, the opportunity is available to make money in it. That job has served me well"—at least up until recently. He now travels as far away as Wyoming and southern Colorado to find work. "We're all fighting for scraps right now."

Over the years, Tom has built a reputation for quality work and efficient and prompt service, as I confirmed in interviews with others in the business. Until recently that was enough to secure a good living. Now though, like a friend of his who recently folded his small landscaping company ("I just can't bid 'em low enough"), Tom is thinking of leaving the business. He is also struggling to find a way to keep up the mortgage payments on his house.

He does not blame immigrants, though. "If you were born in Mexico, and you had to fight for food or clothing, you would do the same thing," Tom tells me. "You would come here."

*

Any immigration policy will have winners and losers. So claims Harvard economist George Borjas, a leading authority on the economic impacts of immigration.[5] My interviews with Javier Morales and Tom Kenney suggest why Borjas is right.

If we enforce our immigration laws, then good people like Javier and his family will have their lives turned upside down. If we limit the numbers of immigrants, then good people in Mexico (and Guatemala, and Vietnam, and the Philippines . . .) will have to forgo opportunities to live better lives in the United States.

On the other hand, if we fail to enforce our immigration laws or repeatedly grant amnesties to people like Javier who are in the country illegally, then we forfeit the ability to set limits to immigration. And if immigration levels remain high, then hard-working men and women like Tom and *his* wife and children will probably continue to see their economic fortunes decline. Economic inequality will continue to increase in America, as it has for the past four decades.

In the abstract neither of these options is appealing. When you talk to the people most directly affected by our immigration policies, the dilemma becomes even more acute. But as we will see further on when we explore the economics of immigration in greater detail, these appear to be the options we have.

Recognizing trade-offs—economic, environmental, social—is indeed the beginning of wisdom on the topic of immigration. We should not exaggerate such conflicts, or imagine conflicts where none exist, but neither can we ignore them. Here are some other trade-offs that immigration decisions may force us to confront:

- Cheaper prices for new houses vs. good wages for construction workers.
- Accommodating more people in the United States vs. preserving wildlife habitat and vital resources.
- Increasing ethnic and racial diversity in America vs. enhancing social solidarity among our citizens.
- More opportunities for Latin Americans to work in the United States vs. greater pressure on Latin American elites to share wealth and opportunities with their fellow citizens.

The best approach to immigration will make such trade-offs explicit, minimize them where possible, and choose fairly between them when necessary.

Since any immigration policy will have winners and losers, at any particular time there probably will be reasonable arguments for changing the mix of immigrants we allow in, or for increasing or decreasing overall immigration, with good people on all sides of these issues. Whatever your current beliefs, by the time you finish this book you should have a much better understanding of the complex trade-offs involved in setting immigration policy. This may cause you to change your views about immigration. It may throw your current views into doubt, making it harder to choose a position on how many immigrants to let into the country each year; or what to do about illegal immigrants; or whether we should emphasize country of origin, educational level, family reunification, or asylum and refugee claims, in choosing whom to let in. In the end, understanding trade-offs ensures that whatever policies we wind up advocating for are more consciously chosen, rationally defensible, and honest. For such a contentious issue, where debate often generates more heat than light, that might have to suffice.

*

Perhaps a few words about my own political orientation will help clarify the argument and goals of this book. I'm a political progressive. I favor a relatively equal distribution of wealth across society, economic security for workers and their families, strong, well-enforced environmental protection laws, and an end to racial discrimination in the United States. I want to maximize the political power of common citizens and limit the influence of large corporations. Among my political heroes are the three Roosevelts (Teddy, Franklin, and Eleanor), Rachel Carson, and Martin Luther King Jr.

I also want to reduce immigration into the United States. If this combination seems odd to you, you are not alone. Friends, political allies, even my mother the social worker shake their heads or worse when I bring up the subject. This book aims to show that this combination of political progressivism and reduced immigration is not odd at all. In fact, it makes more sense than liberals' typical embrace of mass immigration: an embrace shared by many conservatives, from George W. Bush and Orrin Hatch to the editorial board of the *Wall Street Journal* and the US Chamber of Commerce.

In what follows I detail how current immigration levels—the highest in American history—undermine attempts to achieve progressive economic, environmental, and social goals. I have tried not to oversimplify these complex issues, or mislead readers by cherry-picking facts to support pre-established conclusions. I have worked hard to present the experts' views on how immigration affects US population growth, poorer workers' wages, urban sprawl, and so forth. Where the facts are unclear or knowledgeable observers disagree, I report that, too.

This book is divided into four main parts. Chapters 1 and 2 set the stage for us to consider how immigration relates to progressive political goals. Chapter 2, "Immigration by the Numbers," provides a concise history of US immigration policy. It explains current policy, including who gets in under what categories of entry and how many people immigrate annually. It also discusses population projections for the next one hundred years under different immigration scenarios, showing how relatively small annual differences in immigration numbers quickly lead to huge differences in overall population.

Part 2 consists of chapters 3–5, which explore the economics of immigration, showing how flooded labor markets have driven down workers' wages in construction, meatpacking, landscaping, and other economic sectors in recent decades, and increased economic inequality. I ask who wins and who loses economically under current immigration policies and consider how different groups might fare under alternative scenarios. I also consider immigration's contribution to economic growth and argue that unlike fifty or one hundred years ago America today does not need a larger economy, with more economic activity or higher levels of consumption, but rather a fairer economy that better serves the needs of its citizens. Here as elsewhere, the immigration debate can clarify progressive political aspirations; in this case, helping us rethink our support for endless economic growth and develop a more mature understanding of our economic goals.

Part 3, chapters 6–8, focuses on the environment. Mass immigration has increased America's population by tens of millions of people in recent decades and is set to add hundreds of millions more over the twenty-first century. According to Census Bureau data our population now stands at 320 million people, the third-largest in the world, and at current immigration rates could balloon to over 700 million by 2100.[6] This section examines the environmental problems caused by a rapidly growing population, including urban sprawl, overcrowding, habitat loss, species extinctions, and increased greenhouse gas emissions. I chronicle the environmental community's historic retreat from population issues over the past four decades, including the Sierra Club's failed attempts to adopt a consensus policy on immigration, and conclude that this retreat has been a great mistake. Creating an ecologically sustainable society is not just window dressing; it is necessary to pass on a decent future to our descendants and do our part to solve dangerous global environmental problems. Because sustainability is incompatible with an endlessly growing population, Americans can no longer afford to ignore domestic population growth.

Part 4, chapters 9–11, looks for answers. The chapter "Solutions" sketches out a comprehensive proposal for immigration reform in line with progressive political goals, focused on reducing overall immigration levels. I suggest shifting enforcement efforts from border control to employer sanctions—as several European nations have done with great success—and a targeted amnesty for illegal immigrants who have lived in the United States for years and built lives here (Javier and his wife could stay, but their cousins probably would not get to come). I propose changes in US trade and aid policies that could help people create better lives where they are, alleviating some of the pressure to emigrate. In these ways, Americans can meet our global responsibilities without doing so on the backs of our own poor citizens, or sacrificing the interests of future generations. A companion chapter considers a wide range of reasonable progressive "Objections" to this more restrictive immigration policy. I try to answer these objections honestly, focusing on the trade-offs involved. A short concluding chapter reminds readers of all that is at stake in immigration policy, and affirms that we will make better policy with our minds open.

How Many Is Too Many? shows that by thinking through immigration policy progressives can get clearer on our own goals. These do not include having the largest possible percentage of racial and ethnic minorities, but creating a society free of racial discrimination, where diversity is appreciated. They do not include an ever-growing economy, but feature an economy that works for the good of society as a whole. They most certainly do not include a crowded, cooked, polluted, ever-more-tamed environment, but instead a healthy, spacious landscape that supports us with sufficient room for wild nature. Finally our goals should include playing our proper role as global citizens, while still paying attention to our special responsibilities as Americans. Like it or not those responsibilities include setting US immigration policy.

*

Although I hope readers across the political spectrum will find this book interesting, I have written it primarily for my fellow progressives. Frankly, we need to think harder about this issue than we have been. Just because Rush Limbaugh and his ilk want to close our borders does not necessarily mean progressives should be for opening them wider. But this is not an easy topic to discuss and I appreciate your willingness to consider it with me. In fact I come to this topic reluctantly myself. I recognize immigration's contribution to making the United States one of the most dynamic countries in the world. I also find personal meaning in the immigrant experience.

My paternal grandfather came to America from southern Italy when he was twelve years old. As a child I listened entranced to his stories, told in an accent still heavy after half a century in his adopted country. Stories of the trip over and how excited he was to explore everything on the big ship (a sailor, taking advantage of his curiosity, convinced him to lift some newspapers lying on deck, to see what was underneath . . .). Stories of working as a journeyman shoe repairman in cities and towns across up-state New York and Ohio (in one store, the foreman put my grandfather and his lathe in the front window so passers-by would stop to watch how fast and well he did his work). Stories of settling down and starting his own business, marrying Nana, raising a family.

I admired Grandpa's adventurousness in coming to a new world, his self-reliance, his pride in his work, and his willingness to work hard to create a better future for himself and his family, including, eventually, me. Stopping by the store, listening to him chat with his customers, I saw clearly that he was a respected member of his community. When he and the relatives got together for those three-hour meals that grew ever longer over stories, songs, and a little wine, I felt part of something special, something different from my everyday life and beyond the experience of many of my friends.

So this book is not a criticism of immigrants! I know that many of today's immigrants, legal and illegal, share my grandfather's intelligence and initiative. The lives they are creating here are good lives rich in love and achievement. Nor is it an argument against all immigration: I favor reducing immigration into the United States, not ending it. I hope immigrants will continue to enrich America for many years to come. In fact, reducing current immigration levels would be a good way to insure continued widespread support for immigration.[7]

Still, Americans sometimes forget that we can have too much of a good thing. Sometimes when Nana passes the pasta, it's time to say *basta*. Enough.

When to say enough, though, can be a difficult question. How do we know when immigration levels need to be scaled back? And do any of us, as the descendants of immigrants, have the right to do so?

Answering the first question, in detail, is one of the main goals of this book. Speaking generally I think we need to reduce immigration when it seriously harms our society, or its weakest members. The issues are complex, but I think any country should consider reducing immigration:

- When immigration significantly drives down wages for its poorer citizens.
- When immigrants are regularly used to weaken or break unions.

- When immigration appears to increase economic inequality within a society.
- When immigration makes the difference between stabilizing a country's population or doubling it within the next century.
- When immigration-driven population growth makes it impossible to rein in sprawl, decrease greenhouse gas emissions sufficiently, or take the other steps necessary to create an ecologically sustainable society.
- When rapid demographic shifts undermine social solidarity and a sense of communal purpose.
- When most of its citizens *say* that immigration should be reduced.

Of course, there may also be good reasons to continue mass immigration: reasons powerful enough to outweigh such serious social costs or the expressed wishes of a nation's citizens. But they had better be important. And in the case at hand they had better articulate responsibilities that properly belong to the United States and its citizens—and not help our "sender" countries avoid their own problems and responsibilities. Reversing gross economic inequality and creating a sustainable society are the primary political tasks facing this generation of Americans. Progressives should think long and hard before we accept immigration policies that work against these goals.

But what about the second question: do Americans today have a right to reduce immigration? To tell Javier's cousins, perhaps, that they cannot come to America and make better lives for themselves and their families?

Yes, we do. Not only do we have a right to limit immigration into the United States, as citizens we have a responsibility to do so if immigration levels get so high that they harm our fellow citizens, or society as a whole.[8] Meeting this responsibility may be disagreeable, because it means telling good people that they cannot come to America to pursue their dreams. Still, it may need to be done.

Those of us who want to limit immigration are sometimes accused of selfishness: of wanting to hog resources or keep "the American way of life" for ourselves. There may be some truth in this charge, since many Americans' interests are threatened by mass immigration. Still, some of those interests seem worth preserving. The union carpenter taking home $30 an hour who owns his own house, free and clear, or the outdoorsman walking quietly along the edge of a favorite elk meadow or trout stream, may want to continue to enjoy these good things and pass them on to their sons and daughters. What is wrong with that?

Besides, the charge of selfishness cuts both ways. Restaurant owners and software tycoons hardly deserve the Mother Teresa Self-Sacrifice Medal when they lobby Congress for more low-wage workers. The wealthy progressive patting herself on the back for her enlightened views on immigration probably hasn't ever totaled up the many ways she and her family benefit from cheap labor.

In the end our job as citizens is to look beyond our narrow self-interest and consider the common good. Many of us oppose mass immigration not because of what it costs us as individuals, but because we worry about the economic costs to our fellow citizens, or the environmental costs to future generations. Most Americans enjoy sharing our country with foreign visitors and are happy to share economic opportunities with reasonable numbers of newcomers. We just want to make sure we preserve those good things that make this a desirable destination in the first place.

All else being equal, Americans would just as soon not interfere with other people's decisions about where to live and work. In fact such a laissez-faire approach to immigration lasted for much of our nation's history. But today all else is not equal. For one thing this is the age of jet airplanes, not tall-masted sailing ships or coal-fired steamers. It is much quicker and easier to come here than it used to be and the pool of would-be immigrants has increased by an order of magnitude since my grandfather's day. (In 2006, there were 6.4 *million* applications for the 50,000 green cards available under that year's "diversity lottery."[9]) For another, we do not have an abundance of unclaimed land for farmers to homestead, or new factories opening up to provide work for masses of unskilled laborers. Unemployment is high and projected to remain high for the foreseeable future. For a third, we recognize new imperatives to live sustainably and do our part to meet global ecological challenges. Scientists are warning that we run grave risks should we fail to do so.

Americans today overwhelmingly support immigration restrictions. We disagree about the optimal amount of immigration, but almost everyone agrees that setting *some* limits is necessary. Of course, our immigration policies should be fair to all concerned. Javier Morales came to America illegally, but for most of his time here our government just winked at illegal immigration. It also taxed his paychecks. After two and a half decades of hard work that has benefited our country, I think we owe Javier citizenship. But we also owe Tom Kenney something. Perhaps the opportunity to prosper, if he is willing to work hard. Surely, at a minimum, government policies that do not undermine his own attempts to prosper.

*

The progressive vision is alive and well in the United States today. Most Americans want a clean environment with flourishing wildlife, a fair economy that serves all its citizens, and a diverse society that is free from racism. Still, it will take a lot of hard work to make this vision a reality and success is not guaranteed. Progressives cannot shackle our hopes to an outmoded immigration policy that thwarts us at every turn.

Given the difficulties involved in getting 320 million Americans to curb consumption and waste, there is little reason to think we will be able to achieve ecological sustainability while doubling or tripling that number. Mass immigration ensures that our population will continue growing at a rapid rate and that environmentalists will always be playing catch up. Fifty or one hundred years from now we will still be arguing that we should destroy *this* area rather than *that* one, or that we can make the destruction a little more aesthetically appealing—instead of ending the destruction. We will still be trying to slow the growth of air pollution, water use, or carbon emissions—rather than cutting them back.

But the US population would quickly stabilize without mass immigration.[10] We can stop population growth—without coercion or intrusive domestic population policies—simply by returning to pre-1965 immigration levels.

Imagine an environmentalism that was not always looking to meet the next crisis and that could instead look forward to real triumphs. What if we achieved significant energy efficiency gains and were able to enjoy those gains with less pollution, less industrial development on public lands, and an end to oil wars, because those efficiency gains were not swallowed up by growing populations?

Imagine if the push to develop new lands largely ended and habitat for other species *increased* year by year, with a culture of conservation developed around restoring and protecting that habitat. Imagine if our demand for fresh water leveled off and instead of fighting new dam projects we could actually leave more water in our rivers.

And what of the American worker? It is hard to see how progressives will succeed in reversing current powerful trends toward ever greater economic inequality in a context of continued mass immigration, particularly with high numbers of relatively unskilled and poorly educated immigrants. Flooded labor markets will harm poorer workers directly, by driving down wages and driving up unemployment. Mass immigration will also continue to harm workers indirectly by making it harder for them to organize and challenge employers, by reducing the percentage of poor workers who are citizens and thus able to vote for politicians who favor the poor, and by limiting sympathy between the haves and have-nots, since with mass immigration they are more likely to belong to different ethnic groups.

But it does not have to be this way. We can tighten labor markets and get them working *for* working people in this country. Combined with other good progressive egalitarian measures—universal health care; a living minimum wage; a more progressive tax structure—we might even reverse current trends and create a more economically just country.

Imagine meatpacking plants and carpet-cleaning companies competing with one another for scarce workers, bidding up their wages. Imagine unions able to strike those companies without having to worry about scabs taking their members' jobs. Imagine college graduates sifting through numerous job offers, like my father and his friends did fifty years ago during that era's pause in mass immigration, instead of having to wait tables and just hope for something better.

Imagine poor children of color in our inner cities, no longer looked on as a problem to be warehoused in failing schools, or jails, but instead seen as an indispensable resource: the solution to labor shortages in restaurants and software companies.

Well, why not? Why are we progressives always playing catch up? The right immigration policies could help lead us toward a more just, egalitarian, and sustainable future. They could help liberals achieve our immediate goals and drive the long-term political agenda. But we will not win these battles without an inspiring vision for a better society, or with an immigration policy that makes that vision impossible to achieve.

two

IMMIGRATION BY THE NUMBERS

While setting immigration policy depends on our values, it is also a matter of numbers. If we want to make intelligent policy decisions we need to know what our options are and the full implications of choosing one option over another. That means exploring demography: the science of the quantitative measurement of human populations. This chapter reviews America's demographic history. It surveys the evolution of US immigration policy and examines current policies. It also considers projected future population numbers under different immigration scenarios, to get a sense of where we might be heading. All this will help ground the ethical analysis of subsequent chapters.[1]

The first official US census in 1790 returned a national population of a little under 4 million. The most recently completed, in 2010, totaled America's population at 309 million: an increase of 7625%. You can find an up-to-date estimate of our current population on the Census Bureau's website (www.census.gov). When I accessed it on April 9, 2014, it stood at 317,837,224. That makes us the third most populous nation in the world, behind China and India.

Notice that our population trend has been relentlessly upward (Figure 2–1). The largest decadal increases in absolute terms have also been the most recent: from 1990 to 2000 the US population grew by 33 million people, while from 2000 to 2010 our population grew by 28 million. At

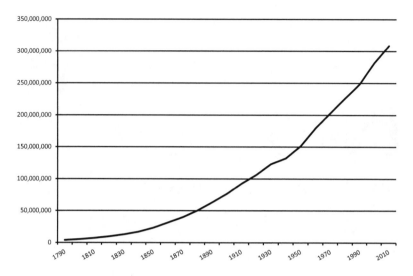

Figure 2-1. United States population, 1790–2010.
Source: US Census Bureau.

13% and 12%, however, these were not the highest decadal *rates* of growth in American history. For example, from 1830 to 1840 the US population grew by 33%, from just under 13 million to more than 17 million people. However, this growth was on a much lower base population. So while the United States grew at a much higher rate over the course of the nineteenth century, by far the most growth in total numbers occurred in the twentieth century. From 1900 to 2010, the US population more than quadrupled, from 76 million to 309 million people (Figure 2–2).

In contrast to the steady rise in total population, immigration numbers have fluctuated throughout American history. Figure 2–3, also based on Census Bureau figures, shows decadal (not annual) immigration numbers since 1820, when the federal government began keeping such figures. There has always been some immigration, but its levels have varied greatly, primarily owing to changes in policy. For example, between 1900 and 1910 net immigration (total immigration into the United States minus emigration from the United States) averaged about 900,000 annually. Between 1950 and 1960 net annual immigration was much lower, at around 250,000. And between 2000 and 2010 expansive immigration policies and lax enforcement of immigration laws pushed immigration numbers

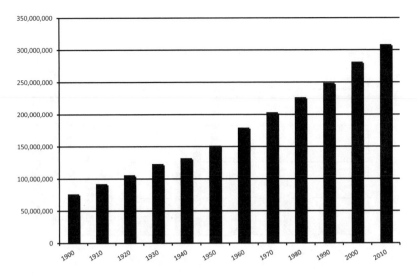

Figure 2-2. United States population, 1900–2010.

Source: US Census Bureau.

to their highest levels ever: total legal immigration averaged more than one million, while illegal immigration fluctuated between a few hundred thousand and half a million, depending on the state of the economy.

As suggested by Figure 2-3, America's immigration history breaks down into four main periods: a laissez-faire century, with initially low and then accelerating numbers of immigrants; the "Great Wave" of mass immigration, primarily from Southern and Eastern Europe, lasting for five decades around the turn of the last century; a Great Pause from large-scale immigration for about four decades during the mid-twentieth century; and a Second Wave of mass immigration over the past fifty years, this time with a majority of immigrants coming from Latin America. This Second Wave continues through the present day. Briefly reviewing this history reminds us of the importance of immigration policy in determining not just who comes to America, but how many immigrants are allowed to come.[2]

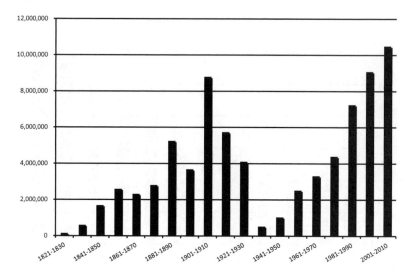

Figure 2-3. Immigration into the United States per decade, 1820–2010.

Source: US Department of Homeland Security, *Yearbook of Immigration Statistics: 2011*, table 1.

IMMIGRATION POLICIES AND TRENDS

1789–1880: LAISSEZ-FAIRE

During our first century American immigration policy was set by the individual states, which largely limited themselves to testing incoming immigrants for communicable diseases in a few major ports and in some instances sending back those deemed a threat to public health. In practice this meant a laissez-faire immigration policy: those who could afford to book passage to America could enter, settle down, and look for work. Acquiring citizenship ("naturalization") when desired was relatively straightforward and in any case the children of immigrants were born citizens, as specified in the Constitution.

Over its first ninety years immigration into the United States rose from a few thousand per year at the start of the period to several hundred thousand per year by its end. Famine in Ireland and political repression in the aftermath of the European revolutions of 1848 briefly drove the numbers from 100,000 to over 400,000 for a few years before the Civil War; the push of Europe's century-long population surge combined with the pull of newly opened agricultural lands and factory jobs returned immigration numbers to that range within a few years of the war's end. Africans transported across the Atlantic into slavery and Native Americans decimated and pushed off their lands suffered grievously during this period, of course: clear examples that any immigration policy creates losers as well as winners.

After the Civil War, large numbers of Chinese immigrants were brought to California, at first to build the railroads and later branching out into other areas of the economy. In the 1870s and 1880s, white settlers in California (many of them recent immigrants from Europe) began agitating against continued immigration of Chinese into the state. Many proponents of restriction argued that Chinese laborers displaced white workers and drove down their wages—a position that resonated particularly strongly during the recurring depressions of the period. Others claimed that the Chinese were racially inferior, or that cultural differences made them difficult to assimilate and hence a threat to social stability and progress. In 1882 Congress heeded these calls and passed the Chinese Exclusion Act, greatly reducing Chinese immigration. Several years earlier the US Supreme Court had ruled that individual states could *not* regulate immigration; the Exclusion Act helped establish the political principle that the federal government *could* make immigration law for the country as a whole, bringing a long period of de facto laissez-faire immigration policy to a close.

1880–1924: THE GREAT WAVE

In 1881, immigration topped half a million for the first time in American history. From the 1880s through the mid-1920s, America experienced an immigration boom, the Great Wave, during which immigration averaged nearly 600,000 annually. This was the period during which the United States fully industrialized, creating a huge demand for factory workers. The demand was filled primarily by American farmers displaced by depressed commodity prices and technological innovations in agriculture, but also by European immigrants, mainly from Southern and Eastern Europe (Italians, Greeks, Poles, Russians, and others). This period of immense wealth creation was, somewhat paradoxically, also a period of great suffering for workers and of greatly increased economic inequality.

Unions were founded and sometimes organized impressive numbers of workers, but they tended to be weak and found it hard to win major concessions. From Pennsylvania's steel mills to Colorado's coal mines, unions struck for better wages, hours, and working conditions—and were usually defeated, often with the help of immigrant strikebreakers.

Throughout this period immigration policy was mostly limited to sending back would-be immigrants for reasons of health or their likelihood of becoming "public charges." No limits were placed on the overall number of immigrants; however, limiting immigration from Europe was debated with ever greater seriousness. Throughout the period many labor leaders argued for reduced immigration into the United States, in order to facilitate their efforts to improve conditions for workers—although then as now some disagreed, believing that opposition to mass immigration risked alienating immigrants they needed to organize. Samuel Gompers, head of the American Federation of Labor and himself an immigrant, over time came to see reducing immigration as essential to creating a strong union movement, because organizing workers or winning concessions was so difficult under flooded labor markets. In a letter to Congress in the 1920s, he wrote:

> Every effort to enact immigration legislation must expect to meet a number of hostile forces and, in particular, two hostile forces of considerable strength.
>
> One of these is composed of corporation employers who desire to employ physical strength (broad backs) at the lowest possible wage and who prefer a rapidly revolving labor supply at low wages to a regular supply of American wage earners at fair wages.
>
> The other is composed of racial groups in the United States who oppose all restrictive legislation because they want the doors left open for an influx of their countrymen regardless of the menace to the people of their adopted country.[3]

Such pro-labor arguments appealed to the left. On the right, cultural and racial arguments were made regarding the swamping of "Anglo-Saxon stock" or the decline of traditional political and social institutions. Meanwhile citizens of all political persuasions often felt that the country was changing too quickly (from rural to urban, northern to southern European, etc.) and saw immigration reduction as one way to hit the brakes. Repeatedly during the first two decades of the twentieth century one or both houses of Congress passed restrictive immigration legislation, only to have it die in the other house or by presidential vetoes. But in 1921 and 1924 the restrictionists succeeded. Congress enacted the first comprehensive quota system to limit overall immigration into the United States and the first Great Wave came to an end.

1924–1965: THE GREAT PAUSE

The system put in place in 1924 had two key features. First, for those concerned about the numbers of immigrants coming to America, it set an annual limit of 155,000 for immigrants from outside the Western hemisphere (interhemispheric immigration made up a small portion of the total at this time and quotas for lands south of the border were not seen as necessary).[4] This represented a huge decrease: six times during the first two decades of the twentieth century annual immigration had topped one million. Second, for those worried about the changing ethnic makeup of the country, the legislation set quotas for individual sender countries on the basis of their contribution to America's ethnic stock as of 1890. During the following decades this led to most available slots being allocated to immigrants from northern Europe. (It is also why I knew my Great-uncle Césare growing up but never met Great-uncle Antonio, who waited too long to try to leave Italy and had to settle for emigrating to Argentina.)

For the next forty years, from 1925 to 1965, this relatively restrictive immigration policy allowed only about 175,000 people into the country annually (numbers that were also held down by depression and war). Demographers sometimes call this period the Great Pause, although at the time most Americans thought of it as permanent. Speaking in 1936 at the ceremony celebrating the 50th anniversary of the unveiling of the Statue of Liberty, President Franklin Roosevelt praised immigrants' contributions to America, saying:

> For over three centuries, a steady stream of men, women and children followed the beacon of liberty which this light symbolizes. They brought to us strength and moral fiber developed in a civilization centuries old but fired anew by the dream of a better life in America. . . . They not only found free-

dom in the new world, but by their effort and devotion they made the new world's freedom safer, richer, more far reaching, more capable of growth.

But Roosevelt also said: "Within this present generation, that stream from abroad has largely stopped. We have within our shores today the materials out of which we shall continue to build an even better home for liberty."[5]

Most Americans shared President Roosevelt's views. Mass immigration had helped build the country and make us who we were. But times had changed and the era of mass immigration was over.

In retrospect, the Great Pause in immigration corresponded with a golden age for American labor, despite encompassing the Depression. Labor markets tightened eventually and union organizing boomed. After World War II salaries rose, unemployment remained low, work hours decreased, and fringe benefits improved, as employers chased relatively scarce labor.[6] This era also included the hiring of African Americans into industrial occupations from which they had previously been excluded, another fruit of tight labor markets. America created the world's first mass middle-class society, with a relatively egalitarian sharing of wealth and relatively prosperous and secure workers throughout most sectors of the economy. Thanks, FDR and the New Deal Congresses! Thanks, Walter Reuther and the striking auto workers at River Rouge! Toward the end of this period the nation took significant steps toward redressing its historic wrongs against African Americans, with President Truman integrating the armed forces, the Supreme Court ruling segregated schooling unconstitutional, and Congress passing major civil rights legislation in 1964 and 1965. Throughout this period there was no groundswell from the general public for a return to the high levels of immigration of half a century earlier.

1965–PRESENT: THE SECOND WAVE

Nevertheless aspects of the "national origins" policy of 1924 rankled, particularly its explicit preference for immigrants from Northern and Western Europe. Although proponents tried to argue that this simply preserved the existing ethnic makeup of the country, opponents succeeded in presenting it as discriminatory against other racial and ethnic groups:

a relic of more racist times, ripe for reform in the civil rights era. (This progressive, for one, agrees. A racially based immigration system is by definition unfair.) In 1965 Congress passed the Hart-Cellar immigration bill, replacing quotas that had favored Europeans with a new system that instead allotted slots to individual countries on the basis of their proportion of total world population. Rather than mirror the existing ethnic or racial makeup of the United States, new immigrants would, at least in theory, mirror the world as a whole.

Proponents of the new policy took pains to assure Americans that it would not substantially increase total immigration, or radically change the ethnic make-up of the country. "Our cities will not be flooded with a million immigrants annually," Ted Kennedy, the bill's chief Senate sponsor, asserted on the Senate floor. "Under the proposed bill, the present level of immigration remains substantially the same."[7] In fact, the new bill nearly doubled official quota levels from 155,000 to 290,000. It removed hard caps regarding refugee resettlement. Most important in hindsight, Hart-Cellar split out "family reunification"—broadly interpreted to include not just spouses and children, but also parents and siblings—as a separate immigration category that no longer counted against annual country quotas and that had no legal limit. Family reunification subsequently became the country's largest immigration category, accounting for over half a million immigrants annually, the majority coming from Mexico in a sort of "chain migration." Within three decades legal immigration into the United States had more than tripled, from 300,000 to 900,000 annually.

Meanwhile *illegal* immigration also increased significantly. In 1986 in response to this increase, Congress for the first time made it a crime for employers to knowingly hire unauthorized workers. It also granted amnesty and citizenship to three million illegal residents, presenting this as a one-time measure to "clear the books." This and subsequent amnesties, however, along with weak enforcement of employer sanctions, encouraged even more illegal immigration, which rose to a peak of half a million annually in the first few years of the twenty-first century. Total numbers of illegal immigrants continued to climb: from an estimated one to two million in 1965 they grew to five to six million in 1986, and then to ten to twelve million illegal residents by 2010.

Subsequent federal legislation has tended to extend this generally expansive immigration policy. Country quotas were increased in 1980 and again in 1990. New categories of legal immigration were created: H1-B visas for highly skilled workers; temporary work visas for agricultural workers (who often overstayed and joined the ranks of the illegal); 50,000 slots in an annual "diversity lottery" directed at citizens from underrepresented sender countries; and numerous others. Over the past three years annual immigration numbers have broken down approximately as follows[8]:

Family-sponsored	710,000
Employment-based	145,000
Diversity programs	50,000
Refugees and asylum seekers	160,000
Other minor categories	25,000
Legal immigration, total:	1,090,000
Illegal immigration (uncertain and highly variable)	~200,000
Total immigration (legal and illegal)	~1,300,000

Again, it seems important to note that these policy changes were not enacted as part of a groundswell of popular support for increased immigration. Quite the contrary: in recent decades, public opinion polls have typically found that 85% to 90% of Americans favor lowering or stabilizing immigration levels, not raising them.[9] In fact, every legislative change that has increased immigration numbers has been sold to the public as something else: in 1965 as a civil rights measure to do away with racist preferences for white Europeans; in 1986 and 1990 as part of more wide-ranging legislative packages supposedly focused on improving the enforcement of immigration laws. In subsequent chapters we will return to this curious disconnect between public views and public policy.[10]

In any event, 1965 initiated a Second Wave of mass immigration that continues today. During the 1990s legal immigration averaged 900,000 annually, increasing to more than one million per year during the next decade. That was the highest number in US history and more than five times the average during the middle of the previous century (although once again it was not the highest *rate* of immigration as a percentage of total US population; rates were higher at the end of the 19th century than they are today). During this time immigration from Mexico and the rest of Latin America has come to predominate, along with relatively high immigration numbers from South and East Asia. Like the era of the first Great Wave, this period has been a time of technological innovation and rapidly expanding wealth, increased racial and ethnic diversity, identity group politics (particularly in larger cities), weak labor unions, stagnating wages for poorer Americans, and increasing economic inequality.

DEMOGRAPHIC NOTE ON THE CAUSES OF POPULATION GROWTH

Comparing this chapter's earlier figures on population growth and immigration numbers might cause some confusion. How is it that the US population has climbed steadily while immigration has varied so greatly over the past two hundred years? The answer is that population growth is a function of both native birthrates and immigration. More precisely, demographers see four primary factors determining the overall growth rate for any population: birthrates, death rates, immigration into a population, and emigration out of it. All four factors help determine whether a population grows or declines, and by how much.

During the first Great Wave from 1880 to the mid-1920s, America's population grew rapidly owing to a combination of high birthrates and high levels of immigration. US population increased from 50 million in 1880 to 116 million in 1925. During the Great Pause the US population continued to grow substantially—from 116 million to 194 million people in 1965—but now primarily owing to high rates of natural increase. During the 1950s for example, American women had an average of 3.5 children each: far above the 2.1 total fertility rate necessary to maintain a stable population for a nation with modern health care and sanitation. Yes, the United States' population grew, but by tens of millions fewer than would have been the case if pre-1925 immigration levels had been retained.

By the 1970s American families were raising fewer children—in 1976 the total fertility rate stood at a lowest-ever 1.7 and it has remained below replacement level since then—and the United States was well positioned to transition from a growing to a stable population. One study found that

Table 2–1 Population increases 1950–2010, selected countries.

	Percentage population increase, 1950–2010	Percentage population increase, 1990–2010
France	55%	11%
Germany	19%	3%
Italy	29%	7%
Japan	52%	3%
United Kingdom	24%	9%
United States	104%	24%

Source: US Census Bureau, "Midyear Population and Density."

without post-1970 immigration the US population would have leveled off below 250 million around 2030.[11] At steady pre-1965 immigration levels America's population would have taken longer to stabilize and would have stabilized at a higher number, but broadly speaking the trajectory would have been the same.

If we had taken such a stabilization path the United States would not have been alone. Germany, Italy, Great Britain, France, Japan, and most countries in the developed world made this "demographic transition" in the decades after World War II and have now either stabilized their populations or reached a relatively slow rate of growth.[12] See Table 2–1.

The United States did not take this path. Instead we ratcheted up immigration just as native birthrates fell below replacement level, bringing in tens of millions of new citizens (see Figure 2–3).[13] Many of them were men and women in their child-raising years coming from countries where large families remained the norm, helping to raise US fertility rates. The number of births to immigrant mothers has risen quickly in recent decades, from 228,000 in 1970 to 916,000 in 2002, according to data from the National Center for Health Statistics.[14] One demographer concludes, "At the very time that the great majority of native-born Americans were voluntarily choosing to limit their family sizes to levels which could have led to the end of US population growth, Congress was making changes in immigration policy which have ensured ever more growth. The result of these changes was the highest sustained immigration and greatest population growth in US history."[15]

As a consequence, since 1965 America's population has climbed from 194 to 320 million. That's an increase of 126 million people, equal to the

Table 2-2 US population projections to 2050 under
different immigration scenarios.

Average annual net immigration	Population in 2050
Zero	323 million
1 million	399 million
1.5 million	423 million
2 million	458 million

Source: Jennifer Ortman and Christine Guarneri, "United
States Population Projections: 2000 to 2050."

total population of the United States in 1933. Just as important, our population continues to grow rapidly with no end in sight. Indeed, the current
annual growth rate for the United States (0.96%) is much closer to that
of developing countries such as Morocco, Vietnam, or Indonesia (all at
1.07%) than to other developed nations such as Denmark (0.25%), Tai-
wan (0.19%), or Belgium (0.07%).[16] The main difference is that population growth in the developing world is driven by high fertility rates, while
US population growth is mostly a function of mass immigration. Another
difference is that many developing countries are working to cut their fertility levels and reduce population growth, while in the United States continued population growth is a function of deliberate government policy.

FUTURE POPULATION GROWTH

Such is our demographic past. What of America's demographic future?

In 2008 the Census Bureau projected US population numbers out to
2050 based on current trends regarding fertility rates, average lifespans,
and immigration numbers. They came up with a medium (or "most
likely") projection of 439 million—a 119 million increase over our current population.[17] The following year the Bureau delivered a further series
of projections, which held fertility rates and longevity constant and varied
immigration levels.[18] These came out as shown in Table 2–2.

Obviously, according to the Census Bureau, immigration makes an immense difference to future US numbers. The difference between zero net
immigration and the Bureau's most likely scenario is 116 million people—

equal to the total US population in 1925. Other studies have confirmed the impact immigration is likely to have on America's future population; one study published by the Pew Research Center estimated that 82% of population growth between 2000 and 2050 will be due to post-2000 immigrants and their descendants.[19]

Immigration's impact on total population becomes even clearer when we take longer views. This is because population growth tends to cumulate and because, in the case of the United States, mass immigration prevents us from ever taking advantage of our replacement-level fertility rate and stabilizing our population. The elders of the Iroquois Confederacy reputedly considered the impacts of their important decisions seven generations into the future. Consider then several one-hundred-year population projections, still only half the seven generations recommended by the Iroquois, as we Americans grapple with important immigration policy decisions.

Demographers employed by the Center for Immigration Studies have created a projection tool that replicates the model created by the Census Bureau for its 2008 and 2009 projections, while allowing users to vary fertility and immigration levels and to run projections out to the year 2100.[20] Holding fertility rates steady at the levels predicted by the Census Bureau and varying immigration in half million person annual increments allowed me to develop the projections graphed in Figure 2–4. The results are striking.

At zero annual net immigration (immigration set equal to emigration), America's population continues to increase for about forty years and then slowly decreases to 343 million total, for an overall increase of 33 million people over 2010. Under this scenario we essentially stabilize our population near where it is today.

If Congress followed the 1997 recommendations of the Jordan Commission on Immigration Reform, cutting immigration to 500,000 annually, the US population would grow significantly, to 415 million by 2100. That would represent an increase of 105 million people. Population stabilization would at least be in sight by then, albeit at a much higher level — provided future leaders chose to cut immigration even further.

In a third scenario, we can imagine Congress holding legal immigration steady near current levels, at one million annually, while succeeding presidential administrations reined in illegal immigration. In that case

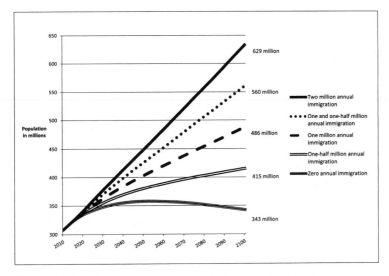

Figure 2-4. US population projections to 2100 under five different immigration scenarios.

Source: Author's projections using population projection tool developed by the Center for Immigration Studies, Washington, DC.

America's population would instead increase by 176 million to 486 million total. Just as important, in 2100 we would still be confronting an upward trajectory with no population stabilization in sight.

In a fourth "no action" scenario, total immigration could continue near its recent heights of 1.5 million annually, through some combination of high legal immigration and continued tolerance for illegal immigration (perhaps regularized through occasional amnesties, as in recent decades). In this scenario America's population would reach 560 million by 2100, increasing by 250 million people, and our growth curve would angle even more steeply upward.

Finally, immigration could be increased to 2 million annually, the highest rate in history, but still less than the increase proposed in the "comprehensive" immigration reform bill that passed the US Senate in 2013. Under this scenario our population would nearly double to 629 million people. As in the previous two scenarios, the population in 2100 would be set to increase by tens of millions more for many years to come.

Once again, at the risk of stating the obvious: which immigration rate we choose will make a huge difference to US population numbers in the coming years. A good rule of thumb is that for every half million immigrants admitted annually we increase America's population at the end of this century by 72 million people. Another is that under all mass immigration scenarios with more than a few hundred thousand net immigrants per year, the US population cannot stabilize and instead continues to grow.

It remains true that major changes to any of four key demographic factors could significantly change the trajectory of US population growth in the twenty-first century. If death rates increase that will slow growth, as AIDS has slowed population growth in some countries in sub-Saharan Africa. Conversely, medical advances that extend life spans could cause our population to grow even more quickly. A mass exodus of American citizens (increased emigration) or a widespread trend to refrain from childbearing (decreased fertility rates) could slow growth and in extreme scenarios even lead to population decreases, despite continued mass immigration. Realistically however, in the short- to mid-term these other possibilities for curbing growth seem unlikely, and except for some reduction in native fertility, unwelcome. They also seem relatively impervious to policy interventions: we are not likely to offer incentives for US citizens to emigrate, while such small inducements to have fewer children as might see the light of day are unlikely to bend the demographic curve significantly. In contrast, immigration policy can be changed quickly and radically via Congressional legislation, as was shown in 1924 and again in 1965. This means that for the foreseeable future immigration policy will remain the primary means to regulate US population growth. In the United States, immigration policy essentially *is* our national population policy.

CONCLUSION

Finally and by way of contrast, let's consider some numbers that have stayed remarkably steady. As both immigration levels and total population have moved ever upward over the past five decades, Americans' *views* regarding immigration have remained relatively constant. Most Americans approve of immigration, within limits, and welcome immigrants into our society. When asked in Gallup polls over the past decade, "On the whole, do you think immigration is a good thing or a bad thing for this country today?" approximately 60% have affirmed immigration "a good thing."[21]

In addition and by much wider margins, Americans disapprove of illegal immigration. They also disapprove of the federal government's perceived failure to enforce immigration laws.[22] Most Americans also oppose amnesties for illegal immigrants; hence the recent use of euphemisms such as "earned legalization" by our political class.

Most important, on the key question of appropriate immigration levels, polls consistently show that Americans overwhelmingly want less or stabilized immigration, not more. When asked over the past twenty-five years, "In your view, should immigration be kept at its present level, increased, or decreased?" on average only 10% to 15% of poll respondents have favored an increase. About 35% wanted to keep immigration at current levels and the majority, averaging 55% of respondents, actually wanted to decrease immigration.[23]

These figures seem important. In a democracy the will of the people presumably should play some role in setting policy. In recent decades it does not seem to have done so regarding immigration policy in the United States. It's true that if a majority of Americans wanted to increase immigration, and the economic and environmental impacts of mass immigration remained what I show them to be in subsequent chapters, I would disagree with the majority. So I do not think that vox populi is everything. But popular opinion should count for something—particularly for progressives, with our commitment to democratic grassroots politics. Yet the voice of the people has consistently been ignored in setting immigration policy in recent years.

I believe this failure to respect the popular will in immigration policy making is a function of excessive corporate influence over government policy in contemporary America. It is also another example of the Democratic party's failure to defend the interests of working-class Americans. I make my case for these conclusions in the following two chapters, which document the economic costs of mass immigration, including stagnating wages, persistently high unemployment, and growing economic inequality. As we will see, these costs have fallen disproportionally on those least able to afford them.

three

THE WAGES OF MASS IMMIGRATION

One hot summer day a few years ago, I spent a morning digging post-holes for a new wooden fence around the house my wife and I had recently bought. I was helping Steve, who does odd jobs when he is not working for a small home-builder here in Fort Collins, Colorado. Steve is a short, powerful man pushing fifty, with deep blue eyes that light up with laughter when he talks. He drives an old, multicolored pickup truck that looks like it's held together with baling wire, but he can fix anything on it himself.

Kris and I had hired Steve to design and build the fence because he seemed like the best choice for a job calling for both creativity and hard physical work. We also knew we could trust him to report his hours honestly and buy several thousand dollars' worth of materials for us without inflating their price.

As we worked that day, Steve talked about how hard it could be to make ends meet working construction. He mentioned a bum knee and a bad back that he was trying to treat himself; he had no health insurance and it wouldn't take many visits to the doctor to wipe out his profits from this fence job. We talked about the going rates for construction workers. I wondered whether he had ever asked his current employer for a raise, or for health benefits.

"Well, yeah," Steve said. "I did. He told me he could hire two Mexicans for what he pays me. And I know it's true." [1]

Steve and I became friends over those postholes. I would like our economy to work for him and people like him—but it does not seem to be. He works more than full-time, lives modestly, and as far as I know has no expensive vices. Steve is a good worker, honest, reliable, and intelligent, yet he is one serious injury or a few missed paychecks away from bankruptcy.

Over the years, Steve has done plenty of hard, dirty, repetitive work—the kind of work one often hears that Americans are no longer willing to do. He is also a real craftsman, imaginative and skilled at working with wood, stone, and plants. But he does not push paper or drive a hard bargain. He is not an "entrepreneur." So he is poor and likely to stay poor. In the twenty-first century, in the richest nation in the world, why should this be?

A TREND TOWARD GREATER INEQUALITY

Some people buck trends; most of us ride them. Leaving aside the specifics of his personality and personal history, I would say Steve is poor because folks like him are poor. Americans with his level of education, working the kinds of jobs he works, do not make a lot of money compared to people with similar jobs and educational levels in other wealthy countries.[2] They have less job security than people doing the same kinds of jobs had in the United States forty years ago. Americans were less likely to have health insurance in 2010 than they were in 1970 (although the Affordable Care Act of 2010 should partially rectify this last problem when it is fully implemented).[3]

Americans do not like to think about ourselves in class terms. But the simplest way to put it is to say that Steve is poor because his class is poor.

The trends are clear. Over the past forty years, technological innovation and hard work have greatly increased overall economic productivity. In constant 2000 dollars, America's gross domestic product was 3191 billion dollars in 1965, 4311 billion dollars in 1975, 6054 billion dollars in 1985, 8032 billion dollars in 1995 and 11,049 billion dollars in 2005.[4] In other words, the US economy generated about 250% more total wealth in 2005 than it did in 1965.

Table 3–1 Annual family incomes in the United States in 1970 and 2005, in constant 2005 dollars.

	Poorest 20%	Second 20%	Middle 20%	Fourth 20%	Richest 20%	Richest 5%
1970	$13,340	$29,500	$42,650	$57,530	$98,930	$150,640
2005	$14,770	$35,140	$56,230	$84,100	$176,290	$308,640

Source: US Census Bureau, "Current Population Survey, Annual Social and Economic Supplements," "Historical Income Tables—Families."

However, poorer Americans have had a hard time gaining a fair share of this rapidly growing pie. Consider Table 3–1, which presents Census Bureau figures for annual family incomes for Americans in 1970 and 2005.[5] Whether we compare percentage increases or absolute increases in income, the results are striking.

From 1970 to 2005 the poorest 20% of Americans increased their annual earnings a measly $1430, a 10.5% increase that came from working longer hours rather than from increased hourly pay. Meanwhile the wealthiest quintile increased their annual incomes by $77,360 for a 78% increase—a fifty-four times greater increase in absolute terms. The wealthiest 5% of Americans did even better: their incomes increased 105%, growing on average by $158,000. That represents a 110 times greater gain compared to the poorest quintile (Figure 3–1).

Increased income inequality has in turn led to greater inequality in overall wealth (see Figure 3–2). Between 1989 and 2010, the wealthiest 1% of Americans saw their share of the nation's total net worth increase from 30.1% to 34.5%. Over the same period, that half of Americans below the median income line saw their share of total net worth decrease from 3.0% to 1.1%.[6] Today the total net worth of the three million wealthiest Americans is approximately 35 times the total net worth of the poorest 160 million Americans. That makes the average "one percenter" a mind-boggling 1855 times wealthier than the average person in the bottom 50%.

In recent decades, the rich got richer and the poor stayed poor. In addition to stagnating or declining wages and much smaller shares of overall wealth, poorer workers are working many more hours per year than they did a generation ago. With outsourcing, weak unions or no unions, high unemployment levels, dismissal from jobs at the discretion of employers (unlike in Europe or Japan), and flooded labor markets, these workers

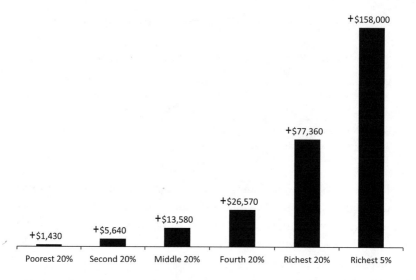

Figure 3-1. Changes in annual family incomes in the US, 1970 to 2005.

Source: US Census Bureau, "Current Population Survey, Annual Social and Economic Supplements."

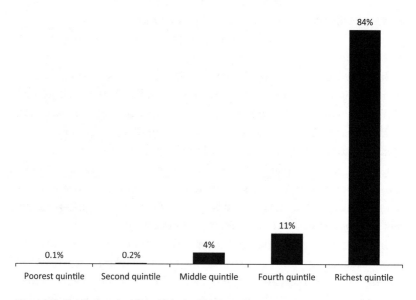

Figure 3-2. Distribution of total wealth in the US in 2010, by quintile.

Source: Dan Ariely, "Americans Want to Live in a Much More Equal Country (They Just Don't Realize It)."

have little job security today. It all adds up to less economic security and greater economic anxiety for many Americans. All this, remember, in a country that is three-and-a-half times richer than it was in 1965.

Just now I said that in recent decades poorer Americans had not succeeded in getting their fair share of America's growing wealth. But what is a fair share?[7] Opinions differ widely. Conservatives are comfortable with immense economic disparities between wealthier and poorer Americans. Big gaps in income and wealth confirm their belief in the workings of a beneficent free market that rewards the really important and productive members of society, and punishes unproductive losers. Progressives seek to decrease disparities in wealth and increase the incomes and economic security of poor and middle-class Americans. We believe that we are all in this economy together and that everyone should benefit from rising prosperity.

In thinking about this question, I find the idea of "economic citizenship" helpful. The American economy is immense and immensely complex, with many kinds of jobs that need doing. Some require rare skills or complex training, while others do not. Some demand extraordinary physical strength or stamina, some unusual mental acuity, others both or neither. Some less glamorous jobs are by any reasonable reckoning necessary—someone has to grow our food, dispose of our garbage, nurse sick patients, educate young children—while others seem dispensable (somewhat paradoxically, dispensable jobs often pay much better than necessary ones). Some jobs are stimulating and enjoyable, while others are dirty, dull, difficult, dangerous, and hard to imagine anyone doing without the stimulus of wages.

I believe that anyone who proves him or herself willing to perform a reasonable amount of useful work over his or her lifetime—work that our society either finds valuable enough to pay for, or that it depends on and cannot do without, such as child rearing—should be considered an economic citizen. Just like political citizenship, economic citizenship as I conceive it involves both rights and responsibilities. In exchange for meeting their economic responsibilities economic citizens should secure a right to basic provisioning and economic security. In a society as advanced and wealthy as the United States this should include rights to primary and secondary education and any additional training necessary to become or remain economically productive; health care adequate to meet most emergencies; sufficient remuneration during one's working life to live decently without having to work excessively long hours; and a pension sufficient to secure a comfortable retirement. In addition to guarantees that such basic material needs will be met, I believe all economic citizens are also entitled to a reasonable share of the growing wealth represented by rising annual GDP, *because they help create that increased wealth.*

I say economic citizens deserve all this as a matter of justice, not charity. Securing basic material needs and a fair share of our society's growing economic wealth can be accomplished in various ways, from minimum wage laws and tighter labor markets to needs-based college scholarships and progressive tax structures. The key point is that they should be effectively guaranteed as fair compensation for an individual's economic contributions. Securing basic economic justice will also keep most Americans invested in the success of our society, which is just as important for the rich as for the poor. After all, without a widely shared prosperity, wealthy citizens' hold on their possessions becomes more tenuous.

Much more might be said regarding what economic basics to guarantee and what would constitute a reasonable or fair share of society's growing wealth, with room for legitimate disagreement. But economic inequality has grown so extreme in the United States in recent decades that I see no need to specify these further for purposes of my argument here. Tens of millions of hard-working Americans find it difficult or impossible to meet their basic economic needs today, the *majority* of Americans have received so little from large productivity gains in recent decades, while the wealthiest one or two percent are squatting on such vast reserves of unearned and undeserved wealth, that the injustice of the current situation is obvious and cries out for redress.

To be clear: I am not advocating some Maoist conception of complete economic equality, which seems to me neither necessary nor just. Arguably some workers deserve somewhat greater compensation than others, due to their greater efforts or economic contributions.[8] Some degree of differential pay incentivizes effort and innovation, leading to greater economic productivity and increased overall wealth. Allowing some amount of excess wealth to accumulate as capital that is then available for productive investment may benefit society as a whole. But the operative word in all these cases is "some." Just as morality and prudence argue against too much enforced economic equality, there are moral and practical limits to acceptable economic inequality.

I do not claim to know what a perfectly fair distribution of the vast wealth Americans have created in recent decades might be, but I do feel confident that its actual distribution has been grossly *unfair*. Too many people who have worked hard and well, performing some of our society's most essential economic roles, have seen their economic fortunes decline, sometimes steeply. We might debate whether the wealthiest 20% of Americans deserved two, three, or even four times as great a reward as the poorest 20% for their greater importance or supposedly higher productivity during this period. But no one can seriously argue that they were *fifty-four times* more important or productive, or deserved *fifty-four times* the reward—which is what they received. No serious argument exists that unless the wealthiest Americans are allowed to keep almost all the increased wealth generated by an expanding economy, important work will be left undone or productivity gains will cease.[9] On the contrary: if the average person becomes convinced that the economic system is rigged against him and that his efforts to get ahead are doomed to failure, that will likely undermine both his own economic efforts and his willingness to let others keep what they have earned through theirs.

If you accept the commonsense view that the purpose of material wealth is to help people live good lives, then America's skewed income and wealth distributions over the past forty years appear not only unjust, but also highly inefficient. That's because increased wealth is more likely to help poor people improve their lives than to help rich people do so.[10] Money, wonderful as it is, appears to have what economists call "diminishing marginal utility."[11] Shifting resources toward the poor often allows them to meet important unmet needs, while funneling more resources to the rich mostly just helps them satisfy their desires in more expensive or elaborate ways. An extra one million dollars in the pocket of someone earning $10 million annually will probably not significantly affect her happiness. But divide that million dollars into fifty $20,000 shares and add it to the annual incomes of fifty men and women currently earning the minimum wage of $15,000 per year, and you have just raised fifty families out of poverty. Whether you do that through taxing the millionaire and cutting checks to the fifty poverty-wage workers, or through other measures which tip the scales in favor of labor over capital, such as increasing the minimum wage or reducing immigration to tighten labor markets, doing so clearly will further the common good.

Beyond their unfairness and their manifest inefficiency, I believe recent trends toward greater economic inequality are bad for our country in other ways. A winner-take-all economic philosophy is not consistent with the core American values of securing opportunities widely across society and rewarding individual hard work.[12] If we truly believe in the dignity and worth of every individual we cannot allow less wealthy Americans to sink into overworked, insecure poverty. If we truly believe in equality and democracy, we cannot accept ever-greater economic inequality, or the political impotence that mass poverty entails. A robust political citizenship demands some protection for economic citizenship as well. Most fundamentally, if we want to have a society at all, one where we cooperate as well as compete with one another, and not just a huge agglomeration of strangers, then we must reverse these trends.

CAUSES OF INCREASED INEQUALITY

This startling juxtaposition—of greatly increased overall wealth with the nearly total failure of poorer Americans to capture a reasonable share of it—is the great economic fact of our time. It cries out for some explanation. Most mainstream accounts focus on technological changes and the shift from manufacturing to a service economy, which have radically changed the skills most in demand in the US economy. These trends, we are told, have devalued brute strength and manual labor and put a premium on "head work."[13] As Treasury Secretary Henry Paulson put this conventional wisdom in 2006: "Market forces work to provide the greatest rewards to those with the needed skills in growth areas. This means that those workers with less education and fewer skills will realize fewer rewards and have fewer opportunities to advance."[14] Other explanations of widening inequality foreground the failure to maintain the real value of the federal minimum wage,[15] or the disproportionate benefits accruing to wealthier Americans from the tax cuts signed into law by Ronald Reagan in 1981 and 1986 and George W. Bush in 2001 and 2003.[16]

There seems to be some truth to all these explanations. The more formal education workers have the better they have done economically in recent decades. The real value of the minimum wage has declined significantly since the 1970s, affecting tens of millions of workers. Numerous studies have shown that the tax cuts of the 1980s and early 2000s benefited upper-income earners much more than poor and middle-class Americans, helping to ratchet up inequality. But all this does not fully explain why less-educated American workers have fared so much worse than their Canadian, Japanese, or Western European counterparts, whose economies have gone through the same changes during the same time. Similarly it leaves unexplained why lawmakers in the United States, from both major political parties, have legislated wage, tax, and benefits policies that have increased inequality, while legislators in other developed countries have often enacted policies designed to reduce inequality.

Another common explanation for increased economic inequality points to weak American labor unions. According to Bruce Western and Jake Rosenfeld, "From 1973 to 2007, private sector union membership in the United States declined from 34 to 8 percent for men and from 16 to 6 percent for women. During this time, wage inequality in the private sector increased by over 40 percent."[17] This precipitous drop in union membership directly undermined efforts to raise wages for millions of previously unionized workers. Strong unions had also been a primary incentive for employers resisting unionization to "buy off" non-union workers with improved wages and benefits. In addition and more broadly, the authors hypothesize that "unions also contribute to a *moral economy* that institutionalizes norms for fair pay, even for nonunion workers. In the early 1970s, when 1 in 3 male workers were organized, unions were often prominent voices for equity, not just for their members, but for all workers. Union decline marks an erosion of the moral economy and its underlying distributional norms. Wage inequality in the nonunion sector increased as a result."[18]

Again there seems to be some truth to this explanation.[19] Smaller union memberships and the weak bargaining power of the remaining private sector unions in the United States do appear to have limited workers' ability to demand higher wages and benefits in recent decades. But this explanation also raises as many questions as it answers. In particular, we need to ask why American unions have declined so precipitously, much more so than unions in Western Europe and Japan. Corruption and poor strategic decisions by union leaders, such as the failure to focus sooner on unionizing service employees, are certainly contributing factors, but cannot be the whole story. And those explanations don't explain why unions' bargaining powers have eroded even where the workforce has remained unionized.

Many economists argue that another important factor in American workers' declining fortunes has been the resumption of mass immigration. Paul Samuelson, a Nobel Prize winner, wrote in the 1964 edition of his best-selling economics textbook: "After World War I, laws were passed severely limiting immigration. Only a trickle of immigrants has been admitted since then . . . By keeping labor supply down, immigration policy tends to keep wages high. Let us underline this basic principle: Limitation of the supply of any grade of labor relative to all other productive factors can be expected to raise its wage rate; an increase in supply will, other things being equal, tend to depress wage rates."[20] Recent history has proved this notion correct.

Starting with the Immigration and Nationality Act of 1965, Congress greatly increased legal immigration levels, from around 250,000 per year to about 1.1 million per year today.[21] Because the 1965 Act encouraged non-European immigration and family reunification while deemphasizing literacy, education, and special skills requirements, most of these new immigrants were relatively unskilled and relatively poorly educated. So are the vast majority of undocumented immigrants in America, who currently number about 12 million people. One study found that from 1980 to 1995 immigration increased the number of college graduates in the US workforce by 4% while increasing the number of workers without a high school diploma by 21%.[22]

The upshot has been that labor markets for less skilled workers in the United States have been flooded with workers: driving down their wages, allowing employers to slash their benefits, and greatly increasing unemployment among poorer Americans.[23] Well-educated, highly skilled workers, by contrast, have mostly been spared strong downward pressure on their own wages. And because they command greater disposable income, these highly-skilled workers have profited more from the lower prices of goods and services made possible by lower labor costs. Doctors, lawyers, and computer software engineers have done pretty well in recent years. Truck drivers, butchers, nurses, cleaning women, and bus boys? Not so well.

Anyone who has spent time looking for work or negotiating a salary knows that it makes a difference whether employers are begging for workers, or workers are begging for work.[24] As most of us learned in Economics 101, in a market economy wages are set by the mutual consent of (potential) employers and (potential) employees. Employers try to hire for as little as possible, to keep their profits up. Workers bargain for the highest possible wages. What they finally agree to is largely determined by supply and demand. Tighten the labor market, either by increasing demand for workers or by reducing the supply, and wages and benefits increase. Reduce demand or flood the market with workers, and wages and benefits decrease. Flooded labor markets also increase unemployment within sectors with excess workers.

It has proven surprisingly difficult to agree on the precise impacts of immigration on poorer workers' wages and opportunities. George Borjas contends that during the 1970s and 1980s each 10% increase in the number of workers in a particular economic field in the United States decreased wages in that field by 3.5% on average.[25] More recently, researching the impacts of immigration on African Americans, Borjas and colleagues have argued that "a 10% immigration-induced increase in the supply of workers in a particular skill group reduced the black wage of that group by 2.5%, lowered the employment rate by 5.9 percentage points, and increased the incarceration rate by 1.3 percentage points."[26]

In contrast, economist David Card maintains that comparisons between US cities with larger and smaller percentages of immigrants show little to no downward pressure on poorer workers' wages in most cases (although he acknowledges evidence of significant downward wage pressure in a few cities with particularly rapid growth in immigrant populations).[27] More recently, Gianmarco Ottaviano and Giovanni Peri have claimed that any immigration-driven downward pressure on poorer workers' wages has been concentrated on previous immigrants, who are more likely to compete with new immigrants. They argue that poorer native-born workers have largely been spared the effects of direct competition with new immigrants and that because such workers benefit from the opportunities provided by a growing economy, immigration may actually improve their economic welfare.[28]

However, arguments for the benign effect of immigration on American workers have lost much of their persuasiveness after a decade of persistently high unemployment among less-educated Americans. A recent study found 4.9 million more working-age, native-born US citizens with no more than a high school education were out of work in 2013 than in 2000, while among those with some college experience but no degree, 6.8 million more were unemployed. During this period many new jobs in the United States were filled by immigrants rather than by unemployed citizens. As the study notes: "The overall size of the working-age native-born population [in the United States] increased by 16.4 million from 2000 to 2013, yet the number of natives actually holding a job was 1.3 million lower in 2013 than 2000." Meanwhile, "over the same time period, the number of immigrants working increased by 5.3 million."[29] Long-term unemployment can be devastating for poorer workers, who often have little savings to cushion difficult economic times, and for older workers, who may feel useless and ashamed over their inability to provide for their families.

Debates on the precise impacts of immigration on workers' wages turn in part on disagreements regarding the relative "substitutability" of different classes of workers. This is an issue that appears to resist easy empirical resolution. Reviewing the economic literature, I think the weight of evidence points to significant downward pressure on poorer workers' earnings by recent immigration. I am particularly impressed by the comparison between the United States and Canada, two countries with high levels of immigration and relatively similar economies, but with very different immigration systems. Canada, which primarily imports well-educated workers with skills that are in high demand, has seen greater downward wage pressure among its more skilled employment classes than the United States, while wages for less-skilled Canadian workers have held up better than they have south of the border.[30] This is what one would expect if the standard Econ 101 view were correct, that rapidly increasing the supply of workers depresses wages.

Similarly, while immigration's impacts on unemployment are difficult to precisely quantify, it appears to be an important factor in the increase and increasing persistence of unemployment. This is particularly true among younger Americans, who may have a hard time getting a foot on the first rung of the work ladder; older Americans, who are easier to discard in a flooded labor market; and poorer Americans, who face greater job competition from immigrants.[31] One might hope that a poor economy would afford some relief from this downward pressure, by leading to less immigration. But because many immigrants come from very difficult economic circumstances, immigration levels seem relatively impervious to economic conditions in the United States. According to Steven Camarota of the Center for Immigration Studies, during the 1990s there was a net growth of 21 million jobs in the United States and 12.1 million new immigrants, while during the following decade even more immigrants arrived (13.1 million) despite two severe recessions and a net *decline* of 1 million jobs between 2000 and 2010.[32]

To state the obvious, long-term unemployment can be an economic catastrophe for working-class or middle-class Americans, while high levels of unemployment increase economic inequality between the poor and middle-class (largely dependent on their jobs for income) and the very wealthy (whose incomes derive primarily from investments). The total number of working-age native-born citizens not working in the United States (unemployed or out of the labor force entirely) was 18 million larger in 2013 than it was in 2000.[33] Not all of that increase can be blamed on mass immigration. But surely some of it can, with immigrants and native-born American citizens competing across the full range of occupations in the United States, according to figures from the US Department of Labor,[34] and *all* of the net gain in employment between 2000 and 2013 going to immigrants.[35]

To conclude, even researchers who find little to no immigration-driven wage suppression among low-wage workers in the United States acknowledge that wealthier Americans have benefited economically a lot more from mass immigration than poorer Americans. Meanwhile even pro-growth advocates for increased immigration who find its overall economic impacts beneficial have to admit that current immigration policies import large numbers of poor people into the United States each year.[36] So even on the most benign reading of the evidence, mass immigration appears to be widening economic inequality in the United States.

Of course, both the causes of increased inequality and the American economy itself are complex. It would be a mistake to dismiss all the other possible factors in working-class wage stagnation over the past four decades and focus exclusively on mass immigration as *the* cause. On the other hand, it would be a mistake to follow many of my fellow progressives and completely discount immigration's effects for ideological reasons, without considering the facts. Let's examine one industry where immigration seems to have made a big difference.

MEATPACKING

My friend Steve grew up in Dubuque, Iowa. After graduating from high school in 1973 he went to work in a packing house there, "cutting cows." Steve remembers the work as repetitive and boring, but he stayed on for seven years. Dubuque Packers, Inc., like most of the American meatpacking industry, was unionized and paid high wages: from $16 to $20 an hour for most jobs at the plant.

"People lived real well," Steve recalls. "They had boats and second homes" on the little lakes that dot east-central Iowa. They also had the time to enjoy them, since work hours were limited by contract. Being unionized their jobs were also secure—or so Steve and his coworkers thought.[37]

Working in a slaughterhouse, then as now, was hard and exhausting. But in the 1970s it paid pretty well throughout the United States, partly as a result of union drives in previous decades. In today's dollars, wages averaged $23.60 per hour at US meatpacking plants in 1975, and health and retirement benefits were generous.[38] The work may have been difficult, but it kept men without college degrees and their families in a comfortable, middle-class existence. Workers saw these as good, permanent jobs. Turnover at the plants was low.

The system worked reasonably well for all the people involved. Workers got steady, well-paid work and a say in working conditions. Meatpacking companies turned a profit. And American consumers bought beef, pork, and chicken at some of the lowest prices in the world.

Today slaughterhouse jobs average $13.30 per hour—*44% less than they did forty years ago*—and salaries start as low as $7 per hour. Benefits have been cut industry-wide, with decent health insurance rare and good retirement plans nonexistent. Workers are now also highly transient. What happened?[39]

Well, corporate profits were high, but apparently not as high as they could be. That meant trouble for meatpackers. Starting in the 1970s and accelerating in the 1980s, big companies like ConAgra and IBP demanded steep wage cuts and other concessions. Small companies, like Dubuque Packers, followed suit or were driven out of business. In plant after plant, town after town, the companies closed down plants and locked out workers, either shifting production elsewhere or bringing in outside workers to replace union members who balked at seeing their wages cut. Workers staged dozens of strikes and fought tenaciously, in some cases for years. In every instance they were forced to make large concessions or lost their jobs altogether.

The meatpacking industry's union-busting tactics worked because unlike in many countries, American labor law allows companies to permanently replace striking workers (and because Democratic politicians have failed to defend workers' rights by changing the law when they have controlled Congress). But crucially, breaking unions also worked because the companies had a large supply of poor, unskilled immigrant workers to use as strikebreakers. Just as Italians and Slavs "fresh off the boat" were used to thwart unions in Chicago slaughterhouses at the turn of the twentieth century (as memorably chronicled in Upton Sinclair's *The Jungle*) packing companies used Hispanics and Southeast Asians to defeat unions in the 1970s and 1980s.

ITEM: STORM LAKE, IOWA

In 1981 the Hygrade hog-processing plant in Storm Lake, Iowa, locked out five hundred unionized workers, replacing them with Laotians, Vietnamese, Mexicans, and other immigrants. The company broke the union, but a few old union members swallowed their pride and later were hired back at half-wages. Since then the plant has relied almost exclusively on immigrant workers. Many of them do not know that experienced line workers there once received six weeks of paid vacation annually.[40]

ITEM: GREELEY, COLORADO

In 1980 the Monfort Company of Greeley, Colorado, locked out four-teen hundred workers and closed their main meatpacking plant. They re-opened two years later with 40% wage cuts and even greater cuts in bene-fits. In 1987 Monfort did the same thing at their four-hundred-person "portion foods" plant. In both cases, bringing in immigrants as replace-ment workers was a key part of company strategy. Union representative Steve Clasen recalled that throughout the 1980s, as immigrants took over more jobs at Monfort plants, "the company would use migrants to justify keeping the wage structure low."[41]

ITEM: AUSTIN, MINNESOTA

In Austin, Minnesota, good wages allowed the Hormel Company's workers and managers to live side-by-side in middle-class neighborhoods during the 1950s, 1960s, and 1970s. But by the 1980s the Hormel family de-cided the company could no longer buck industry trends, and demanded steep wage cuts. Workers staged a bitter strike for a year and a half to preserve their standard of living. They were crushed. Over one thousand workers lost their jobs. Minnesota had a strong tradition of labor soli-darity, so it was particularly important that Hormel could count on bring-ing in hundreds of recent immigrants with no historic ties to the area and with few other economic options. The Hormel strike was widely viewed as the death blow to organized labor in the meatpacking industry.[42]

*

The stories at Storm Lake, Greeley, and Austin were repeated again and again across the United States. After a while, the mere threat to bring in immigrant workers could force concessions from the unions. Workers at one plant or company who successfully resisted wage reductions, work speed-ups, or decertification of their unions, were undermined when these measures succeeded elsewhere. Today the unions are mostly gone and those that remain have little bargaining power. Each individual em-ployee must take whatever the company offers, or take a hike.

What does it mean when a job pays $10 or $12 an hour rather than $20 or $25? Lower wages make it more difficult to save money; combined with reduced benefits, there is less economic cushion if things go wrong. So the family as a whole has less security and a lower quality of life. Mom or Dad may have to take a second job to make ends meet, and neither parent may be able to stay at home and take care of young children. Everyone is more tired. There is less leisure time and less time for being with family. Jobs that once supported a middle-class family have been replaced with jobs that keep that same family in poverty.

The new jobs not only pay much less, they are also more dangerous, since workers no longer negotiate hours, breaks, or working conditions, and cannot effectively challenge supervisors who cut corners on safety. Injury rates have jumped since the 1970s as companies have increased line speeds up to the limits of physical endurance. According to the Occupational Safety and Health Administration (OSHA), slaughterhouse work is now the most dangerous major occupation in the United States.[43]

Today meatpacking jobs are unattractive, even to poor immigrants. Turnover is high: 60% to 70% annually industry-wide and an astounding 700% to 800% per year at some plants.[44] This turnover costs the companies money, and if it wasn't so easy to exploit new workers, this would give them some incentive to improve wages and working conditions. But with high immigration rates there are always newcomers to fill these difficult and dangerous jobs. Wages stay low. Company profits, however, are higher than ever.[45]

*

The transformation I have just described in the meatpacking industry signifies an immense, ongoing transfer of wealth from workers to owners. In the middle of the greatest sustained increase in overall wealth in the nation's history, meatpacking companies successfully drove tens of thousands of American workers performing grueling, necessary work from middle-class prosperity into poverty. This never would have been possible without the 1965 Revisions to the Immigration and Nationality Act. The packing companies could not have replaced tens of thousands of locked-out union members without the ready availability of tens of thousands of poor immigrants desperate for work.

For the same reasons, these low wages and dangerous working conditions could not persist in the meatpacking industry without continuing high levels of immigration. Over and over, today's packinghouse workers describe themselves as "expendable" in the eyes of management. Sadly, they are. As things now stand it is easier and more profitable to use workers up and get new ones, rather than treating them as valued assets, much less as fellow human beings. This may seem like "the harsh logic of the market." Actually it is the harsh logic of a *flooded* labor market; flooded in this case by the deliberate decisions of successive US Congresses, which set annual immigration levels, and successive presidential administrations, which decide whether or not to enforce immigration laws.

In Steve's case, the company lowered the boom in 1979. "They claimed they couldn't hang on with a union," Steve remembers, and with the bigger companies slashing labor costs and aggressively undercutting their competitors' prices, they may have been right.[46] Dubuque Packers locked out their workers and closed the plant for a year, then reopened with a new, non-union, poorly paid, largely immigrant workforce. Steve and his coworkers held out for a while, but every week saw fewer and fewer walking the picket line. Eventually they all gave up and many left their home state for good. Steve headed west to Colorado. When he first arrived in Fort Collins, in 1980, he looked for work at the nearby Monfort slaughterhouses. Ten years earlier this might have been a good bet. Now Monfort, in the process of breaking its own union, was offering even lower pay than Dubuque Packers. Steve went into construction and agricultural work instead.

However, one man's loss may be another man's opportunity—as with my Fort Collins neighbor, Francisco Nevares, for instance. Francisco talks quickly and smiles easily, especially when his eyes light on one of his many grandchildren. He first came to the United States from Mexico over forty years ago, cowboying for years on ranches across the West. In 1984 he found more steady work at Monfort's main slaughterhouse in Greeley, cutting livers and kidneys out of the carcasses at a starting wage of $6.10 an hour. By the time he left, twelve years later, Francisco was making $10.10. He considered that "good pay" with the overtime he earned working twelve-hour shifts, five days a week, for a sixty-hour work week.[47]

I have never met another post-1980 worker who stayed more than a few years at Monfort, where working conditions are now so dangerous that even a lax OSHA fined the company millions of dollars during the 1990s. When I ask Francisco why he stayed so long, he laughs and says:

"*Es necessario trabajar! Hacer dinero, pagar los billes. . . .*" Although he found the work exhausting and eventually left for a job as a school janitor, his Monfort paycheck allowed him to build a good life for himself and his family in the United States. No boat or second home by the lake for Francisco. Still, he was able to buy a modest house, raise four children in relative comfort, and send two of his kids to college. All this was a lot more than most poor men could achieve in Mexico, no matter how hard they worked, and Francisco is grateful for his opportunities in America. Monfort, he says, "always treated me well."

In fact the new regime in meatpacking, miserly as it seems to those who knew the industry in better days, has offered a way up for thousands of poor immigrants. If you talk to residents of the growing Hispanic sections of Greeley or Fort Collins, you can hear many stories similar to Francisco's. Of men and women who came here from Mexico or Central America, often illegally, and found whatever work they could at whatever wages they could get. They saved money and started families. They helped their brothers, sisters, and other relatives come here, finding employers who would offer work visas, or sending money to hire coyotes to smuggle them over the border. For the most part, as soon as they could these immigrants got the hell out of the packing houses. And along the way they worked hard to make better lives for themselves and their families. Leaning across a back fence, or sitting in a crowded living room, sharing a *cerveza fria* and listening to these families' stories, I have sometimes felt a lump grow in my throat. The American dream is alive and well in these immigrants.

All of which suggests a dilemma. What if America's current meatpacking regime, including allowing the packing companies to have access to vast pools of unskilled labor, is good for poor Mexicans and other potential immigrants, but bad for American workers? Bad for native-born citizens, who still make up two-thirds of the slaughterhouse workforce,[48] and even for previous immigrants, who would benefit from a tighter labor market in meatpacking? Good for Francisco, but bad for Steve? Good for Francisco in 1984, but bad for Francisco ten or twenty years later?

*

Meatpacking is an important example, because it is the kind of hard, dirty, physical work that we are often told "Americans won't do," making immigrant labor necessary. In fact, forty years ago this work was done almost exclusively by native-born Americans. It took extraordinary efforts by "Big Meat" to *make* meatpacking a job that is often done by recent immigrants or others desperate for work. Today Americans do try to avoid the industry, but that is because it pays poorly and is so dangerous. Why take a hard, risky job if it does not pay much better than one that is easier and safer? And even today, the majority of meatpacking workers are native-born American citizens—now working for much less than the previous generation of meat-packers.

Not only is meatpacking a job that Americans will do. Barring a mass conversion to vegetarianism, meatpacking is also a job that someone *has* to do. Recent experience teaches us that the American economy can perform just fine with slaughterhouse workers making solid middle-class wages or poverty-level wages, earning good benefits or few benefits, working under safe conditions or dangerous conditions. Which alternatives should we progressives prefer?

My own view is that regardless of who performs them slaughterhouse jobs in America should be as safe as possible and carry high wages and extensive benefits. Well-off professionals whose work is intrinsically rewarding should be especially grateful to people like meat cutters, garbage men, and cleaning ladies, who do society's tough, dangerous, or monotonous work. This work needs to be done. We know that many of our less-educated fellow-citizens wind up doing it and *need* to do it, to earn a living and to secure their own self-respect. So we should do all we can to improve wages and working conditions in these jobs. With labor unions weak and Democratic politicians confused and timid, perhaps the best thing we can do for our fellow workers is to help tighten labor markets, so they can negotiate the best possible wages and working conditions for themselves. That means reducing immigration and perhaps even paying a little more for chicken wings or hamburger meat at the supermarket.

Now I realize the value of those same tough, dangerous, monotonous jobs to new immigrants from Mexico or Cambodia, even at significantly lower wages. I realize the value of their remittances to relatives back home. It is only honest to acknowledge that if we lower immigration levels some would-be immigrants and their families will lose out.

However it seems to me that as Americans, our first responsibility is to create an economically just society that provides decent opportunities for our fellow citizens. If our economy also creates jobs that can benefit new arrivals, so much the better. But we have no right to pursue immigration policies that sacrifice the vital economic interests of poor Americans in order to help poor foreigners. There is something morally wrong in a view that says, "Let's spread native working-class workers' wealth around to poor immigrants, while successful, well-educated professionals like us reap the benefits in terms of cheaper gardeners, nannies, and restaurant meals."

Don't get me wrong. The United States is a wealthy nation and I believe Americans should look for ways to share our wealth so that it benefits poor people overseas. But we should not do it on the backs of those least able to afford it here in our own country. That is unjust to our fellow citizens, who have a special claim on us to set policies that increase their welfare. And in the case of mass immigration, it is helping create a less egalitarian society with an ever-widening gap between rich and poor. If we are not careful, the United States may end up looking like the crummy plutocracies that so many immigrants are fleeing.

Some readers may find such a possibility preposterous. After all, they may opine, America is the land of opportunity and will always remain so. But during the past forty years the United States has become a much less egalitarian society, with greater income stratification and less economic mobility between classes than most other developed nations. In short, we have become more like Mexico and Brazil economically. Let me ask the optimists reading this book what precisely you think is going to change in order to slow or reverse these trends. Are corporate executives going to undergo a mass humanitarian conversion and increase workers' wages and benefits, solely out of the goodness of their hearts? Are the laws of supply and demand going to magically reverse themselves, so that increasing the number of workers drives wages up rather than down? Forgive this progressive for being skeptical. If we want to reverse these negative economic trends, the evidence suggests that we must tighten labor markets for less skilled, less educated workers.

Whatever you think America owes the rest of the world and however much you may join me in admiring immigrants' courage, resourcefulness, and work ethic, it seems wrong to help poor foreigners in ways that harm working-class American citizens. It seems doubly wrong to say, as current policy in effect says: *From now on the one hundred and twenty thousand line workers in a major branch of American industry will be a permanent underclass. No matter how wealthy America becomes, they will continue to make low wages. When their bodies are damaged or worn out, we will send them packing and get new ones. In fact, they will be paid just enough and treated just well enough, so that people from the poorest nations on Earth will continue to take these jobs.*

This has long been America's de facto policy toward agricultural labor. In the past forty years it has infected meatpacking and many other areas of our economy. But watch out, my fellow progressives! Accept this approach and we give up all hope of creating a truly just society, ceding the whole economic realm to the forces of reaction and inequity. I see no reason to think the economic barbarians will stop at the slaughterhouses and the factories, and not gallop on to the offices and cubicles where many of *us* work, hoping to find the prosperity and security that our blue-collar fellow citizens once enjoyed. At the height of the great recession of 2008–2009, former Federal Reserve Board Chairman Alan Greenspan testified before the Senate Subcommittee on Immigration, Refugees, and Border Security in favor of greatly increasing high-skilled immigration, citing as an important benefit that increasing immigration would drive down wages.[49] As the rest of the world becomes more educated and learns English, we may see more and more white-collar jobs going the way of the meatpacking industry. If Upton Sinclair's "jungle" is once again a reality, can Charles Dickens' Bob Cratchit be far behind?

As for my friend Steve, he has worked many jobs since he moved to Colorado, in construction, agriculture, landscaping, and nursing, among others. But he has never held a steady job that paid as well as his first job out of high school with Dubuque Packers. And he probably never will again.

four

WINNERS AND LOSERS

Any immigration policy will have winners and losers: people with more job opportunities and people with fewer; folks with more money in their pockets and folks with less. This is because the people affected by immigration often have conflicting interests, a point that is obscured by discussions that focus on what level of immigration is "good for the economy." Remember that employers generally support high levels of immigration precisely *because* they drive down workers' wages.[1] If they didn't lower wages, the benefits to employers would disappear and they would have no reason to push for more immigration. Over the years Samuel Gompers, A. Philip Randolph, and other titans of the American labor movement pushed for reductions in immigration.[2] Their position would have made no sense if tightening labor markets did not, in fact, improve prospects for organizing workers and for bargaining up wages and benefits.

The story told in the previous chapter is not unique. What happened in meatpacking in recent decades has happened or is happening across many areas of the economy: agriculture, hotel and motel housekeeping, landscaping, restaurant work, janitorial services. In one sector after another where immigrants have come to take a significant portion of jobs, whether primarily through legal or illegal immigration, wages have been driven down and benefits have been lost. This process is largely complete in meatpacking—although curbing immigration could once again make it possible for slaughterhouse workers to organize and improve their lot (in the aftermath of recent US Immigration and Customs Enforcement [ICE] raids which caught thousands of illegal workers, Swift and Company increased wages at six of their plants an average of 8% and offered generous signing bonuses, in order to find new workers and keep their plants running).[3] We can see the same destruction of the middle class halfway complete in today's construction industry, as I learned in dozens of interviews at construction sites across northern Colorado.

*

Jeff Gauthier has seen immigration's impacts on the construction industry up close. A friendly man with a direct, no-nonsense manner, he has been hanging drywall in new houses for thirty years, the last twenty-one running his own business. "We pride ourselves on quality and reliability," Jeff tells me; he still works for some of the same builders as when he started out. He has always had plenty of work, although he has "never gotten real big." Currently he has five men working for him full time, a multiethnic crew (Jeff is white). He warms up quickly to the topic of illegal workers in construction.[4]

"I've got no qualms about people coming here," Jeff says. "It's the American dream." But when there are millions of people here illegally, "that's just wrong. They're breaking the law. Period." He says other small contractors and native workers agree with him, something my own interviews confirm. The bigger companies, though, are "a totally different story. That's all they're hiring"—and not because of their strong commitment to ethnic diversity.

Hanging drywall is typically piece work. Jeff pays his workers $8–$10 per sheet hung, with his total costs running $14–$15 a sheet. Some other contractors pay their illegal workers $3–$4 a sheet, in cash. "I'm fully insured, [including] liability, unemployment insurance," Jeff says. "I guarantee ya, half of their [the big contractors'] labor force is not insured." It is pretty easy for less scrupulous contractors to outbid Jeff and still make a profit. He says he does not even show up anymore to bid for the big jobs, with mega-home builders like US Homes and Centex. His work is now mostly on expensive custom-built houses, where quality work can still earn a premium.

"I think it comes down to nothing but greed," Jeff says, a statement I will hear more than once as I talk to construction workers, landscapers, and cleaning women who have been priced out of former jobs. "They see a lot of dollar signs in front of their faces. . . . You're in business to make money, I know that," he says. But that should not be everything. "I'm making a living, but I'm also doing the right thing," by hiring legal workers and paying them a living wage.

Loyalty to his workers, who average eight years working for him, is important to Jeff. In comparison, the big companies go through workers "like water," he says. Loyalty to his country is also important. He worries that Americans are "selling our souls, just to get a few things cheaper." "I'd be willing to spend more" to help American families earn decent wages, he asserts: another comment I have often heard from people discussing low wages in other industries, from meatpacking to housecleaning. I ask Jeff some direct questions about immigration.

Do immigrants perform jobs that Americans do not want to do? I ask. Answer: "That's a flat-out false statement. In the construction industry, they're taking over our jobs."

Question: Does immigration push down wages? Answer: "There's a lot of complaining out there." He mentions a former employee, a great worker, now employed by South Valley Drywall, one of the big outfits in Denver, who only gets $3 a sheet. "They know they can get the labor cheaper," Jeff says. It's that simple.

Jeff is starting to think about retirement. He mentions that when he discussed the issue recently with Paul, one of his longtime employees, he "got a worried look on his face. He knows that if he has to get a new job, his pay will be less."

"Who wants to go to work for less than fair wages?" Jeff asks.

Or for less than you made twenty years ago? I add.

"Exactly. You think you're climbing the ladder in life. . . ."

Before I leave, Jeff tours me through the nearly finished home he's working on. The drywall work is very well done.

*

Men like Jeff Gauthier and Tom Kenney, whom we met in the first chapter, want to preserve a decent middle-class life for themselves, their families, and their fellow workers. They make it clear that they are not asking for handouts, or special treatment. But they see opportunities drying up for people like themselves in construction—and they do not see politicians doing anything about it. When I mention that I find it odd that many unions and Democratic politicians support increased immigration, given their historic roles in defending the interests of American workers, Jeff and Tom have little to say. Like most American workers, they simply do not expect any help from unions or the Democratic party, who used to be workers' natural political allies.

All this is not just a matter of lost wages and earnings. It also involves losing relationships with long-time clients when they make the jump to cheaper contractors who use immigrant labor. It is about declining quality, as less-skilled drywallers take over more of the work and anyone competing with them is forced to cut corners. Personal relationships and craftsmanship, too, are being eroded by "market forces," as the economists say, or "greed," to use more old-fashioned language. "The country's selling itself for money," says Jeff.

Tom and Jeff blame greedy contractors, out-of-touch politicians, and Americans generally for letting immigration get out of hand. One group they do not blame, interestingly enough, is immigrants themselves, even those here illegally.

Jeff, who has taken several hunting trips to northern Mexico, describes seeing people in Sonora living in "less than a hut. They're so used to being so poor, that anything they can make here, they're happy to make," he says. "A trailer is a big step up."[5]

Tom Kenny recalls his son, then in his early twenties and working for him, talking one day about the "damn Mexicans" who were pricing them out of jobs. "Don't generalize," he says he told his son. "If you were born in Mexico and had to fight for every piece of food, you would do the same thing. You would come here."[6]

I have interviewed a journeyman carpenter, who, as soon as I told him my research topic, volunteered that "Tom Tancredo can s*** my d***" (a reference to the former Colorado Congressman and inveterate foe of mass immigration) before adding that the real problem with immigration was its contribution to population growth and urban sprawl.[7] If I were to ignore Tom Kenny's advice and "generalize," I would say white construction workers and other blue-collar workers are no more racist or "anti-immigrant" than other Americans. My fellow progressives would do well to look beyond the country music on the radio and the gun rack in back of the pickup truck to the human beings represented by these disempowered American workers. They might be surprised at what they see and some of what they don't see, as well.

LIMITS TO TRANSCENDENCE

In deciding what immigration policy to set as a society, it is important to realize the limits to personal generosity and altruistic feelings in mitigating mass immigration's negative impacts on workers. Javier Morale's boss, Andy, prides himself on not taking advantage of his workers. A big part of Jeff Gauthier's sense of his own success is that over the years, his business has helped his workers, who are also his friends, earn a good wage and support their families. But there are limits to what Andy and Jeff can pay their workers before they price themselves out of a job. They are generous, but it is necessarily a *comparative* generosity, circumscribed by limits. At the end of the day, wages in our capitalist system are mostly set by the market.

This holds true for even the smallest, most personal transactions. My wife, Kris, and I tried to pay Steve generously for building our fence. But our sense of what was generous was based largely on what other people were paying for similar work. Even if we had wanted to give Steve more than we did for building our fence, he was not looking for charity; in fact, he prides himself on setting "a fair price" for his work. And that price is not set by us sitting down and reading economic theory or political philosophy together, or figuring out a formula for what is fair, but *by the market*. For that reason, Americans need to think hard about immigration levels. We can help some poor foreigners, like Javier or Francisco, by letting them come here and work. But such help necessarily comes at the expense of our own working-class and middle-class workers, like Steve and Tom Kenny.

In 2006, the average wage for workers across all the construction trades in Colorado was $12.30 an hour.[8] In Mexico, the minimum wage in 2006 was 50 pesos *a day*—a little over $3.60. If we allow these two labor markets to merge, both economic theory and recent experience suggest that wages in America's construction industry will decline sharply. Would that be good for our country?

One thing that keeps me optimistic is that many of the people I have interviewed for this book resist the idea that markets have a determining influence over their lives. Javier and Tom, for example, both want to be seen as individuals, not just problems or victims ("We're not the kind of people who come to a dead end and then stop," says Tom, pondering his economic future). They take pride in their work—it's not just a paycheck—and they seem to find their relationships to their fellow workers and clients as meaningful as the money they make.

Yet we are all caught up in the market. Although we can transcend it in various ways, it also constrains us.

Javier Morales is lucky to have a boss who doesn't take advantage of his illegal status, but instead pays him the prevailing wage for legal electricians' assistants. But he cannot expect to earn a much higher wage than that. If high immigration levels decrease wages, his wages probably will also decrease.

Tom Kenney was able to build strong relationships with contractors and a thriving business, owing to his own abilities and hard work. But one by one, those relationships are fraying, as contractors choose to "go cheap." In the current labor market, he probably will not be able to keep his business going. That is a reality that Tom has to face; he does not have the luxury of ignoring it if he wants to avoid personal bankruptcy.

CUI BONO?

No immigration policy can maximize benefits for everyone. If we keep this insight in mind, we can avoid much of the confusion that impedes serious attempts to get to the bottom of this issue. So let's ask a simple question: who benefits and who is harmed, economically, by mass immigration into the United States?

Three groups are big economic winners. First, the very wealthy: not just "the 1%" but even more the top 0.1% or 0.01%, who tend to be large stockholders. The more stock an individual owns in publicly traded companies, the larger his or her potential winnings from a growing economy. With tens of millions of Americans invested in the stock market through their retirement accounts, there are tens of millions of potential beneficiaries, but the biggest benefits are reserved for the wealthy. If you are a teacher or construction worker, a nurse or a policeman with a small 401(k) retirement account, what you gain in the stock market through immigration-driven growth is probably more than made up for by what you lose through having your wages driven down by increased labor competition. But if you are truly wealthy and do not depend on a wage for most of your income, it is a very different story. In pure monetary terms the wealthy elite benefit the most from high levels of immigration into the United States.

A second group benefiting from mass immigration is employers and business owners.[9] Anne, a small landscaper I interviewed at a new construction site in Fort Collins, is an enthusiastic proponent of mass immigration, for obvious reasons. Immigration allows her to lower her labor costs and pocket more profit per job. Lower labor costs may also allow her to lower costs to her customers, increasing the number of customers who can afford her services and helping her business to grow.[10] Of course, the bigger the business, the greater the potential winnings. Anne might be a few thousand dollars richer this year because of mass immigration. The partner owners of TruGreen lawn care services may be many millions of dollars richer. In this way, the first and second groups of beneficiaries show considerable overlap.

A third group benefiting from mass immigration is immigrants themselves, who enjoy greater wealth and economic opportunities in the US than they would in their home countries. Here is a list of America's ten largest immigration "source" countries in numerical order:

1. Mexico	6. El Salvador
2. China & Taiwan	7. Cuba
3. India	8. South Korea
4. The Philippines	9. The Dominican Republic
5. Vietnam	10. Guatemala[11]

These ten countries provide about 60% of all immigrants into the United States; Mexico alone accounts for almost 30%. With the exception of South Korea they are all much poorer than the United States. Many of them suffer from gross systemic corruption and poor public education systems. Most are overpopulated with relatively large cohorts of young people, leading to high unemployment and underemployment. All this makes it hard for the average man or woman to thrive economically in Mexico or El Salvador, China or the Philippines, Vietnam or India. Even where progress is being made, opportunities are much greater in America for average people without connections.

Simply put, the greatest beneficiaries of mass immigration are the very rich (who are mostly US citizens) and the very poor (who come from other countries).

*

Who are the big losers from high levels of immigration? Once again three groups stand out.

First, working-class Americans, whose modest wages are driven down in economic sectors with lots of immigrant workers, and who are much more likely to suffer unemployment or underemployment as a result of competition with immigrants.[12] I'm speaking here of meat-packers, supermarket checkout clerks, and janitors. Construction workers, secretaries, and nurses' aides. Backhoe operators, waiters, and garbage men. Mechanics, roofers, and day laborers. These folks may see some immigration-related relief through lower prices for consumer goods, but generally this does not make up for smaller and fewer paychecks, and less job security.

Recent studies suggest that some professionals have also taken a wage hit from mass immigration: the laws of supply and demand hold for computer programmers and engineers, as well as janitors and cleaning women.[13] But higher salaries and lower numbers of immigrants have insulated most professionals from the harsher effects of immigrant competition. As noted earlier, in recent decades immigration has increased the percentages of less skilled, less educated workers much more than the percentages of highly skilled, well-educated workers in the United States.[14]

Immigration has had different effects on wages among different classes of Americans. Even researchers who find little to no detrimental impacts on poorer workers' wages acknowledge that immigration's economic *benefits* accrue disproportionately to wealthier citizens.[15] Meanwhile, many researchers do find significant harms to poorer Americans. According to one study, during the 1980s and 1990s, immigration reduced the wages of high school dropouts 7.4%, high school graduates 2.1%, workers with some college experience 2.3%, and college graduates 3.6%.[16] Strikingly, the least-educated workers suffered more than double the loss of the most-educated workers, as a percentage of their salaries. And since the salaries of high school dropouts average less than half the salaries for college graduates, these percentage losses translate into even greater losses in quality of life. The college graduate's 3.6% decrease in wages might mean the difference between buying a BMW or a Chevy, or determine whether or not she takes a European vacation this year. The high school dropout's 7.4% pay cut might mean she cannot afford to rent an apartment in a safer part of town, or fix her teeth.[17]

Working-class Americans are also more likely to be rendered unemployed or underemployed due to mass immigration than wealthier Americans—a simple function of their more direct and intense job competition with immigrants. In a recent study, Steven Camarota and Karen Ziegler found that in occupations in the United States where immigrants fill 25% or more of the jobs, unemployment from 2009 to 2011 averaged 14%, compared to 8% unemployment for occupations with lower percentages of immigrants. "In high-immigrant occupations," they write, "59 percent of the natives have no education beyond high school, compared to 31 percent of the rest of the labor force."[18] These are precisely the people for whom even relatively brief spells of unemployment can be economically devastating.

African Americans comprise a second important group generally harmed by mass immigration.[19] This is not surprising, given that owing to past and present discrimination they tend to be less educated, less skilled, and poorer than their white counterparts. African Americans are therefore more likely than whites to compete directly in immigrant-rich sectors of the economy. One detailed study of immigration's impacts on African Americans found "a strong correlation between immigration, black wages, black employment rates, and black incarceration rates." Its authors concluded that an immigration-induced 10 percent increase in the supply of workers in a particular skill group would reduce wages for African Americans in that group 2.5 percent, lower their employment rate 5.9 percent, and increase their incarceration rate by 1.3 percent.[20]

Vernon Briggs, professor emeritus of labor economics at Cornell University, points out that African Americans are more likely to suffer unemployment than the average citizen, partly because unemployment tends to be higher among the poor. "In February 2008," he notes, "the national unemployment rate was 4.8 percent, but the unemployment rate for adults without a high school diploma was 7.3 percent" and the unemployment rate for African Americans without a diploma topped 12%. Because most immigrants seek less-skilled work, where the black labor force is disproportionately concentrated, Briggs believes "there is little doubt that there is significant overlap in competition for jobs in this sector of the labor market." "Given the inordinately high unemployment rates for low-skilled black workers," he writes, "it is obvious that the major losers in this competition are low-skilled black workers."[21]

Younger African Americans may also be harmed because mass immigration alleviates the need to train them for more skilled work. "Cast down your bucket where you are," pleaded Booker T. Washington to the nation's industrialists, a century and a quarter ago. Like Frederick Douglass before him and W.E.B. DuBois and A. Philip Randolph afterwards, Washington urged American employers to hire African Americans rather than import workers from abroad. [22] Today corporate leaders in high tech industries speak of the urgent need for a more educated workforce. But rather than mounting a serious effort to train minority children for these "jobs of the future," they prefer to import workers from other countries, because it is cheaper and quicker. Silicon Valley CEOs have spent tens of millions of dollars to lobby for increased immigration in the past few years. That money could have been spent improving educational opportunities for minority youth. Ask yourself: if "the economy" needed more educated workers and we could find them only among America's own young people, would we continue to tolerate failing inner city schools?

A third group harmed by mass immigration is previous immigrants themselves. Because they are less educated and less skilled than the average American worker, immigrants disproportionately incur the economic costs of continuing immigration.[23] Of course, without earlier immigration, they would not be here in the first place. But once established, immigrants have a strong interest in limiting further immigration and the wage depression and unemployment that goes along with it. This explains the surprising fact that when asked, many immigrants actually support reducing immigration levels. If you want to increase your wages at the carpet factory or the meatpacking plant, you know that a tight labor market is your friend.

I recall a recent interview with Paul, the foreman of a large planned subdivision in Fort Collins.[24] We talked right after a local crackdown on illegal workers in the construction industry. His current framing crew, immigrants based out of Albuquerque, all had papers, he said, and they "were all asking for more money." "My foundation guy [the subcontractor in charge of pouring concrete foundations] says his guys who are legal went to work somewhere else, where they paid them $4 an hour more." Paul and his subcontractors were scrambling to increase wages in order to hold on to good workers and keep their project on schedule. With two-thirds of his workers immigrants, most of the benefits of this government crackdown on illegal workers were actually going to other, legal immigrants already here.

FAIRNESS AND EQUITY

Mass immigration's biggest winners among US citizens are the wealthy, while its biggest losers are found disproportionately among the nation's poor. Under our current immigration system, the less our fellow citizens can afford it, the larger the burden we ask them to shoulder in paying the inevitable costs of mass immigration. On its face this seems unjust.[25]

Of course, US citizens are not the only group with an important stake in US immigration policy. There are immigrants themselves and would-be immigrants around the world: people who may greatly improve their lives by moving to the United States. With our preferential concern for the poor, progressives naturally want to help these people. We often support mass immigration for that very reason. But if the preceding analysis holds true, mass immigration is a bad way to help poor foreigners, precisely because it unfairly burdens America's poor, rather than asking more from wealthy Americans who can better afford to help.

Think of it this way. Let's say you are a political progressive who believes the United States can and should do more to help the world's poor. We are a wealthy nation, after all. President Obama's administration devoted X billion dollars this past year to foreign aid and various global anti-poverty initiatives; you believe we should devote 2X billion, 5X billion, or even 10X billion to such measures. Well, whatever the figure, if you are a progressive you do not want that money coming solely out of the pockets of poor and middle-class Americans, with a disproportionate amount coming from the poor. For example, you would never support a special tax to help poor people overseas that broke down as follows: 5% tax on income for Americans making less than $30,000 a year, 2% for people making $30,000–$60,000 per year and 0% on those making over $60,000 a year—with half the tax money collected not distributed to poor foreigners at all, but instead redistributed to Americans with annual incomes greater than $100,000. But that, effectively, is the kind of regressive "tax" on wages and benefits that high levels of immigration impose on poorer Americans today. This injustice is why progressives should not support our current immigration policy, or proposals to make it even more expansive.

Neither, I believe, should anyone else. Americans differ greatly regarding what we see as our moral responsibilities toward poor people in other countries and these differences do not line up neatly along a liberal/conservative axis. Some conservatives, particularly conservative Christians, generously support overseas health and poverty initiatives; some progressives focus largely on securing economic justice here at home. But however we define our responsibilities toward the world's poor and however much we as a nation are willing to spend to help them, Americans should all be able to agree that we should not meet our responsibilities on the backs of our own poor citizens.[26]

*

Another argument for reducing immigration into the United States is that policies that widen income inequality harm our society and hence should be changed. This is not the same point as the previous one, that current immigration policies are unjust because they benefit wealthy Americans and concentrate harms among poor Americans. The argument now is that in addition to this injustice toward the poor, increased economic inequality is bad for our society as a whole. It is bad most simply because Americans believe in a fundamental moral equality among people and are committed to a democratic political system. When economic inequalities become too great, the differing opportunities available to rich and poor make a mockery of moral equality. When economic inequalities become too great and are allowed free rein within our political process, the resulting power differential between rich and poor makes a mockery of democracy.

Note again that I am not advocating for complete economic equality. Even if it were possible, there is no need to try to ensure that everyone makes the same salary, has the same income, or owns the same kind, number, or quality of possessions. But there is no denying that when individuals are driven into insecure poverty, their opportunities for personal development, political action, and full and equal participation in society are greatly diminished. When other individuals are allowed to concentrate and deploy large amounts of wealth, they will tend to dominate their fellow citizens. For these reasons, economic inequality must be limited in a society like ours with a commitment to moral equality and to equal opportunity and political participation.

Mass immigration widens economic inequality in the United States in three main ways. First, as we have seen, high immigration rates make rich Americans richer and poor Americans poorer. The wages of many American workers have stagnated for the past forty years and wages for some of the poorest Americans have actually declined in real terms, while persistent unemployment for poorer Americans has increased greatly. According to one account, "Earnings for the median man with a high school diploma and no further schooling fell by 41 percent from 1970 to 2010."[27] During this same time the income of the wealthiest Americans has skyrocketed. Not all of this income disparity can be laid at the door of mass immigration, but some of it clearly can be.[28]

Second, mass immigration, as currently organized in the United States, provides a continual influx of poor people. By increasing the numbers of poor people much faster than the numbers of middle-class or rich people, immigration directly increases overall economic inequality.[29]

This is one of those obvious points rarely mentioned in popular or scholarly analyses of persistent poverty in America. For example, once a year or so, my hometown newspaper, the Fort Collins *Coloradoan*, reliably runs a series of articles on the growth of poverty in our region, complete with earnest editorials about how residents should remain committed to fighting poverty. It never mentions that many of the people swelling the ranks of the poor in Colorado are recent arrivals. They are poor not through any failure of ours, but because they came here poor. Furthermore, no matter how many poor people are named Gonzales or Hernandez, these articles almost always focus on a poor person named Smith or Jones. Poverty affects everyone, right? We would not want to give the impression that it only affects Hispanics, or immigrants.

This is all very sweet, but more than a little misleading. Under the best scenarios, poor immigrants swell the ranks of the poor until they can work themselves out of poverty. Yet because poor immigrants are generally less educated and less skilled, they often remain in poverty. Statistics show that while they may do much better than they would have in their native countries, poor immigrants tend to remain poor by American standards.[30] Their children and grandchildren partially close the income gap between themselves and native-born Americans, but remain somewhat poorer than the children and grandchildren of natives. All this contributes to inequality here in America. But this should not come as a surprise. By importing poor people and setting them in competition with other poor people, we ensure this very result.

A third way mass immigration widens inequality is by increasing the percentage of poor Americans who are not citizens. It is a lot easier for politicians to ignore poor people's interests when they do not have to worry about attracting their votes. In many American cities a quarter or more of the population may not be citizens and a majority of the poor may not be.[31] We should not be surprised that during recent decades, as the numbers of US resident noncitizens doubled, and doubled again, and doubled yet again,[32] government policy has shifted away from helping the poor, or that discussions of "urban policy" have become rare and big cities have lost a lot of political clout.

These problems are compounded when large numbers of workers are here illegally. Illegal workers cannot challenge dishonest and abusive employers, much less fight effectively in the political realm for a fair share of government services. But even legal immigrant workers cannot band together effectively without the prerogatives and the mindsets of citizens, including the background belief, foreign to so many immigrants' experience, that government should be working for them. That is why expanding "guest worker" programs from agriculture, where they are bad enough, into landscaping, construction, or other areas, is such a bad idea. It would create more sectors of the economy where we accept the permanent impoverishment of lower-level workers, as Americans now accept the permanent impoverishment of agricultural laborers.

*

To sum up my argument so far: over the past forty years, the American economy sustained tremendous increases in wealth. But that wealth has mostly been captured by wealthier Americans and economic inequality has increased greatly. If we continue to allow mass immigration into the United States, this inequality seems likely to worsen. This is particularly true since supposedly progressive politicians show little willingness to fight for policies that redistribute wealth from the rich to the poor, or to explicitly articulate the need to do so. Political timidity on the left makes it even more important to ensure that labor markets do not work against poor and middle-class Americans.

OBJECTIONS

An immigration policy that benefits rich citizens at the expense of poor ones is prima facie unjust, while an immigration policy that increases economic inequality in the United States, even if it generates greater over-all wealth, seems a poor policy choice for Americans today. These considerations suggest the proper answers to several economic objections that are commonly made against reducing immigration into the United States.

Objection: the answer to wage stagnation and income inequality in the United States is improved education.[33] *That will make the next generation of Americans more productive and allow them to compete better in the global marketplace. Increased and improved education is the answer to these problems, not reducing immigration.*

Response: improving American education is sound public policy for many reasons and the advice to secure more education or specialized training is often good career advice for individuals. But we need an economy that works for all Americans, including that half of the population who are less educated or less skilled than the other half. Simply funneling more educated or highly skilled people into our existing economic system seems unlikely to lead to greater economic equality. According to Rebecca Thiess, "An analysis of the education and training levels projected to be necessary for the labor force of 2020 shows that jobs will *not* require a significantly greater level of education or training than workers currently possess. Therefore, a simple increase in the share of workers with a college degree will not ensure that tomorrow's economy generates better and more equitable outcomes than today's economy."[34] Meanwhile flooded labor markets are harming American workers right now, particularly those with less education and skills, who can least afford it.

Objection: the answers to wage stagnation and income inequality are stronger labor unions, repealing the Taft/Hartley Act to make it easier to unionize workers, increasing the minimum wage, and a more progressive tax structure.[35] Not reducing immigration.

Response: I agree that the suggested policy changes are crucially important in addressing wage stagnation and income inequality in the United States, particularly the proposal to reverse half a century of erosion of progressive taxation principles.[36] Reducing immigration will help achieve these policy changes, by strengthening the constituency advocating for them. If poorer workers are citizens rather than resident aliens or "guest workers," they will be better able to unionize and fight for their fair economic share. In addition, politicians are more likely to enact legislation that helps them, in exchange for their votes. At the same time, reducing immigration will directly drive up wages and improve job opportunities for poorer workers by tightening up job markets. If union members make their demands in a tight labor market, they will be more likely to succeed.

Objection: Americans are no longer willing to pick lettuce in sweltering fields, dig ditches, or empty bedpans. Immigrants do the jobs that Americans don't want. So they do not take jobs from US citizens, or drive down their wages through direct competition.

Response: This is one of the most common objections to reducing immigration into the US. It is also the easiest to counter, since it is simply false. Less than 2% of all immigrant workers in the US pick agricultural crops. US citizens work alongside immigrants across all sectors of the economy, as illustrated by Table 4–1.

In factories and office buildings, restaurants and construction sites, native-born workers compete for jobs with immigrants. That this objection is so common among progressives suggests how disconnected many

Table 4-1 Immigrants' occupational share by sector in the United States in 2004.

	Share of jobs filled by immigrants	Native unemployment rate
Farming, fishing, and forestry	36%	11.9%
Building cleaning and maintenance	35%	10.9%
Construction and extraction	24%	12.7%
Food preparation	23%	9.3%
Production manufacturing	22%	7.2%
Computer and mathematical	19%	5.0%
Healthcare support	17%	6.6%
Healthcare practitioner	12%	1.5%
Sales	12%	6.1%
Arts, entertainment, and media	11%	5.9%
Management	10%	2.6%
Business and financial	10%	3.3%
Education and training	8%	1.3%
Legal occupations	7%	2.7%

Source: Steven Camarota, "A Jobless Recovery? Immigrant Gains and Native Losses," table 5.

of us are from the lives and concerns of our poorer fellow citizens. It is probably also a function of how competition with immigrants is much less intense for politicians, members of the media, and the business and policy-making elites, than among nurses, janitors, construction workers, and waitresses. Note the strong correlation in Table 4-1 between the occupational share taken by immigrants in particular economic sectors and the unemployment rate for native workers within those sectors.

Objection: as Americans have fewer children, we need (or will need) immigrants to fill jobs that are (or will be) going begging.[37] *Who is going to work in our nursing homes, paint and roof our homes, or cut up cows and pigs in our slaughterhouses, as America ages?*

Response: please note that whatever *might* be the case regarding *future* labor shortages, just now the situation is precisely the opposite. Currently the United States has tens of millions of unemployed people, many with low skill and education levels, who desperately need jobs. According to government figures, in the fourth quarter of 2013, "the broader U-6 measure of unemployment—which includes those want to work, but have not looked recently, and those forced to work part-time—was 28.7 percent for native-born adults who have not completed high school and 16.5 percent for those with only a high school education."[38] If this situation changes in ten or twenty years, we can always bring in more immigrants as needed. For now, I believe we should force US businesses to fill all available positions with our own unemployed residents. We want to reduce unemployment and drive up wages. We want employers to train young US citizens for jobs, or take a chance on older workers whom they can discount or ignore when immigrant labor is abundant. In making these suggestions, I am of course asking readers to think of themselves as citizens focused on the common good, rather than consumers, whose overriding concern for cheap goods and services might lead to different conclusions.

Objection: the main problem with current immigration policy is not primarily the high numbers of immigrants, but their skill set. We should shift the immigrant mix to bring in more educated, highly skilled immigrants and fewer unskilled ones, like Australia and Canada. This will reduce the fiscal burden on taxpayers, since poorly educated immigrants pay less in taxes and are more likely to rely on government safety net services. It will also increase economic growth, since better-educated immigrants contribute much more to economic growth than do poorly educated ones.

Response: such a shift would be an improvement over current immigration policy, decreasing the harms that policy inflicts on poorer Americans. Nevertheless I believe we should decrease the numbers of unskilled, poorly educated immigrants without replacing them with greater numbers of more skilled, highly educated ones, for two reasons. First, with immigration slots limited, I think we should reserve as many as possible for those whose desperation gives them the strongest moral claim on our generosity and who will fare the worst if they cannot come to America.

Second, in a warming world, amid strong signs that global ecosystems are starting to unravel, it seems clear that continued economic growth is environmentally toxic. Evidence that an immigration policy is likely to increase economic growth should therefore count against that policy, not for it. I believe forward-thinking progressives need to get out in front of this issue and not just tolerate but embrace limits to growth. We need to figure out how to create flourishing, just societies that do not depend on economic growth. Those of us thinking seriously about immigration need to take this into account and not continue to uncritically assume that "growth is good." I discuss this in greater detail in the next chapter.

A MASTER/SERVANT ECONOMY

We can see increasing economic inequality in the figures for wages and income over the past forty years, but also in signs of a burgeoning servant economy in the United States.[39] More people are hiring lawn care services to cut their grass and trim their hedges. We eat out a lot more than we used to. More people are hiring nannies to take care of their children. All these services rely heavily on immigrant labor.

A mainstream economist would find little to criticize in these trends and much to praise. Contracting out grass cutting relieves some people of a tedious chore and creates jobs for others who need them. Eating out at restaurants is a harmless enjoyment that again creates jobs. Hiring nannies allows educated, busy professionals to make the best (read: "most lucrative") use of their time. All this activity registers positively on the GDP tally sheet, so many feel it is "good for the economy" and therefore good, period. But isn't this way of thinking a gross oversimplification? I do not see busboys and nannies as sinister figures, but I am wary of these trends. In the nineteenth century, servants were a lot more common in America than they are today. During the twentieth century, the rise of the middle class and the related high cost of labor mostly did away with them. Now servants are making a comeback, and aside from the occasional re-run of *Downton Abbey*, I think this is a bad thing.

Where there are servants, there will be masters. There will be some measure of deference on one side and some feeling of entitlement on the other. This contradicts the egalitarian spirit at the heart of progressivism and of America itself.

Where there are servants and masters, the masters will run the show politically. The servants will hardly have the time, inclination, or organization to engage in politics. They also may not have the required citizenship. This contradicts our democratic political system.

Where there are masters, servants do the hard, physical work, as a matter of course. With Americans facing an obesity epidemic, this might not be the right time to cut back on chores like cutting grass and trimming trees that help keep us physically active.

But my main concern is not with our bodies but with our souls, or rather, with the souls of our communities. Americans who are doing fairly well economically need to ask ourselves what sort of society we want to live in. Do we want to live among neighbors, people with the same general status as ourselves—or among deferential domestics, who take care of all our "dirty work"? Do we want fellow citizens, with the interest and the time to get involved in community matters and local politics—or "guest workers" who shut up and do what they are told? And let's not kid ourselves that such programs will provide such effective safeguards that these "guests" will be able to stand up for their rights, successfully unionize, or even have the time and energy to live fully human lives. The goal of such programs is to provide *workers*—not neighbors, not citizens. Employers have these workers over a barrel and the bosses like it that way.

Mass immigration moves us in a less egalitarian, more hierarchical direction: in part through the economic forces we have been discussing, in part by creating linguistic and cultural barriers between different economic classes. When we combine the attitudes and expectations of a servant economy with declining wages for manual workers and less-educated workers, we find ourselves falling into a less egalitarian society. Now meatpackers and garbage men, waitresses and busboys, bus drivers and janitors, roofers and construction workers, are in effect pitted against doctors, lawyers, engineers, and other professionals, as a separate class. They are no longer our equals in terms of wealth, security, education, influence, leisure time, or power. We are the ones with influential professional associations; their unions are weak or gone. We are the ones with stock portfolios and health insurance. We are the ones who can change our jobs or have our teeth fixed, when necessary.

I do not like this new hierarchical America growing up before my eyes—even if I can find Thai food and sushi in places where a dinner out once meant the local diner. If progressivism in America means anything, it means fighting to turn this situation around and get a fairer deal for American workers. And if we are being honest, the answer cannot be for everyone in America to go back to school, get advanced degrees, and enter the professions.[40] That's not going to happen.

We are constantly told that the answer to stagnating incomes is education and the acquisition of new, marketable skills. According to President Obama, "In a global economy where the most valuable skill you can sell is your knowledge, a good education is no longer just a pathway to opportunity—it is a prerequisite." Politicians from both parties regularly offer similar advice, which conveniently lets them off the hook for the growing inequality between more-educated and less-educated citizens.[41] It may be good advice for many individuals, but it is woefully limited as a political prescription. Currently only 35% to 40% of Americans earn four-year college degrees. It is not realistic to imagine this percentage doubling, and even if it did, what about the remaining 20% to 30% of society?

There will always be people who do poorly in school or who get less education, for one reason or another, and for the foreseeable future our society will have plenty of hard, physical labor and repetitive grunt work that needs to be done. Are we saying that the people who wind up doing this work should be poor? Why? Perhaps they deserve to be punished for not being as smart as they should have been. Perhaps their poverty makes us, the successful professionals, feel that much more satisfied with our own lives.

Sound a little ugly? Then join me in saying the opposite. People who are willing to work hard and do the dirty work of this world should be well paid. They should have the same economic security, the same opportunities for leisure, the same basic middle-class comforts as any businessman. I have found that it offends many people's sense of the cosmic order of things to imagine garbage collectors being paid as much as lawyers or professors, so I will not insist on that. Let the professionals make two or three times as much as manual laborers (although I do not see why they should). Let successful businessmen and businesswomen pile up as much wealth as they can if that makes them happy. But then, as a matter of basic fairness, let the garbage man and the janitor, the secretary and the security guard, make a decent middle-class living as well. Let my friend Steve have health insurance, so he can get treatment for his aching back after a hard day's work.

CONCLUSION

I think achieving a more economically just society is the most important political challenge facing us today in America. Do we want to meet our fellow citizens as friends and equals as we go about our economic lives? Or should we magnify economic distinctions so that some of us—the smart, the lucky, the ruthless—can lord it over the peons?

We like to think of the towns and cities we live in as communities, the United States itself as a union of citizens pledged to protect one another's welfare. On our patriotic holidays, we remember the words "all men are created equal . . . endowed by their Creator with certain unalienable Rights." In our churches, we hear how all men and women are precious in God's sight. I think being a progressive means working to create an economy that upholds these noble ideals.

But it does little good to pursue piecemeal reforms if we are not willing to look economic realities squarely in the face. Mass immigration of unskilled workers is a powerful force pushing us toward greater inequality. Cutting back on immigration is one of the most obvious and important actions Americans can take to begin rebuilding a more egalitarian society.

five

GROWTH, OR WHAT IS AN ECONOMY FOR?

In the previous two chapters, we saw that mass immigration has serious economic costs. But it also provides important economic benefits. For many people, immigration's most important impacts can be summed up in a single, magical word: growth. Immigration spurs economic growth and for that reason they believe that immigration is a good thing. That is why some of the most conservative members of Congress support increasing immigration, their efforts cheered on by the US Chamber of Commerce and other free market boosters.

But does immigration really make an important contribution to economic growth? If it does, is economic growth a good thing? If it is, how do we balance the pursuit of growth against other good things with which it may conflict, like economic equality or environmental protection? We need to answer these questions and get clear on what we think about economic growth if we hope to come up with the right immigration policy. This, however, might be easier said than done.

When it comes to economics, Americans are fed a constant diet of "more = better." Evening newscasts note the daily stock market trends as a matter of course; the media report the latest figures on gross domestic product or job creation as important stories. There is rarely any question raised about whether *more* jobs, *higher* stock prices, or a *larger* GDP are good things.[1] This is the basic framework within which Americans think about economic matters.

If you think I am exaggerating the difficulties of thinking clearly about whether more is better, consider that $144 billion in advertising was aimed at the American public in 2011: over 28% of global advertising expenditures directed at less than 4.5% of the world's population.[2] This was not done to make us more informed consumers, but to keep us consuming as much as possible of the advertisers' products. A strong case can be made that this ubiquitous advertising undermines Americans' ability to think intelligently about the roles wealth and consumption really play in living a good life, or the role economic growth plays in improving society. Nevertheless, getting clear about growth and clarifying our fundamental economic goals turn out to be keys to understanding our immigration options. So that is what we will try to do in this chapter.

THE GROWTH ARGUMENT FOR MASS IMMIGRATION

Let's begin by looking briefly at immigration's relationship to economic growth. Tamar Jacoby put the pro-growth case well in an article published several years ago in *Foreign Affairs*. Although "immigrants' overall contribution to economic growth is hard to measure," she writes:

> there is no doubt among economists that newcomers enlarge the economic pie. Foreign workers emerging at the end of the day from the meatpacking plant or the carpet factory buy groceries and shoes for their children; on Saturday, they buy washing machines and then hire plumbers to install them. The companies where they work are more likely to stay in the United States, rather than move operations to another country where labor is cheaper. Readily available immigrant workers allow these businesses to expand, which keeps other Americans on the job and other US businesses, both up- and downstream, afloat . . . no one disputes that [this] results in a bigger, more productive economy.[3]

For Jacoby, as for many of her readers, the goodness of a "bigger, more productive economy" is beyond serious question.

Jacoby's account suggests three main ways in which immigration increases economic growth. First, immigration brings in more workers, helping businesses meet their labor needs and grow. Many of these are poor, unskilled workers willing to work physically demanding jobs for relatively little money. A ready source of cheap labor means a restaurant at the "break even" point may remain open, or a landscaper poised to expand his business may take the plunge. Other immigrants are highly trained professionals—engineers, computer programmers, PhD biologists—with the specialized skills needed by high-tech companies. That is why, as Congress considered whether to increase visas for high tech jobs in 2006, Bill Gates made a rare trip to Washington to testify in favor of the measure. The CEOs of Google and Intel (immigrants themselves), and of Oracle and Cisco Systems, have also argued that access to the world's most talented "knowledge workers" is crucial to their companies' growth. As Congress debated immigration reform in 2013, lobbyists for high tech industries were out in force, pushing for expanded numbers of visas.

Second, immigration fuels economic growth by creating more domestic consumers. Many immigrants come here poor, but they do not necessarily stay poor, and in the meantime they still have to feed, clothe, shelter, entertain, and support themselves and their dependents. Remember the purchases of those meatpackers and carpet factory workers, not to mention Bill Gates' and Sergey Brin's computer programmers. Consumer spending accounts for approximately two-thirds of the American economy. More consumers equal more consumer spending.

Third, immigration reduces the cost of many goods and services, since it reduces the labor costs necessary to produce them. This also increases overall consumption and encourages growth, since the same wage now buys more stuff. If immigration lowers the cost of the average restaurant meal fifty cents (plausible, given the large numbers of immigrants working in the food service industry) people will eat out more often. If immigrant labor lowers the price of the average home in Colorado, more people will be able to buy a house, increasing housing starts and profits in the home construction industry.

All three of these factors can work together to increase economic growth. In construction in the United States today, for example, 22 to 30 percent of workers are foreign born, with approximately 2.4 million immigrant construction workers. "You take 30 percent of the labor out of any sector and you're going to have a serious impact," says Jerry Howard, CEO of the National Association of Home Builders. "The [labor] costs would go up and it would suppress demand to some extent because of the higher costs."[4] Just as important, industry analysts see immigration-driven population growth as one of the spurs for new home construction in many parts of the country. Take away that population growth and the future demand for new houses will shrink dramatically.[5]

There is a highly technical debate about just how much immigration and its attendant population growth actually do increase economic growth. Some economists argue that its role is exaggerated and that the cost of immigration in lowered wages and increased government services (schools, hospitals, jails) actually decreases growth. One study estimates immigration's net contribution to economic growth in recent years at $35 billion annually; relatively small at only 0.2% of the roughly $15 trillion annual US GDP.[6] Certainly mass immigration is not a *requirement* for economic growth.[7] In recent decades some Western European countries, like Norway and Germany, have had relatively low immigration, fairly flat population numbers, and robust economic growth. Still, these countries' economies have grown at slower rates than the United States economy and $35 billion a year is not nothing. It can compound pretty quickly, increasing the base upon which further economic expansion occurs. In any event, most economists agree that recent immigration into the United States has increased economic growth.[8]

For some, that is all they need to know in order to know where they stand on immigration. In an editorial titled "In Praise of Huddled Masses," published July 3 thirty years ago and patriotically reaffirmed on subsequent national anniversaries, the *Wall Street Journal* wrote that "people are the great resource, and so long as we keep our economy free, more people means more growth, the more the merrier." The *Journal* continued:

If anyone doubts that the immigration and growth issue touches the fundamental character of a nation, he should look to recent experience in Europe. Some European governments are taken in by the no-growth nonsense that economic pies no longer grow, and must be sliced. They are actually paying immigrants and guest workers to go home . . . It was this dour view of people as liabilities, not assets, that led to the great European emigration to the U.S. in the first place. Meanwhile, Europe today settles into long-term unemployment for millions while the US economy is booming with new jobs.

"If Washington still wants to 'do something' about immigration," the *Journal* concluded, "we propose a five-word constitutional amendment: There shall be open borders."[9]

Note that those who want to limit immigration are described as "dour." Elsewhere in the editorial, immigration "restrictionists" are described as "pessimistic" and having a "cramped" vision and a "zero-sum mentality." We are filled with irrational fears and we hate people, seeing them as a burden rather than a resource: "More people, the worry runs, will lead to overcrowding; will use up all our 'resources,' and will cause unemployment. Trembling no-growthers cry that we'll never feed, house or clothe all the immigrants—though the immigrants want to feed, house and clothe themselves."[10] In contrast, those who side with the *Journal* on expanding immigration are real Americans, since "America, above all, is a nation founded upon optimism." Proponents of open borders are brave: unafraid of competition and unafraid of the future, which is filled with endless opportunity and, of course, endless economic growth.

Immigration expansionists often use this rhetorical strategy. Tamar Jacoby speaks of the "naysayers" who block "reasonable solutions" to our immigration problems while failing to offer real alternatives.[11] Ben Wattenberg, in his book *The Birth Dearth*, paints a grim picture of economic deterioration without a growing population: "low growth, no growth, shrinkage."[12] This way of arguing is clever and effective, since Americans love "can-do" optimism and find it hard to imagine appealing alternatives to an endlessly growing economy.

Allow me to present a different view. I think those of us arguing for less immigration will have to specify an alternative to the splendor of more: one built around other values, like permanence, stability, and community; and around the possibility that *less* pursuit of material wealth will open up space for Americans to acquire *more* of what we really want. Less radically and perhaps of more use in the immediate political context, we need to remind people that economic growth is possible *without* demographic growth and that a growing population has its own financial, social, and ecological costs. First, though, let's define growth more clearly and distinguish it from some other things with which it is often confused.

WHAT ECONOMIC GROWTH IS AND WHAT IT IS NOT

Economic growth is conventionally defined as an increase in the amount of goods and services produced by an economy over time. It is often specified as a percent change in an economy's gross domestic product (GDP), adjusted for inflation and expressed in dollars.[13] A standard reference notes that "measuring GDP is complicated . . . but at its most basic, the calculation can be done in one of two ways: either by adding up what everyone earned in a year (income approach), or by adding up what everyone spent (expenditure method). Logically, both measures should arrive at roughly the same total."[14]

There is an important sense in which "economic growth" is equivalent to "increased wealth," since it focuses on changes in the monetary value of a country's economic activities. When US or French GDP increases 2%, then 2% more wealth has been created by these national economies. However, several cautions are in order.[15]

For one thing, noting that economic growth has occurred says nothing about how that increased wealth has been divided up. For another, we are talking only about wealth that can be captured in monetary terms; other kinds of wealth are explicitly excluded.[16] GDP sums up wage work but not other important kinds of work, like parents taking care of their own children, or home gardeners growing food for themselves and their neighbors. Such work (or play) may be meaningful or enjoyable to us. But replacing it as quickly as possible with alternatives that may be less efficient or less conducive to human happiness, but that involve transfers of money, is one way to increase economic growth.

As a matter of fact, human losses may well show up as economic gains when we calculate GDP growth. When poor children work in factories, rather than going to school, that shows up positively on national balance sheets (at least in the short term). When Dad or Mom takes a second job as a Walmart greeter and spends less time with the children, that also shows up positively. When air pollution increases asthma and heart disease, that too may go into the plus column as increased economic activity: more industrial production, more money spent on health care, more sports cars sold to doctors specializing in pulmonology and heart surgery.

Of course, not all economic growth is bad. When a young couple saves enough money to buy their first house, starting a family and putting down roots in a community, they contribute to economic growth. So does a wind power company that builds a new turbine factory, or a school district that hires more teachers in order to provide Head Start classes for poor children.

Here is an interesting question: what percentage of US economic growth in the past five decades was tied to undeniably negative trends like increased obesity leading to higher health care expenditures, or poor workers taking a second job to pay the bills? What percentage was tied to positive trends, like improvements in education or increased numbers of family members vacationing together? These kinds of questions never seem to get asked when radio and television announcers report the latest GDP figures. If they were, they might help their listeners think more clearly about the value of growth.[17]

Roughly speaking, then, economic growth means more material wealth and increased economic activity. Let us talk a little now about what economic growth does not mean, at least not necessarily.

Economic growth does not mean growth in average per capita wealth. If a country's GDP is increasing 1% per year while its population is increasing 1.5% per year, then its per capita GDP is decreasing, not increasing, and the average person is likely worse off, not better. This is important, since most people probably value economic growth because of its perceived benefits to average folks. Most of us would prefer a scenario where our state or nation achieved a modest 1% increase in GDP and a 1% increase in per capita income, because our population was stable, over one where the economy grew 2% but we saw no increase in average per capita income, since our population also grew 2%.

Economic growth does not mean increased wealth for the poorest members of society. In the presidential campaigns of 1960 and 1980, John F. Kennedy and Ronald Reagan each stated that "a rising tide floats all boats." They were wrong. Since 1980, the US economy has grown enormously while the incomes of the poorest quarter of Americans arguably have declined.[18] Growth does generate resources that may be captured by poor people directly, or by governments that transfer it to them through tax rebates or government services. But there is nothing inherent in the process of wealth creation that assures that increased wealth actually flows to the poor.

This is because *economic growth does not mean greater economic equality*. Indeed, growth often leads to increased inequality, as the wealthy capture a greater share of the increased wealth. Once again, the recent experience of the United States proves this. Overall wealth has grown rapidly in the last four decades, while economic inequality has increased to levels not seen in America since the Gilded Age.[19] Inequality also grew in Europe, Japan, and other industrial democracies during this time, although not to the same extent as in the United States.[20]

The editorial I quoted earlier suggested a stark choice: either the pie grows, or we have to slice it; either overall economic wealth increases, or we worry about whether it is divided up fairly. This is a false dichotomy typical of free market fundamentalists. Whether the pie is growing, shrinking, or staying the same size, we still need to ask whether it is being divided up fairly. And surely no matter what size the pie, we do have to slice it—unless we all just plan to stand around gaping at the magical, ever-growing pie and basking in its delicious aroma without taking a bite for ourselves. No doubt the 1% dearly hope we will leave this inevitable slicing to the whims of "the market." But progressives disagree, partly because we know that we can have larger pies with smaller slices for most of the eaters, partly because we think pies turn rotten when they are not properly sliced, no matter how big they are.

Before we go on to consider one last thing that economic growth is not, let's remind ourselves why all this might be important from an immigration standpoint. America's current immigration policies, which bring in large numbers of relatively unskilled and uneducated immigrants, make a real contribution to economic growth. They certainly increase the size of the American economy and increase the wealth of already-wealthy Americans. But as we have seen, current immigration policies also harm the poorest members of society and increase economic inequality. It turns out, though, that highly educated immigrants contribute much more, on average, to economic growth than poorly educated ones.[21] So it might be possible to capture much of our current immigration-generated economic growth while limiting downward pressure on poor workers' wages, by increasing "high tech" immigration while cutting immigration overall.

Alternatively, we might choose to limit immigration even if it slows growth. That is because, most importantly, *economic growth does not mean increased happiness*, at least not for the average American, or for most citizens of modern industrial democracies. Americans' average family incomes increased from $13,300 in 1950 to $50,700 in 2000 (in constant dollars).[22] During this same time whole new categories of consumer goods were created, such as cell phones and personal computers, while others were upgraded or transformed. Yet the percentage of Americans who describe ourselves as "happy" or "very happy" has declined since its high in the early 1960s.[23] Greatly increased wealth and greatly increased opportunities to spend it apparently have not made Americans any happier overall. True, wealthier *individuals* do tend to be happier than poorer ones, in the United States and elsewhere.[24] However, this appears to have more to do with a status bonus regarding relative wealth, a zero sum game if ever there was one, rather than indicating the power of increased absolute wealth to improve most people's happiness.[25]

What holds for Americans also seems to hold worldwide. Psychologists at the World Values Study Group have measured the "life satisfaction" of people from over two dozen countries and compared it with their average purchasing power. As Ed Diener and Martin Seligman summarize their findings: "Overall purchasing power and average life satisfaction go strongly in the same general direction," at first. "Once the gross national product exceeds $8000 per person, however, the correlation disappears, and added wealth brings no further satisfaction. So the wealthy Swiss are happier than the poor Bulgarians, but it hardly matters if one is Irish, Italian, Norwegian, or American."[26] In fact, the Irish, with about half the average American's purchasing power, tend to be a little more satisfied with life (maybe it's the music). While some recent studies have found a more robust correlation between wealth and subjective well-being worldwide, they also tend to confirm the finding that poorer societies can sustain equal or superior happiness among their members, provided these societies are safe, relatively noncorrupt, and relatively egalitarian in overall wealth distribution.[27]

The reasons for the relative disconnect between wealth and happiness turn out to be complex and only incompletely understood.[28] Partly it appears to stem from what psychologists and behavioral economists call, with a nice poetry, "the hedonic treadmill."[29] When it comes to material goods we quickly get used to a certain level of wealth, and this just feels like what we should have. That first car or big-screen, high-definition television gives you a real thrill. But soon enough, you become used to it. It does not thrill you anymore, but you feel deprived if you do not have it. Hence the treadmill effect. You can run faster and faster (acquire more stuff) but you never seem to get anywhere (feel lastingly happier). Slow down, though, start to earn or consume less, and you will likely feel worse—particularly if this downsizing is not by choice.

But the more fundamental reason why money does not buy happiness appears to be that the things that make for real, lasting fulfillment are not things that depend primarily on money. These are health, security, a sense of purpose in life, and above all, friendly relations with other people.[30] Research shows that the most important determinant of personal happiness is strong, fulfilling personal relationships. People with more friends and acquaintances are happier than people with fewer. Those who are married tend to be happier than those who are single. True, studies show that how much money a person earns does correlate with her happiness up to a point, but how well she gets along with her coworkers correlates more strongly. Not only can't money ensure sufficient friends or a good marriage, research shows that a materialistic *orientation* toward life tends to undermine personal relationships and lead to greater unhappiness.[31]

The primacy of relationships over wealth in determining happiness means that the endless growth economy is not just endless, but also largely fruitless, if the fruit we are seeking is more meaningful and flourishing lives. If the goal was promoting our happiness, the $144 billion spent annually to convince Americans to buy more stuff would be much better spent reminding us to spend time with our children, get to know our neighbors, call an old friend or make a new one. *If* the goal was promoting our happiness! Of course, that is not the goal at all. The goal of advertising is to increase consumption and corporate profits, not happiness.

When we consider population growth as part of the overall package, as we should in thinking about immigration, the benefits of economic growth appear to recede as wealth increases, while its costs tend to increase. Demographic growth leads to a more impersonal lifestyle, as our daily contacts in larger communities more often involve strangers. It pushes up taxes, as more people require more government services and infrastructure maintenance costs increase. Growth in human numbers and affluence also increases our environmental problems, including more pollution, diminished wildlife habitat, and fewer opportunities to connect to wild nature.[32] Growth likewise worsens modern headaches like increased crowding and traffic. Many Americans have tried to avoid these problems by moving to greener, less populous suburbs and exurbs— inevitably bringing more crowding, more traffic, higher taxes, and increased environmental degradation along with them.

The upshot is that wealth (and hence economic growth) appears to be subject to a law of diminishing returns. For poor individuals and poor societies, more wealth can greatly improve people's lives. For middle-class members of wealthy societies, more wealth may provide modest, short-lived gains, but it is largely irrelevant to most people's long-term happiness. And for the wealthy, piling up more wealth may be valuable as a means to increase their power, status, or influence, but these goods are essentially prizes in a zero-sum game within particular societies. All in all, economic growth does not appear necessary or even useful if the goal is to increase happiness and well-being in wealthy nations such as the United States.

A PROGRESSIVE VIEW OF GROWTH

Progressives need to recognize economic growth's intrinsic insignificance. Its consequences are what is important, particularly whether it furthers or retards human flourishing. We should feel great when growth puts more food into the mouths of people who have not been getting enough to eat; we should treat growth with indifference when it provides millions of iPods for the ears of American teenagers; and we should fight growth when it means higher sales of harmful products like cigarettes or gas-guzzling SUVs.

Progressives should put growth to the test of our principles, asking whether it furthers those goals that we believe are important. Earlier I defined these as a relatively equal distribution of wealth across society, economic security for workers and their families, environmental protection, an end to racial discrimination, and maximizing the political power of common citizens while limiting the influence of large corporations. Growth appears to be at best neutral in helping us achieve these progressive goals, and in some cases detrimental.

Economic growth contributes nothing toward a more equitable distribution of wealth across society. Furthermore, the kind of growth we have pursued in recent decades in America, relying on high numbers of poorly skilled, poorly educated immigrants, has actually increased economic inequality, as we saw in the previous chapters. It is widely recognized by progressives that our current political economy is increasing inequality in the United States.[33] But we rarely stop to consider that escalating growth within the current system therefore *intensifies* economic inequality.

Growth does not increase economic security for workers and their families. Four and five decades ago, Americans were a lot poorer on average, but more economically secure, due to tight labor markets, secure pensions, readily available employer-supplied health care, and a Democratic party that generally fought for their economic interests. After half a century of economic growth, we are a lot wealthier on average, but less economically secure. Unlike most other industrialized nations, we have not invested our increased wealth in ways that have increased economic security: by guaranteeing universal health care, for example, or by saving more as individuals. Despite the Affordable Care Act, American adults are hardly more likely to have health insurance today than they were forty years ago. They are less likely to have a guaranteed pension; less likely to work for the same company they did ten years previously; and less likely to have enough money in the bank to weather prolonged hard times. All this is significant because for most people, economic security contributes more to their happiness than increased wealth.[34]

Economic growth is neutral regarding racial discrimination. And as we saw in the previous chapter, current immigration policy is economically detrimental to African Americans. Thus the kind of growth we promote undercuts attempts to make up for our country's past racial injustices.

Economic growth is very harmful to the environment, since human economic activity is the primary driver of ecological degradation. Habitat loss, air and water pollution, indeed all our main environmental problems are made worse by economic growth. We saw a good example of this recently, when both US and worldwide greenhouse gas emissions declined significantly during the 2008–2009 recession.[35]

Finally, economic growth does not seem to have empowered common citizens or limited the influence of large corporations in the United States. The relative balance of power has shifted toward big business in recent decades, although the precise relationship of this to growth remains obscure. Certainly as our population grows, the relative importance of each individual citizen diminishes, in terms of political decision-making. The greater the number of people who vote for a Congressman or City Council member, the less important any one voter becomes and the more important money, which is needed to reach large masses of people through expensive media campaigns.[36] As money's political importance increases, so does the power of corporations relative to citizens.

On balance, when we consider its effects on progressive goals, economic growth is bad—at least the version of growth prevalent in the United States. Economic growth makes society less equal, fostering envy in the poor and vanity in the rich. It makes our cities, towns, and highways more crowded. It harms other species while failing to deliver substantial benefits to most people. And American progressives have a further, important reason to actively oppose "Growthism." In recent years, the possibility that progressive policies might slow growth has often been used as an excuse to shoot them down. Consider three examples.

ITEM: UNIVERSAL HEALTH CARE

In America, unlike the rest of the developed world, basic health care is not yet accepted as a guaranteed right. Instead the debate is often over whether health care reforms will "benefit the economy." For the past fifty years, while every other industrialized country in the world has enacted universal health care, we have not. As of this writing, forty-eight million Americans lack health insurance, including millions of children.[37]

ITEM: PROGRESSIVE TAXATION

Over the past half-century in the United States, the highest federal tax brackets have been significantly lowered. "We do not want to take away rich people's incentive to make more money" or "penalize success," the argument runs. "That might slow growth—and everyone benefits from growth." Progressive taxation has gone from being the near-consensus approach to providing necessary government funding, seen by most Americans two generations ago as the obviously fair approach to taxation, to a hotly debated position today. More states now rely on regressive sales taxes and user fees, rather than progressive state income taxes. Inequality has increased by leaps and bounds.[38]

ITEM: GREENHOUSE GAS EMISSIONS

With 4.5% of the world's population, the United States generates about 20% of its greenhouse gas emissions. Given the dangers of global climate disruption, it is obvious that Americans need to get cracking on emission cuts, even if it costs significant amounts of money. As a matter of basic fairness, we cannot outsource the job to other nations who are less wealthy than us and have done less to cause the problem. And yet we dither and obfuscate. The main excuse of industry apologists? That serious measures to combat global warming might slow economic growth.

*

Growthism typically works against progressives in these debates. Maybe it's time to consider a different economic approach.

BUT WHAT IS THE ALTERNATIVE?

At this point, though, some readers may want more specification of economic alternatives—especially since the endless growth economy, for all its problems, is at least familiar. What would a progressive, sustainable economy look like? Would it generally discourage economic growth, or just be more selective in the growth it encourages? Would it set strict limits to growth, or just ease up on the accelerator and quit using government to maximize growth? Clearly a more progressive society would have a stronger, more comprehensive "safety net" (and would need to pay for it): the United States has a lot to learn from Western Europe in this respect.[39] But how far should this safety net extend? Clearly a more progressive society would strive for greater equality in incomes and wealth, but what is the right balance between providing sufficient resources for everyone (excluding those who are just too lazy to work, of course) and allowing people to keep their just rewards?[40]

I can understand the reluctance to take the plunge into a less growth-focused approach to economics without answers to these important questions. And I am not claiming to know all the right answers. Still, I think progressives need to move beyond just playing defense and reversing recent economic losses, and specify positive alternatives to our current ecologically destructive, winner-take-all economy. So here goes.[41]

I start from the basic premise that the main purpose of any economy is to promote human flourishing. It should aim to provide the resources necessary to sustain individuals and allow them to develop all their human capabilities: physical, mental, social, and spiritual. And it should be fair, so that anyone willing to do his or her share of the world's necessary work is able to live decently and comfortably. "Decent" and "comfortable" are relative terms, of course, and should be defined relative to the lives of well-off members of the same society. This does not mean that poor or middle-class people need to have all the superfluous possessions of the rich. It means that with reasonable effort and a little luck, they can live comfortably and pleasantly, with time and opportunity to engage in a full range of human activities, including work, play, politics, the arts, recreation, study, and religion, along with a decent amount of lounging, lollygagging, and skylarking.

Our economy should allow us to live fully human lives. However, we do not want to live those lives on a completely humanized planet. While any economy transforms and appropriates nature, no economy should drive other species completely off the landscape, or degrade resources that future human generations will need to live their own good lives. Human flourishing should not (and in the long run cannot) come at the expense of nature's flourishing. This sets limits to the scale of any plausible human economy: both the number of people it can support and their degree of affluence.[42] A good economy must be sustainable, as well as just.

As I envision it, a progressive economy would do a much better job than our current economy of providing for human necessities, including meaningful work, but would avoid fueling the desire for luxuries. Society's grunt work would be better paid and more respected than it is today, or shared more equitably, or both. Advertising would be significantly curtailed (no ads directed at younger children, for example, who deserve to have their minds free of commercial clutter and insatiable desires[43]). There would be more security for the average worker, but perhaps fewer advantages extended to entrepreneurs.

A truly progressive economy would be richer in culture, education, and community than our current economy.[44] Its members would be richer in *time* to pursue life's most valuable experiences, but would probably have fewer consumer goods and less material wealth. The reality of ecological limits means that a truly sustainable economy must focus on providing enough of what a finite number of people need, rather than ever more of what an infinite number of people want.

Let me be clear that I am not advocating asceticism, or heavy-handed government regulation of people's daily economic activities. I assume no drastic changes in human nature under a more progressive, sustainable economy, which means that many people would still chase after money and material goods in ways that would seem, to a philosopher, unwise. On the other hand, the right economic system would make it easier for people to live less materialistic lives if they chose to do so.[45] More sharply progressive taxes would be used to provide guaranteed health care, good public schools for all children, cheap and accessible mass transit, more parks, and more beautiful public spaces. These kinds of improvements in securing public goods would make it easier for people to abandon the pursuit of great private wealth, while still living securely and well. This, in turn, should lead to greater happiness at less ecological cost.

I am well aware that this perspective is very different from our current endless growth economy. However, I am not alone in thinking along these lines; in fact, I'm in pretty good company. Development economist and 1998 Nobel laureate Amartya Sen asks that we replace gross national product and per capita GNP with measurements that more carefully track improvements in the lives and "capabilities" of poor countries' citizens.[46] Political scientist Robert Lane argues that advanced economies should be judged by the happiness of their participants and the opportunities for self-development they provide, rather than solely by their capacity to create wealth.[47] Ecological economist Herman Daly goes further and argues that any economy that undermines local communities or environmental health is a failure, regardless of "the bottom line."[48]

These thinkers engage the root question of economics: what is the purpose of the production and consumption that make up our economic lives? And their diverse answers all reject wealth or increased consumption as the whole of that purpose. Instead they try to define economic success with reference to true human happiness and the development of just, sustainable societies.

My vision of a progressive economy also harmonizes well with many of our society's most important ethical and religious beliefs; better, in fact, than the endless growth economy, which tends to encourage greed, envy, and selfishness in its members.[49] East and West, ethicists have long argued that human lives can be improved through decreasing economic activity: consuming less and worrying less about money and material possessions. For Plato and Aristotle, Seneca and Epicurus, Lao-tzu and Confucius, the good life was equally a life devoted to right living and a life *not* devoted to luxury or the pursuit of wealth.[50] Aristotle distinguished between *chrematistics*, "the manipulation of property and wealth so as to maximize short-term monetary exchange value to the owner," and *oikonomia*, or true economy, "the management of a household (*oikos*) so as to increase its use value to all members of the household over the long run." He saw economy, thus defined, as key to achieving *eudaimonia*, a term variously translated as "happiness," "blessedness," or "human flourishing."[51]

The Christian gospels are also filled with commands to put economics in its proper, limited perspective. The Sermon on the Mount warns us that we "cannot serve two masters . . . God and Mammon" (Matthew 6:24). It tells us to give to all who are in need and that if someone asks for our shirt, we should give him our coat, too (Matthew 5:40). Jesus returns to these themes often, showing generosity himself and enjoining his followers to do likewise. "Do not store up for yourselves treasures on earth," he advises, "where moth and rust consume and where thieves break in and steal; but store up for yourselves treasures in heaven . . . For where your treasure is, there your heart will be also" (Matthew 6:19–21). No virtues are praised more often in the gospels than material simplicity, generosity, and gratitude; no dangers are warned against more often than avarice and a focus on piling up wealth, rather than on living a good, or godly, life.

So whether you look to Plato, Jesus, or Amartya Sen for inspiration, you can find support for the approach to economics I have been outlining.

Of course, how to get there from here is a difficult question, which is why more economists currently tending the altars of orthodoxy and revving the engines of growth should shift gears and help guide us toward a more just, sustainable future. Honest citizens will also differ over the extent of the economic changes needed and how fast they should happen. These few speculative pages have merely raised such questions, not answered them. However, I hope to have suggested that there are indeed alternatives to the endless growth economy, that they may be superior alternatives, and that exploring them may be exciting and help us lead more fulfilling lives.

In the meantime, maybe all we need to remember for purposes of our discussion of immigration is that conventional economic growth is not moving us forward; that in fact, in the United States in the second decade of the twenty-first century, growth is moving us further from a just, generous, sustainable society. This much seems clear. So Americans who believe that we need mass immigration to sustain or accelerate economic growth should think again. Such growth is neither necessary nor desirable. Perhaps another example will help underline why.

LANDSCAPING

Consider landscaping, an industry that has grown substantially in recent decades and whose growth is heavily dependent on a growing population. Not only do more people equal more landscaping needs overall, but each newly built house is a landscaping bonanza that gets a complete makeover: trees, grass, maybe a koi pond, all from scratch.

Landscaping has also evolved into an industry that relies heavily on immigrant workers. National estimates of the percentage of basic laborers in landscaping who are immigrants range from 70% on up.[52] When I interviewed Tim, a landscaping superintendent at a new construction site in northern Colorado, he told me that there had been a complete turnover during his career, from 5% immigrant labor 20 years ago to 85% or 90% today.[53] Curious to learn more about immigrants in landscaping, I drove around my hometown of Fort Collins, asking questions.

James, the owner of a small landscaping business, is trimming trees down the street with an older assistant who speaks only Spanish and seems reluctant to talk. James is in his mid-twenties and has been in the business seven years. A recent graduate from the university where I teach, he is short and muscular, friendly and open, and interested in the topic of immigration. He says that immigrant workers are "willing and capable."[54]

Are these jobs that Americans don't want to do? I ask.

"Immigrant workers are not so choosy," he responds. "They don't usually complain." They are more willing to do the grunt work, dig a trench in the freezing rain with the water pooling over their shoes, if necessary. "I'm sorry to say, but sometimes we take advantage of them."

Do immigrant workers drive down wages?

"Yes," James replies. Not only that, but using *illegal* workers can also increase profits. "Sometimes you put a little more under-the-table to these guys [undocumented workers] because you can produce a little more capital with them." He professes not to know the legal status of his worker on this job and I do not press either of them about it.

A mile and a half to the west, at a big new development down by Spring Creek, I come across Tim, directing work at a new home site. Natives are better workers than immigrants, he thinks, but "we've spoiled our kids too much. They don't want to do landscaping."

So, these are jobs we don't want?

"Yeah," he responds. Ten years ago he would go through eight or ten Americans for every immigrant worker, although nowadays few Americans bother to apply. He uses the H2-B visa program that guarantees temporary workers from Mexico forty hours of work a week at $8.88 an hour.

Does immigration drive down wages? I ask.

"I agree with that. You get to a point where you've got so many immigrant workers. . . ." His voice trails off.

Has your company ever hired undocumented workers?

"Oh yeah."

Do you have a problem with that?

"Actually, I prefer the illegals," Tim says. With native workers or legal immigrants who come in through the visa program, "they know they've got a little bit more rights than the illegals." H2-B guys can get flighty, especially toward the end of their temporary stays, when you do not have much leverage over them. "Whereas the illegals want to keep their good names, keep their jobs. . . ."

This is the flip side of the comments you frequently hear about "hard-working immigrants." Their bosses, even the good ones, have them over a barrel, in conditions that can approach indentured servitude.[55] "Employers of immigrants will tell you that these workers are some of their best and hardest-working employees," states the website for the California Landscape Contractors Association: "and, in many cases, that their business couldn't function without them. In addition to landscaping and construction, reasonably priced and dependable immigrant labor is essential to restaurants, hotels, nursing homes, and scores of other businesses that need to fill jobs that Americans often don't want."[56]

But who will a landscaping foreman choose as his "best and hardest-working employee": one who demands an increase in wages, or an extra fifteen minutes for lunch, and who threatens to quit if his requests are not met? Or a worker who meekly does what he is told? And how can these be jobs that "Americans don't want," when according to the US Census Bureau, millions of native-born Americans are working right alongside immigrants in these industries?[57] (See Table 4–1.) These are jobs that many Americans *do* want and that they *need*, for the money and for their own self-respect. When they go to ask for a raise, or a few days off to nurse an injured family member, it makes a difference whether someone else is waiting, eager to take their place. It matters whether that someone else is desperate and willing to take whatever work they can get, regardless of wages and working conditions.

This issue of bargaining power is not confined to manual laborers. An article in the *New York Times*, on the influx of foreign priests into Catholic parishes in the United States, quotes one recruiter in Kentucky, a priest himself, saying: "From a strictly personnel perspective, the international priests are easier to work with than the local priests. If they mess up, you just say, 'See you.' You withdraw your permission for them to stay."[58] The article goes on to note that in many parishes foreign priests are paid considerably less than native-born priests (although how the bishops justify this ethically is left unexplained). Without this influx of foreign priests, the American Catholic hierarchy might have to confront questions about why fewer and fewer Americans want to enter the priesthood. It might have to consider improving working conditions by allowing clergy to marry, or reconsider the ordination of women. Importing priests allows church leaders to avoid these issues.

In the same way, importing workers allows landscapers to avoid paying higher wages or improving benefits. In some "talking points on immigration reform" on their website, the California Landscape Contractors Association makes the following helpful clarification:

> Paying higher wages to attract more workers is not the answer. The demographic projections show that job growth is outstripping the supply of workers. It's not just a matter of offering landscape workers more pay. Supply and demand play a role, but there is an upper limit to how much an employer can charge for their product or service, and thus there is an upper limit to what employers can pay their employees. There really are some jobs that US workers just aren't willing to do at any reasonable price.[59]

Self-serving comments from the landscaping industry notwithstanding, workers and employers have been known to disagree on a "reasonable price" for a day's work. In a free market economy one might have thought a reasonable wage was the wage on which workers and employers could agree, and that it might be all right if wages sometimes went up. Granted there will be some upper price a business owner can get for her product or service, which means that there will be a limit to how much she can pay her workers. But that simply means that if employers can't find workers at a price they can afford to pay and still make a profit, they will hold off on hiring workers and contracting for jobs. In this case, fewer lawns might get mowed or trees trimmed than if wages were one or two dollars an hour less.

To hear the California Landscape Contractors Association tell it, that would be a tragic "failure to meet the needs of a growing economy." But now it sounds as if people are serving the economy, rather than the other way around. "Immigrant labor is essential to the functioning of many service industries and to the overall health of the US economy," they assert boldly.[60] But this brings us back to the main point in contention: must a "healthily functioning" economy always be growing? The answer is no. The more important question is whether or not that economy is providing essential goods and services to its members: efficiently, equitably, and sustainably. No doubt landscapers could cut more grass, trim more trees, and increase profits even more if we brought back slavery, too. But those are hardly sufficient reasons for doing so.

I do not doubt that immigrants may be "better workers" from the perspective of Tim, the Catholic bishops, or other bosses. Still, Americans work longer hours than the citizens of most other developed industrial democracies; we work more hours each year than our parents worked a generation ago.[61] Our economy is very productive, measured in conventional monetary terms if not in the satisfaction it generates. How much harder should we work?

As Adam Smith and Ben Franklin taught us long ago, work in a modern capitalist economy disciplines us, and poorer American workers may indeed have become more disciplined in recent decades, if also more tired and beaten down. But there is an unsettling corollary to this: owners and bosses are *less* disciplined by labor transactions in a flooded labor market. They are less likely to be forced to act civilly or respond generously to their workers, when those workers are easy to replace and have fewer options. The Walmart greeter who wants to tell off his superintendent, the waitress who might prefer *not* to smile today, will need to shape up or ship out. The laborer in landscaping needs to swing his shovel more quickly, and he needs to swing it with a smile.

These trends are a function of high immigration levels. Should our society encourage them? Should we put up with them if it turns out they are necessary to maximize economic growth? Progressives should answer with an emphatic no.

*

Let's put the question in its most general form. Landscaping is currently a $53 billion industry in the United States. It supports almost 300,000 businesses. In 2008, it provided jobs for 1,180,000 workers, generating wages of over $19 billion.[62] Do we want this industry to grow? Orthodox economic thinking says, "Of course." I disagree.

For what does all this work, this "industry," really amount to? Much of it involves able-bodied men and women paying other men and women to cut their grass and trim their shrubs. But most homeowners could easily do this work themselves. As Americans get ever fatter, we need more excuses for exercise, not fewer. As our country becomes more economically stratified, we could do with fewer occasions for the conspicuous consumption of status-enhancing services like professional lawn care.

Landscaping labor does not pay particularly well. In order to grow this sector of the economy, we will need to keep the wage differential high between potential customers and potential workers. The lower laborers' wages, the lower the cost for landscaping services, and the higher wealthy Americans' incomes, the more likely they are to spring for landscaping. So the recipe for a landscaping boom is flooded labor markets and growing inequality.

What would it mean if this industry contracted? It sounds bad, doesn't it: "contraction," "recession." But what would it mean in practice? Well, just that more people would cut their own lawns and trim their own shrubs. They would get more exercise. Instead of hiring strangers to cut your lawn, you might hire the neighbor kid and have one more neighborly interaction. With wages and prices higher, some lawns probably would not get cut and some shrubs would not be trimmed, or they would be trimmed less frequently. There would be fewer "bodies" for hire and less economic inequality between manual laborers and the "knowledge workers" who have caught all the economic breaks for the past forty years. All this sounds pretty positive to me.

Contraction would also be good for the environment, despite landscaping's self-proclaimed title as "the green industry." Lawns use more fertilizers and pesticides, per acre, than farm fields, and professional landscapers tend to go heavier on these products than private homeowners.[63] Expansion of managed landscapes at the expense of farms and natural areas, due to population growth, has another name: sprawl. The name suggests that we do not want the whole landscape landscaped. But if that's true, then let's face it: at some point growth in the landscaping industry will have to cease.[64]

In many ways shrinking the landscaping industry would appear to be good for American society. The real loss in such a contraction would be fewer jobs for the Mexicans, Guatemalans, Salvadorans, and others pouring into the industry. True, wages for those remaining, including many recent immigrants, would likely rise, if this contraction were achieved through restricting further immigration. Still, such job losses are not to be trivialized; we are talking about poor people, some with families to feed. Yet I cannot help but think that many of these men and women would be better off back in their own countries, rather than working thousands of miles from home. Some will say as much, if you ask them. "I miss my land, my parents, even my dog," said Jamie Garcia, a landscape worker who has been in the United States for over ten years, bringing laughs and knowing smiles from the rest of his crew.[65]

The problem is that there is not enough work in Mexico or Central America for all these displaced workers. Yet the inhabitants of their home countries are mostly poor, with plenty of unmet needs. There should be a way to get these people working to meet the real needs of their neighbors and fellow citizens, rather than the superfluous wants of Americans. Perhaps too, wealthy Mexicans, Guatemalans, and Salvadorans need to be forced to share their countries' wealth and opportunities more fairly. Without the "safety valve" of the United States, rich landowners and tycoons in Mexico and Central America might be obliged to confront the injustices that send so many of their fellow citizens northward in the first place.

What brought you to America? I ask Jamie Garcia. He seems eager to talk, resting on his shovel; it is a hot day and the break seems welcome.

"Looking for the opportunity to make more money and to make a better life. . . . Something that doesn't happen there [in Mexico] because of corruption and crime."

What is "corruption"?

"If you have money, you have friends, you have everything. . . . If you have no money, no influence, you don't have a chance. Even if you are the smartest man in the world."

I have heard this comment too often to doubt that it contains some truth, yet its fatalism bothers me. I press on with my questions.

If everyone leaves Mexico, there won't be any pressure to improve things. Right?

"Improve things?"

Improve conditions there, fight to make things better. End corruption.

"If you don't have money, what can you do?"[66]

Truthfully, I don't know. Maybe poor Mexicans need to get together with their fellow workers and take back what is rightfully theirs. Americans should not pretend to have all the answers to Mexico's problems. But I think Mexicans need to face them, rather than run away from them to the United States. That too is part of my progressive faith: the belief that citizens have the right and the responsibility to work to improve their own societies. It is condescending to assume otherwise.

There is no real answer to the problem of endlessly more people needing work. Lately, through climate change, burning forests, and bleaching coral reefs, the Earth seems to be reminding us that it cannot accommodate an infinite number of people. And our current answer to this problem—inviting the world to come to America and cut our grass, wash our dishes, and diaper our children—is a particularly bad answer, for immigrants and American citizens alike. It is bad for Mexican fathers or Salvadoran mothers to separate from their own children, just to make money. It is bad for Americans to sit on our duffs while other people cut our grass. It is bad to create a society where, more and more, we are divided into the haves and the have nots, the big shots and the servants. After all, that is what much of Latin America is like and a major reason why so many people emigrate from there in the first place.

More growth—at least here in the United States—will not solve any of these problems. Still, the appeal to growth is ubiquitous in the immigration debate: a conversation stopper when every other challenge to mass immigration has been met.[67] Even Jamie, who never finished high school or took a class in economics, was ready with it when I suggested that maybe America needed a brief time-out from mass immigration.

"The US is a land of opportunity," he asserted. "You need workers everywhere you go. The economy is growing, thanks to many immigrants." And unlike most business owners who sound off on the issue, Jamie was happy to admit that immigration reduced wages. *That was one of its benefits.* "If you have no people, people will be asking about $25, $30 an hour, because they are unique," Jamie told me. "If you have lots of people, you can pay $10 per hour, and get the same work, and increase your economy."[68]

When I questioned whether knocking down workers' wages was good for America as a whole, Jamie reminded me that if labor costs are high, prices will be higher. Cheap labor keeps prices down, encouraging consumption and—economic growth! The circle was closed; end of story. The *Wall Street Journal* could not have explained it any more clearly.

Still, my proposal for this industry would be much different: tighten labor markets by cutting immigration, and meet the reduced need for landscaping primarily with American workers. Even with a somewhat smaller industry, there would still be lots of landscaping work to be done. There would still be rich people, old people, disabled people, and lazy people, who want or need their grass cut and their trees trimmed, and corporate properties that need tending. Meeting these needs with the workers already here would undoubtedly drive up the price of landscaping and decrease business. Fewer people would work in landscaping, but their salaries would be higher. That's the kind of "growth" I'd like to see.

Smaller profits and less activity in the landscaping industry would show up negatively in the figures for US gross domestic product. But that would be okay, since economic activity in itself has no value. The question should always be whether more economic activity would improve society, and in this case the answer is probably "no." Here again, less would be more.

CONCLUSION

Ask yourself what you need to live a good life: one that is enjoyable and meaningful and of which you can be proud.

Do you need nicer clothes? A new Lexus or Maserati? A trip to Bali over Christmas?

Do you need a servant? Three servants? Twelve servants?

Do you need to be richer than you were growing up? Richer than you are today? Richer than your neighbors? So rich that no matter how unintelligent your conversation or how poor your personal hygiene, people will still be interested in you?

Do you need a pony?

I assume that like me, many readers would accept and enjoy some of these things, should they come their way. But few of us would be willing to say that living a good life depends on any of them. This comes down to saying that we do not have to be rich to live happy, meaningful, good lives.

But if that is the case for us as individuals, why do we take it for granted that creating a better society depends on economic growth and increased riches? It most certainly does not. It depends on creating a better society, with no masters and no servants, only free and equal citizens, whose temperance and sane views on wealth allow them to treat one another with justice and generosity. We need immigration policies that foster the evolution of such a society, not policies that focus on increasing economic growth.

Ninety years ago, in a talk to the Albuquerque Chamber of Commerce, the great conservationist Aldo Leopold asked: "What, concretely, is our ambition as a city? '100,000 by 1930'—we have blazoned it forth like an army with banners. . . . Can anyone deny that the vast fund of time, brains and money now devoted to making our city big would actually make it better if diverted to betterment instead of bigness?" Civic-mindedness may be a force for good, Leopold added, but went on to ask his "boosters," somewhat plaintively: "Is it too much to hope that this force, harnessed to a finer ideal, may someday accomplish good as well as big things? That our future standard of civic values may even exclude quantity, obtained at the expense of quality, as not worthwhile?"[69]

No, this is not too much to hope. Without such a society-wide re-valuation of economic values, progressives will not succeed in creating a just and sustainable society. We must redefine "the good life" in less materialistic terms and create economies designed to sustain such good lives—not to grow indefinitely. These are daunting tasks, but they are not optional for serious progressives. In America, where we habitually mistake quantity for quality, these tasks are even more urgent.

To sum up the past three chapters, I contend that economic consider-ations strongly support my immigration policy proposals—on a proper understanding of "economy." As Henry Thoreau noted in his own discus-sion of economic matters one hundred and sixty years ago, "in the long run, men hit only what they aim at. Therefore . . . they had better aim at something high."[70] That remains good economic advice. Our immigra-tion policies should be designed to further the key economic goals of the twenty-first century: greater economic equality and genuine ecological sustainability. Achieving these goals demands greatly reducing immigra-tion into the United States.

six

POPULATION MATTERS

I have been an environmental activist for over twenty-five years. I vividly remember the issue that made me one: a proposal to dam the Oconee River, a lovely, lazy river that runs for a hundred miles through the Georgia piedmont.

I had moved to Athens, Georgia, in 1986, from Chicago. I came to study American history at the state university, but the main effect of moving to the South was to open my eyes to the great variety of landscapes in our country. Here, in a very different environment from the one I had grown up in, I came to realize the beauty and importance of the natural world.

A friend taught me bird watching, during the spring warbler migration. Another took me for my first canoe ride, and soon I was floating my own canoe on two- and three-day trips down the Oconee, the Ogeechee, and other nearby rivers. Before long I was immersed in learning about the local landscape. I wrote my master's thesis in the then-new field of environmental history.

But as is often the case, I had hardly started to learn about the environment when I began to learn about threats to it. New highways. New sprawling subdivisions. The issue that really catalyzed my activism, though, was the scheme to dam the Oconee, which flows through Athens. Its stated purpose was to provide flood control and drinking water to local residents, but its real purpose was to encourage continued economic and demographic growth. A dozen miles of the river were to be inundated, its lovely streamside forests drowned, its playful river otters displaced, to accommodate more of the bland sprawl spreading across north Georgia.

A number of us in the local Sierra Club group sprang into action. We wrote articles. We lobbied public officials. We took reporters on canoe trips down the river to show them what would be destroyed. As part of this effort I read my first environmental impact statement on the proposal, prepared for the US Army Corps of Engineers.

I've read dozens of environmental impact statements in subsequent years, but you always remember your first one, don't you? I still recall my sinking feeling, as toward the start of the report, I reviewed its 50-year population projections for the northeast Georgia region. Was it possible that our population was going to grow *that* fast? Perhaps the numbers were inflated, examples of what people wanted to happen, not what was likely to happen.

Possible—but the numbers came from the US Census Bureau. Our little group was hardly in a position to challenge federal demographers. Besides, houses were springing up daily all around the area. Project that out a few decades and why wouldn't we double or triple our population?

In the ensuing months, as I talked to county commissioners, water engineers, and other decision makers, I noticed a pattern. My fellow greenies and I would talk about the river: its beauty and its history; the forests, fish, and other wildlife that would be displaced by the reservoir. Our listeners would express sympathy and say that of course they didn't want to harm the river, either. Many of them had fished it or hunted along its banks as kids. But more people were coming to north Georgia, lots more, and all those people would need water. . . .

In the end, we fought the dam builders to a kind of a draw. Instead of a huge dam inundating a dozen miles of the Oconee River, the local communities pitched in and built a smaller reservoir on a tributary, destroying 3 or 4 miles of Bear Creek. With a stable population, the original reservoir never would have been proposed. There would have been no need. *With* those population projections from the Census Bureau, a smaller reservoir was really the best we environmentalists could hope for.

In other words, we were going to lose, one way or the other. The only questions were how big and how quickly we would lose.

Bear Creek Reservoir took nearly a dozen years to build. It came on line only twelve years ago and almost immediately it was being cited as inadequate to meet regional drinking water needs. The Bear Creek Reservoir was built to accommodate new water demands for the next fifty years at the "middle" or "moderate" growth projections from the Census Bureau. But it turned out that the counties around Athens were among the fastest growing in the state. They actually grew faster than even the "high" Census Bureau projections.[1]

Now there is talk of building a system of huge regional reservoirs in north Georgia to handle all this growth—including that river-killer on the main stem of the Oconee River. Environmentalists, of course, oppose these plans. A new generation of activists will write earnest letters to the editor. They will lobby their public officials on behalf of the river they love. And then they will probably lose.

*

I was thinking of this history recently, as I sat through a public hearing held by the Corps of Engineers on another reservoir proposal, the Northern Integrated Supply Project. These days I live two thousand miles from Georgia, in Colorado. Once again a lovely river flows through my town, the Cache la Poudre. Water is a scarce commodity here in the West and river flows are sadly reduced from earlier times.

Still, there is usually some water in the river and it supports a lot of life along its banks. I've helped the local Audubon Society census its bird populations and co-wrote a proposal to have the river corridor designated a state Important Bird Area. I've pointed out kingfishers, osprey, and foxes to my sons on our river walks. When I proposed to my wife, Kris, the natural choice was along the banks of the Poudre.

I love the Cache and so do many people here. Fort Collins has spent millions of dollars to buy land and preserve parks and open space along the river. And like a lot of people, I hate plans to siphon off its last unallocated flows and pump them into a new storage reservoir, drying up our river in order to promote more development in the boom towns east and south of Fort Collins. I've already lobbied my city council members on the issue, trying to put into words what the river means to me and reminding them of the many benefits that it gives to residents of our city: economic, aesthetic, recreational, and spiritual.

Now one by one, dozens and dozens of my fellow citizens walk up to the microphone at the Corps of Engineers hearing. Many are obviously nervous, but they overcome their fear in order to speak up for their river. Again and again I hear, in a variety of voices, that they love this river and that they want it to live.

The four hundred people who have gathered in this immense hall have spent countless hours poring over the proposal and assorted technical documents. Their testimony is by turns analytical, personal, passionate, funny, and even a little nutty. Overall the message is clear: my fellow citizens want us to build a community that respects and protects the river and that leaves enough water in it for the fish, the birds, and the trees that grow along its banks.

Their testimony is inspiring. But of course the reservoir's proponents also get to tell their side of the story. Their spokeswoman begins a fancy PowerPoint presentation. And here they are, two slides into the proceedings . . . oh, no . . .

The population projections! Again, looking thirty to fifty years out from the present. Again: low-, medium-, and high-growth projections. And again, it is obvious. We are going to have more people and they are going to need water. The whole rest of the presentation flows from that one slide and with those numbers on their side, the dam proposal will be very tough to defeat.

Nevertheless local environmentalists have formed the Save the Poudre coalition to fight the dam project and we have gained some early victories, successfully challenging the initial draft of the environmental impact statement and forcing proponents to acknowledge hidden costs and potential environmental harms. It turned out to be easy enough to show that the towns that are proposing the reservoir have not done much to conserve water and that there are lots of options for doing so. "Don't dry up the river until you've done the most with what you've already got," we argued in presenting our own "healthy rivers" alternative. "You can even save millions of dollars by conserving water, rather than building expensive new dams, pumps, and other infrastructure."

The problem is that reservoir proponents can easily plug more water conservation into their models and by looking another ten or fifteen years down the line, see the same looming water shortages. More people will need more water. It's as simple as that.

If our population were not growing, no one would be proposing this reservoir. In fact, there are plenty of opportunities to save water through conservation and put more of it back in the river, where it belongs. But an ever-growing population takes those conservation measures, swallows them with hardly a thank you, and demands more. At some point that means new dams and reservoirs, and a dried-out Cache la Poudre River. We may well be able to defeat this reservoir proposal, but others are in the pipeline. As along the Oconee, environmentalists cannot hope to keep sufficient water flowing freely in the Cache in the context of endless population growth.

POPULATION GROWTH AND ENVIRONMENTAL PROBLEMS

The two fights I have described should sound familiar to environmentalists. Environmentalism often involves attempts to defend beloved places from destruction that masquerades as "development." People naturally bond with the wild or pastoral places around them. Making such connections is part of what makes life worth living. Certainly a healthy, flourishing Cache la Poudre River is important to the quality of life of the residents of Fort Collins. I imagine most readers could probably name their own beloved wild places, and also some places that *were* near and dear but that have since been paved over in the name of progress. In societies with growing populations such natural oases are often threatened. After all, the landscape itself is not growing. We aren't creating new rivers or forests, new mountains or prairies. Hence the imperative to defend the places we love and the continual minting of new environmentalists.

In the early days of the environmental movement, there was a popular slogan that went: "Any cause is a lost cause, without population control." As we will see below, subsequent history has borne out its truth. Environmental problems are primarily caused by people going about our economic business: buying and selling, producing and consuming, discarding and excreting. Because every person, no matter how poor or abstemious, puts some economic demands on the biosphere, each extra person adds to the environmental impacts we are trying to mitigate. You would be hard pressed to imagine a single environmental problem that would not be easier to solve with a smaller population than a larger one, or with a stable population rather than with a growing one. In fact, if we look at the focus of American environmental efforts in recent decades, the pattern is often "one step forward, one step back," owing to continued population growth.

We begin by looking at two areas where population growth has *not* prevented considerable environmental improvement in the United States: air and water pollution. Even here, however, it appears population growth has limited the improvements we would likely have seen with a stable population and that a growing population threatens future gains. When we move on to consider species loss, sprawl, and greenhouse gas emissions, we will see clearly how continued population growth undermines efforts to create a sustainable society.

ITEM: AIR AND WATER POLLUTION

A main focus of the environmental movement over the past half-century has been cleaning the air we breathe. Nothing is more important in terms of human health, and great strides have been made: the Clean Air Act of 1970 was a landmark US environmental law and the Clean Air Act Amendments of 1992 were arguably the last major victory for American environmentalists at the federal level. Most residents in US cities and towns today breathe cleaner air than residents thirty and forty years ago, the result primarily of aggressive efforts to clean up factory emissions and improve fuel economy and pollution technologies on automobiles. According to the EPA, emissions of most major air pollutants have declined significantly in recent decades. Between 1980 and 2010, carbon monoxide (CO) emissions declined 71%, nitrogen oxides (NO_x) emissions declined 52%, sulfur dioxide (SO_2) emissions declined 69%, and emissions of large organic particulates (PM_{10}) declined 83%. Most impressive of all, lead emissions declined a whopping 97% as lead was phased out as a common additive in gasoline.[2]

Environmentalists can take great pride in these successes, which translate directly into improved health, longevity, and quality of life for all Americans. (You're welcome!) Research shows that these improvements have led to tens of thousands of fewer deaths annually due to cancers and other diseases, and that the "bad air days" avoided have allowed millions of children to play outside who would have been prevented from doing so. Still, according to the EPA, "despite great progress in air quality improvement, approximately 124 million people nationwide lived in counties with pollution levels above the primary national ambient air quality standards in 2010," primarily owing to excessive ground ozone levels.[3] So more remains to be done, and it is clear that continued population increase makes achieving healthy air more difficult.

Reviewing the American Lung Association's "State of the Air 2012" report and comparing different localities, one is struck by how many of the metropolitan areas that received a "D" or "F" grade for ozone pollution, elevated particulate levels, or both, were either highly populous or rapidly growing in population.[4] The worst levels of air pollution are typically found in the most highly populated areas. Los Angeles, with the nation's worst air quality, provides an instructive example.

Starting in the 1970s, Los Angeles put rudimentary "scrubbers" on many of its plastics and aerospace factories and reaped the benefits from smaller cars with catalytic converters. The air cleaned up considerably in the 1970s and 1980s, and it has continued to improve since then, albeit more slowly. But as the population of the LA basin has continued to grow, from 10 million people in 1970 to 18 million in 2010, more expensive and intrusive efforts have been needed to continue to drive down air pollution numbers. In the 1990s, factories were required to install more elaborate, expensive scrubbing technology; rather than do so, many simply closed, taking their jobs and their pollution to Mexico or China. Small dry cleaners were told to change the chemicals they used, builders were encouraged to use new kinds of paints that have less "off-gassing," etc. Some of the proposed changes have been phased in, others have been judged too intrusive or not worth the trouble.

According to figures from the South Coast Air Quality Management District, improvements in air quality in the LA basin have slowed in the past decade and they appear to be flattening out at levels that remain unhealthy. In 2012, smog exceeded the acceptable levels set by the EPA approximately 120 days during the year.[5] Given the immense technology and efficiency improvements achieved since 1970, it seems likely that an LA basin with 10 million people today would have achieved substantial compliance with the requirements of the Clean Air Act. An LA basin with 18 million people has not.

Similar trends become apparent when we review efforts to rein in water pollution. When Congress passed the Clean Water Act in 1972, many waterways across the United States were filthy, toxic, even occasionally flammable. The Act's primary stated goal was to render all US rivers and streams "fishable and swimmable": that is, usable by people without threat to their health. Initially, great improvements were made. Factories that had been dumping chemicals directly into rivers were now forced to dispose of them more safely. Cities and towns were put on a timeline to construct adequate sewer systems and treat their wastes. Detergents were reformulated to contain less phosphorus. Streams running through agricultural lands were fenced off from cattle. All these measures paid off. Phosphorus, nitrogen, and suspended solid levels decreased in many rivers and streams, and significant numbers were restored to "swimmable" or "fishable" conditions.[6]

Unfortunately improvements have slowed and in some areas water quality has begun to deteriorate again. Scientists have learned that in addition to the obvious examples of "point-source" water polluters, such as factories and municipal sewer pipes, water quality is impacted by "non–point-source" pollution as well: the millions of individual actions that send pollutants into our water. The back-yard mechanic changing his oil and dumping it into a storm sewer; the farmer spreading fertilizer on his fields; you or I absent-mindedly tossing expired medicines down the bathroom sink. These activities, it turns out, also add tremendous amounts of contaminants to our water. But because they are so dispersed, they are hard to target and reduce. While we can imagine reducing major point-sources to almost nothing with sufficient money and ingenuity, non–point-sources are more intractable. There are too many activities that go into making them up; it is too hard to police the little infractions that add up to serious pollution; and life would become much more difficult if we worried constantly about all of them.

Basically a certain amount of non–point-source pollution is just a function of people existing and doing what we do. It is not going away and so the more people we add to our population, the more such pollution we will have. Add another million people to the LA basin or the Front Range of Colorado and some of them will put fertilizers and pesticides on their lawns, toss expired medicines down the sink, spill oil when they change it, etc. The various other people who service their needs also will generate significant non–point-source pollutants. The farmers growing food for an extra million people will fertilize fields and some of that fertilizer will find its way into the water. The extra trucks driving to restock the shelves at Walmart will belch chemicals, some of which children will wind up breathing. People can pollute less, but everyone pollutes some. It is a lesson no serious environmentalist can afford to neglect.

According to the EPA's most recent "Wadeable Streams Assessment," which looked at the physical, chemical, and biological condition of the nation's rivers and streams, "28% of US stream miles are in good condition, compared to the best available reference sites in their regions, 25% are in fair condition, and 42% are in poor condition" (5% were not assessed). Significantly, less densely populated parts of the country tended to have biologically healthier rivers and superior water quality. While 45% of western rivers were found in "good" condition, in the more populous eastern highlands only 18% were found to be in "good" condition and over half were in "poor" condition.[7]

In sum, the United States has made solid progress combating air and water pollution since the first Earth Day, despite rapid population growth. But that progress has slowed in recent decades, in part because the easier steps have been taken and in part because of continued population growth. Americans appear unlikely to fully achieve our stated air quality and water quality goals without stabilizing or reducing our population.

ITEM: SPECIES LOSS

Perhaps the strongest environmental law in the United States is the Endangered Species Act of 1973, which clearly mandates that when any native species of plant or animal is driven to the brink of extinction, it is our duty to act to prevent that extinction from occurring. As originally written, the Endangered Species Act specifically stated that the threat of extinction should trump any economic interests that were causing a species to go extinct. Congress subsequently amended the law to allow some projects of great economic value to go through, provided a committee of cabinet officers (the so-called God squad) voted to do so. To date, however, only one such vote to allow extinction has occurred, perhaps in recognition of the fact that extinction is forever and that there is something selfish and impious in sacrificing a natural life-form on the altar of commerce.[8]

The Endangered Species Act has helped bring back several species from the brink of extinction, including such iconic American wildlife as the bald eagle, the American alligator, and the grey wolf. Its protections have helped hold the line on species extinctions. However, only a handful of endangered species have recovered sufficiently to take them off the threatened and endangered list, which currently contains over 1400 species. Why?

When we think of an endangered species, we often imagine direct, purposive activities that are harming them. Hunters are killing alligators for their skins and selling them to make handbags; wolves are being poisoned by ranchers. End the direct killing and the species can flourish again. Sometimes this is exactly how it works. Alligators, which can reproduce quickly, staged a terrific comeback across much of the southeastern United States once people quit slaughtering them, and they have since been de-listed. Wolves could provide a similar success story, if ranchers manage to overcome their irrational hatred of them, relinquish a few calves each year, and share the landscape more generously.

But many cases are not like this. People are not directly killing wildlife; instead, they are competing with them for habitat or other essential resources. This is a more intractable problem, and one that other species are generally going to lose by attrition.[9]

The causes of extinction are complex; often a species faces multiple or uncertain threats. But scientists who have studied the matter agree that habitat loss is the primary threat to species, and habitat loss is directly tied to human numbers. In a thorough study of Endangered Species Act information published in the US Federal Register, D. S. Wilcove and colleagues found habitat degradation or loss implicated as a cause for 85% of threatened and endangered species in the United States, making habitat loss by far the number one cause of species endangerment in the United States.[10] Studies looking at worldwide species endangerment have come to similar conclusions.

Consider Table 6–1, from another study, this one by Brian Czech and associates, on the leading causes of endangerment for American species classified as threatened or endangered by the US Fish and Wildlife Service. We see that a wide variety of human activities contribute to the displacement of other species, but few of them appear objectionable in themselves.

Table 6–1 Leading causes of species endangerment in the United States.

Cause of endangerment	Number of species harmed
Interactions with nonnative species	305
Urbanization	275
Row-crop agriculture	224
Outdoor recreation and tourism development	186
Domestic livestock and ranching activities	182
Reservoirs and other running water diversions	161
Modified fire regimes and silviculture	144
Pollution of water, air, or soil	144
Mineral, gas, oil, and geothermal extraction or exploration	140
Industrial, institutional, and military activities	131
Harvest (hunting, collecting)	120
Logging	109
Road presence, construction, and maintenance	94

Source: B. Czech, R. Krausman, and P. K. Devers, "Economic Associations among Causes of Species Endangerment in the United States."

They are simply the economic pursuits that sustain human well-being, whether that means growing food, providing people with water or energy, or allowing them to recreate in enjoyable places. In other words, these are activities that to some degree are part and parcel of people existing at all. Bring in more people and you will need to work the landscape harder or use more of it in order to provide these things for them.

So, for example, alligators have made a great comeback in the southeastern United States. But as more people settle in Florida, Georgia, and the Carolinas, human/alligator conflicts become more common and alligators and other wildlife get displaced. As more people move into Colorado's mountains to "get close to nature," human/bear conflicts increase and "problem bears" tend to be relocated, or if that does not work, shot. In the communities along Colorado's growing Front Range, indiscriminate shooting and poisoning of prairie dogs when the area was primarily agricultural has given way to an appreciation for these intelligent little animals, a keystone species that provides food for several dozen other animal species that cannot flourish without them. Children learn about prairie dogs in grade school now, but these fine sentiments are not leading to increased numbers of prairie dogs on the ground. That is because as these communities grow, prairie dog colonies are paved over for new houses, new roads, new Walmarts and Targets. To some extent, Colorado's wildlife is being overrun by wildlife lovers.

The bottom line is that more people means less wildlife.[11] Strong sentiments, strong laws, and serious efforts to live and let live with wildlife are commendable and necessary. But they all will prove insufficient if people are not willing to limit our numbers, thereby limiting how much habitat and resources we take from other species. Without limiting our numbers we will, inevitably, replace *them* with *us* and our economic support systems.

ITEM: SPRAWL

In the past three decades, stopping sprawl, defined as new development on the fringes of existing urban and suburban areas, has become a leading goal for environmentalists across the United States. Sprawl is an environmental problem for numerous reasons, including increased energy and water consumption, increased air and water pollution, and decreased open space and wildlife habitat. Since habitat loss is a leading cause of species endangerment, it's no surprise that some of the nation's worst sprawl centers, such as Southern Florida and the Los Angeles basin, also contain large numbers of endangered species. Between 1982 and 2001, the United States converted 34 million acres of forest, cropland, and pasture to developed uses, an area the size of Illinois. The average annual rate of land conversion increased from 1.4 million acres to 2.2 million acres over this time.[12]

What causes sprawl? Transportation policies that favor building roads over mass transit appear to be important sprawl generators. So are zoning laws that encourage "leapfrog" developments far out into the country and tax policies that allow builders to pass many of the costs of new development on to current taxpayers rather than new home buyers. Between 1970 and 1990, these and other factors caused Americans' *per capita* land use in the hundred largest metropolitan areas to increase 22.6 percent. In these same areas during this same period, however, the amount of developed land increased 51.5 percent.[13]

What accounts for this discrepancy? Population growth: by far the single most important cause of sprawl. New houses, new shopping centers, and new roads are being built for new residents. As Figure 6–1 illus-

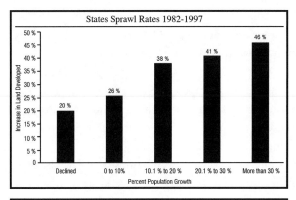

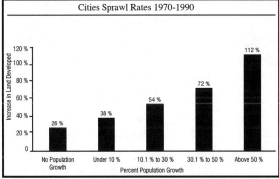

Figure 6-1. US state sprawl rates, 1982–1997, and US city sprawl rates, 1970–1990.

Source: Roy Beck, Leon Kolankiewicz, and Steven Camarota, *Outsmarting Smart Growth: Population Growth, Immigration, and the Problem of Sprawl,* 5.

trates, in recent decades, cities and states with the highest population growth rates have also sprawled the most.

The most thorough study to date on the causes of sprawl in the United States analyzed several dozen possible factors. Grouping together all those factors that can increase per capita land use and comparing these with the single factor of more "capitas," it found that between 1982 and 1997 in America, 52 percent of sprawl was attributable to population increase while 48 percent was attributable to misguided policies that increased land use per person.[14]

Some "smart growth" advocates resist the conclusion that population growth is an important sprawl factor: partly because they do not want to obscure the need for good planning and land use policies, partly because they are uncomfortable talking about population growth. They point out that several metropolitan areas that lost population in recent decades exhibited significant sprawl, including St. Louis, Detroit, and Pittsburgh. Of America's 100 largest metropolitan areas, 11 lost population between 1970 and 1990, yet they sprawled an average of 26 percent (see Figure 6–1). This shows that poor land use planning and bad transportation, zoning, and tax policies are indeed important in generating sprawl. Population growth is not everything.

On the other hand, cities with growing populations sprawled a lot more than ones with stable or declining populations. Several states that managed to decrease per capita land use during this period also sprawled, due to high rates of population growth. From 1982 to 1995, Nevada decreased its per capita land use 26 percent while sprawling 37 percent, due to a whopping 90 percent population increase. Arizona decreased per capita land use 13 percent while its population increased 58 percent, generating a 40 percent increase in developed land.[15] The facts are clear: population growth also causes sprawl.

The bottom line is that if we want to stop sprawl, we must change the population policies that cause it, in addition to reforming misguided transportation, tax, and zoning policies. We will not stop sprawl if we simply accept population increase as inevitable, when the best research shows that it accounts for half of the problem. Nor are we likely to solve our other important environmental problems without stabilizing or reducing our population. The impact of population growth is just too powerful.

*

The twin forces driving increased environmental pressures in the United States in the twentieth century have been demographic and economic growth; they remain the main drivers today. Between 1900 and 2000, a four-times-bigger population and twenty-five-times-bigger economy led to approximately ten times more water use,[16] fifteen times more fossil fuel use,[17] and thirty times more agricultural fertilizer use[18] by the end of the period (see Figure 6–2). These increases in production and consumption have placed unprecedented demands on the ability of the American landscape, our soils and waters, to assimilate our wastes while simultaneously providing necessary resources. They have also greatly increased the percentage of those resources commandeered by a single species—us—at the expense of all the other species that depend on them for their existence.

In many cases, these levels of resource use already appear to exceed what is sustainable over the long term. In others, continued growth seems likely to drive such resource use into overshoot mode relatively soon. In no case have Americans formally recognized a *limit* regarding how much of a particular resource we can use and put in place effective measures to remain below that limit. In all cases, we seem to be taking more than our fair share of resources and sheer ecological space vis-à-vis the non-human world.

IN THEORY . . .

Now in theory, many of our environmental problems could be solved, at least temporarily, while still continuing to increase our population. For example, let's imagine that Colorado's state and local governments enacted the full wish list of smart growth proponents. These include new rail lines up and down the Front Range and mass transit within our cities, strong zoning rules that prevent development in rural and wild areas, and large tax incentives for "infill" building on parcels within current urban areas and for building tall apartment buildings. With all these steps, we could imagine funneling considerably more people into existing developed areas, while slowing the growth of new sprawling developments.

One problem with this scenario is how difficult it is to win even modest smart growth improvements. This is partly because many people *like* sprawling, car-oriented subdivisions and want to live in them, and partly because there is a lot of money to be made promoting sprawl, so development interests typically block any improvements. A statewide growth-management plan that was put before Colorado voters through a citizens' initiative in 2000 started out with an 80%+ approval rating; after $10 million in negative advertising by builders and the real estate industry, it went down to defeat by a margin of two to one. A few cities and towns around the country have managed to implement good growth management plans, but the main result has been to create nicer communities where the plans are in place and to funnel "dumb growth" into nearby communities that are anxious to have it. It seems safe to assume that if we have growth, a lot of it will be dumb.

A second problem is that even smart growth is growth, which inevitably increases ecological impacts and displaces wild nature. Funneling new houses onto inner city lots can spare land out in the country. But the people moving into those houses still need to eat, shop, travel, and recreate. Site new developments along rail lines, rather than highways, and you can cut down on the car use of new residents, but you cannot eliminate it completely. That means those developments will increase regional air pollution. If you add another million people to the Denver metropolitan area, it is better to do it with smart growth rather than dumb growth.[19] But from an environmental perspective, it is better not to add a million people at all.

These two problems should be enough to convince committed environmentalists to support population stabilization in the United States. But there is a third problem that is even more fundamental. It is that "sustainable growth" is an oxymoron, a contradiction in terms.[20] No physical thing can grow forever in a limited area, such as on the surface of the Earth or within the political boundaries of the United States. So pure efficiency solutions to our environmental problems at best can be only temporary expedients, as long as we continue to grow. Yet these solutions themselves are typically put forward as *alternatives* to limiting growth. They help facilitate continued growth while shutting down discussions

---

Figure 6-2 (opposite). Twentieth century environmental trends, United States.

Notes: A, Population in millions, 1900–2010. US Census Bureau figures. *B*, Real GDP per capita, 1900 to 2010, in constant 2009 dollars. Louis Johnston and Samuel Williamson, "What Was the US GDP Then?" *C*, Annual fossil fuel consumption in quadrillion BTUs. US Energy Information Administration, "Energy Sources Have Changed throughout the History of the United States." *D*, Annual CO_2 emissions in millions of metric tons of carbon. T. A. Boden, G. Marland, and R. J. Andres, "Global, Regional, and National Fossil-Fuel CO_2 Emissions." *E*, Annual fertilizer use (nitrogen and phosphorus) in millions of kilograms, 1945–85. Richard Alexander and Richard Smith, "County-Level Estimates of Nitrogen and Phosphorus Fertilizer Use in the United States, 1945 to 1985." *F*, Annual water withdrawals in cubic kilometers, 1940–2000. Personal communication, Reagan Waskom, Colorado State University Water Institute, Fort Collins, December 2013. *G*, Annual paper consumption in millions of metric tons. Iddo Wernick, Robert Herman, Shekhar Govind, and Jesse Ausubel, "Materialization and Dematerialization: Measures and Trends." *H*, Annual cement consumption in millions of metric tons. Thomas Kelly and Grecia Matos, "Historical Statistics for Mineral and Material Commodities in the United States." US Geological Survey, Data Series 140, 2013 online version.

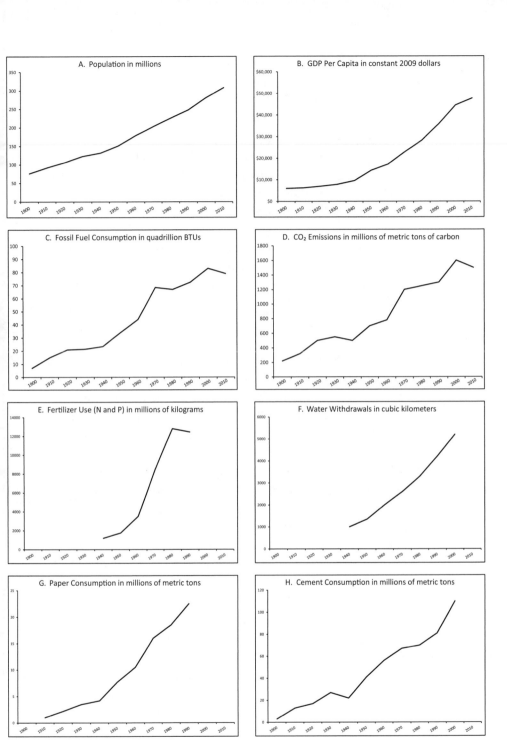

A. Population in millions

B. GDP Per Capita in constant 2009 dollars

C. Fossil Fuel Consumption in quadrillion BTUs

D. CO$_2$ Emissions in millions of metric tons of carbon

E. Fertilizer Use (N and P) in millions of kilograms

F. Water Withdrawals in cubic kilometers

G. Paper Consumption in millions of metric tons

H. Cement Consumption in millions of metric tons

about limiting it. In this way pure efficiency solutions seem bound to lead us astray in our thinking and policymaking.

Lest readers object that this third problem is merely theoretical, a difficulty for our distant descendants that perhaps might be alleviated by space colonization, I remind you of the power of exponential growth. At 2% annual growth, a population doubles every 35 years and is nearly eight times larger after one hundred years. Even small annual growth rates lead in a surprisingly short time to staggeringly large numbers. If we have evidence that something cannot keep growing for long without harming us, whether carbon emissions or our own numbers, then sustainability advocates have good reasons to try to end that growth as soon as possible. Meanwhile evidence continues to accumulate that human numbers and economic activity are bumping up against global ecological limits right now.

*

In theory, we can double our population and still provide increased habitat for the more than fourteen hundred species we have pushed to the edge of extinction in the United States. In practice, doubling our population will increase human demands for the resources and habitat they need to survive. So it will probably help extinguish, forever, many species on the endangered species list.

In theory, we can double our population while so improving our behavior as consumers that we decrease water pollution and clean up our rivers and streams. In practice, the same lack of discipline that leads us to refuse to limit our numbers undermines efforts to get us to consume more conscientiously. The same selfish unwillingness to change will reappear in our unwillingness to spend the money needed to prevent excessive pollution.

Environmentalists need to be pragmatic idealists. We should remain open to new ways of doing things and on the lookout for new technologies that can help reduce our ecological footprints. We should challenge our fellow citizens to consume less, in order to do right by nature and future generations. But we also need to be realistic about how far and how fast societies can change. I hope Americans fifty or one hundred years from now will show some willingness to sacrifice for the common good; perhaps they will even define the common good to include other species.

Still, we may be sure that then, as now, their primary focus will remain furthering their own immediate happiness. For that reason alone, we have to limit our numbers if we hope to create a sustainable society.

Those who think such an analysis lets Americans off the hook for excessive consumerism or deficient altruism need to remember that even a nation of eco-saints can become too populous. Furthermore, because even small annual growth rates lead relatively quickly to large absolute increases in population, environmentalists' calls for an end to growth do not really depend on the details of how environmentally well countries are behaving. A commitment to sustainability implies population limits, and respecting those limits implies not just slowing but *ending* population growth.

THE NUMBERS

At this point, a brief review of the numbers is in order. As we saw earlier, fertility rates in the United States are currently just under the replacement rate of 2.1 children per woman. That means that without immigration, America's population would likely peak in thirty to forty years (first we need to finish digesting "the baby boomlet": the childbearing years of the children of the postwar baby boomers). It would then either fluctuate within a few tens of millions above our current population, or slowly decrease, back towards the 300 million population reached in the first few years of the twenty-first century.

While most recent population growth in the United States is tied to post-1965 immigration, with fertility rates now below replacement rate, almost all our future growth will be immigration-driven. This is clearly shown in the US population projections to 2100 shown in Figure 6–3.[21] The five scenarios graphed vary immigration in half-million increments, from zero to 2 million net annual immigration.

Note that every extra half-million immigrants admitted annually increases America's population in 2100 by about 72 million people. Note too that under any mass immigration scenario, the US population cannot stabilize and instead continues to grow. Both of these points should be of grave concern to serious environmentalists. Given Americans' failure to create a sustainable society of 320 million people, creating one with hun-

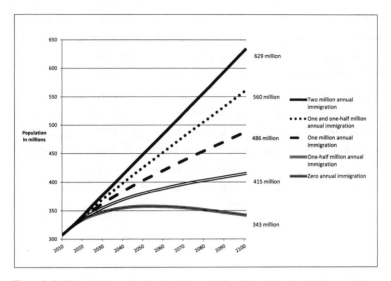

Figure 6-3. US population projections to 2100 under five different immigration scenarios.

Source: Author's projections using population projection tool developed by the Center for Immigration Studies, Washington, DC.

dreds of millions more inhabitants is even more unlikely.[22] And even if we managed to stumble to the year 2100 with 500 million or 600 million inhabitants, our unpromising trajectory with continued mass immigration would be for further immense population growth in the following century.

Fortunately such growth is not inevitable. We need to remember that the American people have voluntarily chosen to stabilize our population, through our choices to have fewer children than our parents and grandparents. We can build on this by choosing to reduce immigration rates as well and stabilize our population. This can be shown by graphing population projections under three alternative immigration scenarios: 250,000 annually, 1.25 million annually, and 2.25 million annually. These correspond roughly to the US immigration rate during the four decades around the middle of the previous century; to our current annual immigration rate; and to the annual immigration levels likely under the immigration reform bill passed by the US Senate in 2013, respectively (see Figure 6-4).

These projections show that the United States has a clear path to population stabilization (although whether stabilization around 380 million people is still too high for ecological sustainability is a valid question). They also show that our current path is likely to lead to massive population growth: over 200 million more Americans by 2100 at current immigration levels. Finally, they show that recent "comprehensive immigration reform" proposals have the potential to drive US population growth even higher, potentially more than doubling our population by the end of this century.

Unfortunately people's short-term focus tends to blind us to the importance of immigration in determining future US population size. For example, the Census Bureau rarely projects population growth out more than forty or fifty years. Compare the previous graph of US population growth to 2100 with one to 2050 under the same three immigration scenarios (Figure 6–5).

This shorter projection does show a significant difference in US population by 2050 under our three scenarios. However, the difference is "only" about 45 million people between each scenario: seemingly manageable, perhaps, in the context of total populations between 369 and 460 million people. All three scenarios in this shorter projection show an upward trending population, although the low-immigration scenario

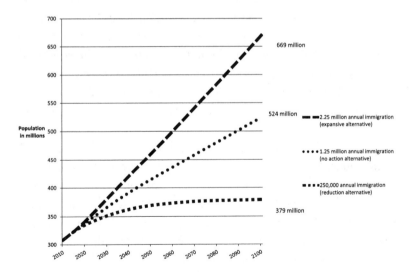

Figure 6–4. US population projections to 2100 under three different immigration scenarios.

Source: Author's projections using population projection tool developed by the Center for Immigration Studies, Washington, DC.

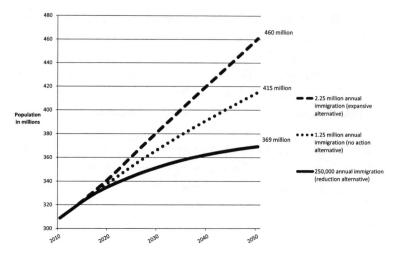

Figure 6–5. US population projections to 2050 under three different immigration scenarios.

Source: Author's projections using population projection tool developed by the Center for Immigration Studies, Washington, DC.

is much gentler than the other two; this obscures the fact that reducing immigration levels would likely eventually stabilize America's population. In the projections to 2100, on the other hand, it is clear that the low-immigration scenario is also a population stabilization scenario, while the two mass immigration scenarios commit the United States to continued rapid population increase. It is also clear that this increase will total hundreds of millions more people within two or three generations. Reviewing population projections out to 2200, as shown in Figure 6–6, makes these points even more forcefully.

Only when contemplating this last graph are we considering the demographic implications "seven generations out" of current US immigration policy. Doing so allows us to see how that policy could limit Americans' environmental options down the road and doom any efforts to create a sustainable society. Only by not pondering these numbers can environmentalists ignore immigration-driven population growth, or Congress seriously consider immigration reform bills that would increase our already record-high immigration levels.

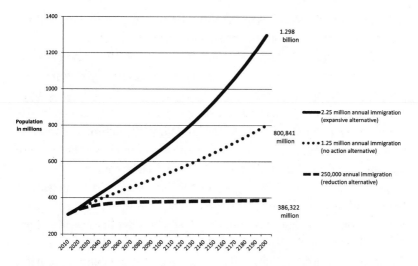

Figure 6-6. US population projections to 2200 under three different immigration scenarios.

Source: Author's projections using population projection tool developed by the Center for Immigration Studies, Washington, DC.

NECESSARY BUT NOT SUFFICIENT

In order to seriously address environmental problems at home and across the globe, we must stop US population growth. Of course, it's possible to spin out scenarios in which America's population doubles, triples, or quadruples and yet we still manage, through miracles of technological creativity or ethical self-sacrifice, to become ecologically sustainable. Perhaps we will begin building farms in high rises,[23] colonize Mars, or discover the secret of perpetual motion. Perhaps Americans will start taking seriously Jesus' advice about the unimportance of wealth and material possessions and focus instead on what is really important in life ("for where your treasure is, there will your heart be also"; Matthew 6:21). Meanwhile, back on planet Earth, such scenarios are implausible. They are therefore morally suspect as a basis for action, or inaction.

Environmentalists often appear to assume an infinite elasticity in our ability to reduce environmentally harmful consumption. This might have made sense 30 years ago when our paradigm for such consumption was burning leaded gasoline or spraying deodorants that contained ozone-depleting chlorofluorocarbons. We could spend some money, remove lead or chlorofluorocarbons from those particular products, and continue happily consuming, minus the negative environmental effects.

Today, as human beings cook the Earth and cause the sixth great extinction episode in our planet's history, we measure environmentally harmful consumption in terms of our carbon footprints and the hectares of land necessary to sustain our consumption choices; land which then is not available as habitat for other species. Our personal impacts can and should be reduced, but because carbon emissions and basic resource use are implicated in almost all our consumption acts, they cannot be reduced to zero. As the cost of greener substitutes increases, the general public and then environmentalists themselves refuse to pay them. As we move beyond *changing* consumption patterns in ways that perhaps more efficiently provide the benefits people want, and instead ask them to *reduce* their consumption of goods and services, sustainability becomes a much harder sell. Even environmentalists tend to fade to a lighter shade of green when consuming less would seriously harm what we consider our quality of life.

Consider your humble author. I bicycle to work every day. My wife and I have spent many thousands of dollars retrofitting our house with solar panels and a super efficient heating system. I buy organic food and try to support local farms. I mostly recreate close to home in ways that are easy on the land and I am teaching my children to do likewise. Still, I drive a car when that is necessary or convenient. I eat a fairly conventional diet. I occasionally fly on airplanes to visit relatives or attend scholarly conferences. I would definitely be willing to do without some amenities in order to help create a sustainable society. Still, there are limits to what I will sacrifice, and I suspect that long before I reach mine, my fellow citizens will have reached theirs.

In other words, I can imagine Americans living and consuming at the lower levels of Western European or Japanese citizens. I see this as a goal worth working for politically. I cannot imagine Americans (or Western Europeans or Japanese) voluntarily living and consuming at the level of the average citizen of Nigeria or Bangladesh. Barring universal enlightenment or dire catastrophe, these are not live political options, regardless of whether a few thousand or even a few million hard-core environmentalists succeed in creating ultra-low consumption lifestyles in the midst of our high consumption culture. Nevertheless, it is urgent that the United States move toward creating a sustainable society now.

By itself population stabilization will not guarantee sustainability. But it would make it possible. The other necessary pieces of the puzzle are limiting excessive per capita consumption and reducing pollution and resource use through technological improvements (rather than using these improvements to facilitate greater consumption or larger populations). Together these efforts make up a sensible environmentalism. Without all three, however, we are setting ourselves up to fail. On the fiftieth Earth Day as on the first one, any environmental cause is a lost cause in the context of an endlessly growing population. The next chapter discusses how American environmentalists came to forget this key truth.

seven

ENVIRONMENTALISTS' RETREAT
FROM DEMOGRAPHY

Several years ago, demographer Leon Bouvier calculated what the population of the United States would have been in 2000 if immigration had
ceased in 1950. He came up with a figure of 232 million people, 50 million fewer than the eventual 2000 census count of 282 million.[1] Table 7–1
summarizes his results.

Reviewing the column marked "Immigration's Share of Growth," you
can see that the initial impact of immigration on population growth is
relatively slight. But that impact increases over time, for three reasons.

First, each year adds new immigrants, some of whom have children.
Eventually those children have children. Immigration thus has a built-in
"multiplier effect." Three million new citizens in the 1950s has meant ten
to twelve million additional citizens two generations later. Second, starting in the late 1950s, Americans began to have smaller families. While
the average American woman had 3.5 children in the mid-1950s, the total
fertility rate declined to 1.7 children per woman by the mid-1970s (it has
since risen to 2.05, in large part due to the higher average fertility rates of
immigrants). With native births contributing less to population growth,
immigration's relative share rose.

Third and most important, there has been a huge increase in immigration, both legal and illegal. In 1965 and several times since then, Congress passed legislation that increased legal immigration from 300,000

Table 7-1 Population of the United States 1950–2000, with and without immigration, in millions.

	Actual population	Actual growth	Population with no immigration	Growth with no immigration	Immigration's share of growth (% of growth)
1950	152	. . .	152	. . .	. . .
1960	181	14.7	176	11.6	3.1 (21.2%)
1970	205	10.7	193	6.9	3.8 (35.8%)
1980	228	11.8	206	6.0	5.7 (48.75)
1990	249	10.4	219	6.7	3.7 (35.5%)
2000	275	11.8	232	5.7	6.1 (51.5%)
Total	. . .	**122.9**	. . .	**79.9**	**43.0 (35.0%)**

Source: Leon Bouvier, "The Impact of Immigration on United States' Population Size: 1950–2050," table 1.

per year to today's 1.1 million. Legal immigrants living in the United States increased from 9 million in 1960 to 42 million in 2012—the most in our history and by far the highest number in the world. Meanwhile, half a dozen Congressional amnesties added 6 million new citizens to the United States and served as a powerful magnet for further illegal immigration, as the undocumented resident population ballooned from 1.5 million in 1960 to roughly 12 million today. Currently 1.3 to 1.5 million new immigrants settle in the United States each year.

Lower immigration scenarios were certainly possible in the United States in the second half of the twentieth century. Other Western democracies that followed such a path, such as Italy and Germany, largely stabilized their populations by the end of the century. I once amused myself by writing an imaginary news article reporting the results from the 2000 US Census in such an alternative reality:

US Population Soon to Stabilize

February 27, 2002, Washington, DC (AP)—The United States population now stands at 240 million, the US Census Bureau reported today. Americans' numbers grew by 5 million during the 1990s, 4 million less than during the preceding decade. If current trends continue, the US population will reach its maximum size during the next ten to fifteen years, at around 244 million, and gradually decline over the next few decades.

President Gore welcomed the news, stating that a smaller population would help the United States meet its goals for reducing greenhouse gas emissions. "Global warming is the moral challenge of our generation," said the President. "This will help us meet that challenge." When asked whether he would encourage his daughters to have fewer children than the four he and Tipper had, the President laughed and said: "I think that would be a good idea."

But stock prices closed sharply down on the news and business spokesmen reacted negatively. CEO Hal I. McGreedy said the population slowdown would make Walmart's growth targets for the coming years harder to reach. The head of the US Chamber of Commerce called for increased immigration and new tax breaks to encourage Americans to have more children. He also urged Congress to study the possibility of annexing Mexico.

Environmental leaders universally welcomed the news. Said Sierra Club Executive Director Carl Pope, "It remains as true today as it was in 1970: any environmental cause is a lost cause without population control." Audubon Society President John Flicker added, "Habitat loss is by far the number one cause of species endangerment. More people equal fewer birds. It's just that simple."

Alas, such articles never got written. This was the good news that never came. Instead, as the US population grew, American environmentalists sat through repeated presentations for the next dam, subdivision, or road-widening, and toward the start of each presentation we watched in silence and swallowed *the projections*: US Census Bureau projections of population increases for our town, region, or state over the next twenty or thirty years, invariably used to justify the new development proposals being considered.[2] This was the *bad* news. Often the proposals we environmentalists opposed were successful (more bad news). Because after all, more people do need more water, houses, and roads, all else being equal.

Now imagine if environmentalists had been the ones introducing the population projections, and that they had showed a rapidly stabilizing US population. How many of those bad projects would have been defeated, or never even brought up for consideration? How much of our own intellectual energy would have been freed up to imagine and implement *good* projects, rather than just react to bad ones?

I'm afraid that the past few decades have taught American environmentalists how to be noble losers. Too often our best hope has been to slow the destruction and help nature unravel a little more gradually.[3] Environmentalists have identified the large-scale ecological problems facing humanity and chipped away at them around the edges. But we have failed to address these challenges comprehensively, much less solve them. The United States has tens of millions fewer acres of farmland and wildlife habitat than we did forty years ago at the start of the environmental movement. We generate over a trillion pounds more greenhouse gases per year than we did twenty-five years ago, when Americans were first widely alerted to the dangers of global warming.[4]

All this might have been quite different under a different demographic scenario; we will never know for sure. Instead, the United States chose continued population growth. Or rather, American *citizens* chose to stabilize our population by having fewer children, while American *politicians* overruled that choice and voted for more population growth via a greatly expanded immigration policy. Successive legislative measures that drastically increased immigration numbers after 1965 were presented initially as a means to create a racially fairer immigration system, and later as part of larger efforts designed to decrease illegal immigration (neither of which they accomplished). Ordinary Americans during this time never asked for continued population growth, regardless of what the business and political elites might have desired.

Today, having recorded four decades of sub-replacement level fertility rates for native-born citizens, we can confidently say that current US population growth is largely driven by immigration. (This fact is typically obscured because discussions of future population growth tend to start from the present and attribute recent immigration-driven population growth to native fertility. "Present" population momentum is divorced from immigration, but of course that momentum would not exist, or would be less, if recent immigration rates had been lower.) Figure 7–1 illustrates the role immigration will play in future population growth, with population projections to 2100 under zero annual net migration and four other immigration scenarios.

At zero annual net migration, the US population levels off around 2050 and then decreases to a little over 340 million people by 2100. Each additional half million in annual immigration will instead add an additional 72 million people to America's population by 2100. Continuing current

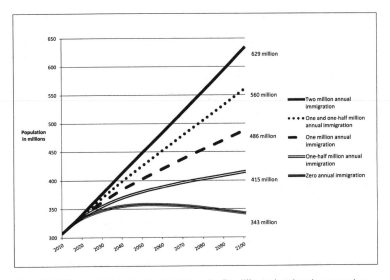

Figure 7-1. US population projections to 2100 under five different immigration scenarios.

Source: Author's projections using population projection tool developed by the Center for Immigration Studies, Washington, DC.

annual immigration levels of 1.1 million legal immigrants and several hundred thousand illegal immigrants (periodically legalized and in any case contributing children to the general population) will add hundreds of millions more people by the end of the century. Just as important, under any demographic scenario of continued mass immigration, the US population will still be growing rapidly in 2100 with no end in sight.

Immigration policy will thus determine whether America's population stabilizes or continues to grow during the current century, helping determine what the next several generations of American environmentalists will be able to accomplish. Problems like limiting greenhouse gas emissions or stopping habitat loss look very different depending on whether or not our population is growing, as we saw in the previous chapter. Whether American environmentalism will be pessimistic and reactive, or optimistic and agenda-setting in the coming decades also depends on underlying demographic realities. We seem unlikely to achieve our highest ambitions, such as restoring significant water flows to the lower Colorado River, in the context of a rapidly growing population.

Fortunately, America's demographic future is largely up to us, its citizens. With a current fertility rate slightly below replacement level, the

United States can achieve a stable population gradually, without coercion and without compromising our values or endangering important national interests. Furthermore, because almost half of all US births are unplanned or involve young single mothers, increased funding and better family planning services could well drive fertility rates even lower and allow us to gradually *reduce* our population, as part of an overall commitment to sustainability.

Many other countries do not have such a smooth path to population stabilization. Many developing nations have large juvenile age cohorts that will have to be digested (like our own baby boom had to be) before their populations can level off; some countries, particularly in Africa and the Middle East, labor under patriarchal cultural values that undermine family planning efforts.[5] Thankfully the United States does not have these problems. We have swallowed our baby boom and in recent decades, economic opportunities for women have increased markedly and relations between the sexes have become more egalitarian. Meanwhile after *Roe v. Wade*, American citizens are largely free to choose when and whether to have children (although barriers to free reproductive choice remain unacceptably high in some states). We have the opportunity to stabilize our population relatively quickly and easily. That is good news if we are serious about creating a sustainable society in the United States! Sadly, we have not taken advantage of this opportunity. To understand why, we must consider the conflicted history of the American environmental movement concerning population matters.

FROM EARLY CONCERN TO CURRENT SILENCE

US environmentalists' shunning of population issues is a relatively recent phenomenon. In the 1960s and 1970s, proponents saw US population stabilization as a key part of a complete environmentalism. Many of the founders of the environmental movement were biologists, who then as now tended to explain biological phenomena in terms of competition for finite resources. Wildlife biologists spoke of the "carrying capacity" of a given piece of land, meaning the number of elk or grouse that it could support given available resources such as food, cover, or nesting sites. It was natural for these writers to think of people as potentially pushing beyond nature's *human* carrying capacity and thus causing environmental problems. In addition, many of these scientists-turned-advocates were field biologists, intimately acquainted with wild nature. Love for the wild led many of them to question the justice of human over-appropriation of the habitat and resources that other species needed for their survival. Aldo Leopold, for example, wrote in *A Sand County Almanac* that a true "land ethic" must affirm every other species' "right to continued existence, and, at least in spots, their continued existence in a natural state."

The best-selling environmental tract of the 1960s was Paul Ehrlich's *The Population Bomb*, published in 1968. Ehrlich, an avian biologist at Stanford, had been encouraged to write the book by Sierra Club executive director David Brower. Environmental issues were its central focus, along with a concern with whether humanity would have adequate resources to feed a growing world population.

In Ehrlich's view, humanity's rapidly expanding numbers were at the root of our ever-increasing demands on the biosphere. These demands drove increased consumption and pollution that were likely to harm both future generations of people and many other species that competed for the same resources. Ehrlich and John Holdren (subsequently President Obama's senior advisor for science and technology issues) popularized a standard formula for considering human beings' environmental impacts: $I = P \times A \times T$, where P equals population, A equals per capita consumption or "affluence," and T represents the technologies used to provide our goods and services. Increasing either a nation's numbers or its affluence will tend to increase the human impact on the environment; increasing both intensifies that impact even more. Technological changes can help mitigate environmental impacts: witness catalytic converters, which have allowed the phasing out of leaded gasoline. But T (technology) cannot drive I (environmental impact) down to zero. Furthermore, technological innovations often *increase* impacts, as new technologies generate new pollutants or create new ways for people to use energy (as with the surge in electronic home appliances since the 1960s). Ehrlich emphasized that technology cannot be our environmental savior, particularly since technological changes are not typically driven by sustainability concerns, but rather by human desires and the profit motive.[6]

The Population Bomb had an enormous impact. Many people first learned about environmental problems through the book, thus emphasizing the connection between population stabilization and environmental protection. Paul Ehrlich appeared numerous times with Johnny Carson on the Tonight Show and became something of a celebrity. When the first Earth Day was held in 1970, many speakers around the country discussed the need for US population stabilization (this at a time when the US population stood at 208 million people, 112 million fewer than today).

In the late 1960s, Ehrlich and other environmentalists founded the group Zero Population Growth. ZPG's main goal was to work for population stabilization in the United States and around the world. As Roy Beck and Leon Kolankiewicz note in a study of the rise and fall of Americans' concern for overpopulation, during its early years ZPG was committed to an inclusive US population stabilization policy. "In the 1970s," Beck and Kolankiewicz write, "ZPG's population policy recommendations covered every contribution to U.S. population growth. It included stands on contraceptives, sex education for teenagers, equality for women, abortion, opposition to illegal immigration, and proposals to reduce legal immigration from about 400,000 a year to 150,000 a year by 1985 in order to reach zero population growth by 2008."[7] ZPG grew quickly and within a few years the group had hundreds of chapters on college campuses across the country.

Environmental groups in the 1960s and 1970s often took strong stands in favor of population stabilization. In 1969, for example, the board of directors of the Sierra Club "urged the people of the United States to abandon population growth as a pattern and goal; to commit themselves to limit the total population of the United States in order to achieve a balance between population and resources; and to achieve a stable population no later than the year 1990."[8] In 1978, the Club's board of directors urged the federal government to conduct a thorough examination of US immigration policies, their impact on US population trends, and how those trends affected the nation's environmental resources. Explicitly rejecting the notion that population growth was solely a Third World problem, the board stated: "All regions of the world must reach a balance between their populations and resources."[9]

Once again, in 1980, Sierra Club representatives argued for immigration reduction, this time before the US Select Committee on Immigration and Refugee Reform (popularly known as the Hesburgh Committee). "It is obvious," they testified, "that the numbers of immigrants the

United States accepts affects our population size and growth rate. It is perhaps less well known the extent to which immigration policy, even more than the number of children per family, is the determinant of future numbers of Americans." It is an "important question," Club representatives continued, "how many immigrants the United States wants to accept and the criteria we choose as the basis for answering that question." And they stood up for an *ecological* criterion, stating, "Immigration to the U.S. should be no greater than that which will permit achievement of population stabilization in the U.S."[10]

*

How times have changed! Today American environmental groups are largely silent regarding US population growth. Of the five or six "majors" (the largest, most influential national environmental groups), most take no position on domestic population growth; it simply goes unmentioned. Several do have general statements regarding the need for US population stabilization, but they do not detail their positions on what domestic population policy should look like. This is in great contrast to energy policy, transportation policy, or natural lands management policy. Although they are mostly headquartered in Washington, DC, and employ staff to lobby Congress, none of these groups lobby on behalf of domestic population stabilization.

Above all, environmental groups big or small almost never touch immigration issues. In 1996 the Sierra Club Board of Directors quietly moved to reverse club policy on immigration, passing a resolution stating: "The Sierra Club will take no position on the issue of immigration into the United States." Around the same time, the group Zero Population Growth dropped most of its work on US population issues and altered its stated goal from "stopping" to "slowing" world population growth. ZPG also changed its name, one of the most vivid and well recognized among nonprofit advocacy groups, to the anodyne Population Connection ("PC" for short).[11]

When the US population crossed the 300 million mark in 2006, no major environmental group issued a statement expressing worry about this slide away from sustainability. In 2007, as Congress considered supposedly "comprehensive" immigration reform legislation, environmental impacts were not among the issues addressed. None of the majors weighed in on the competing proposals, although which one was actually enacted could have made a difference of hundreds of millions more or fewer Americans by the end of this century. In 2013, the Sierra Club and several smaller groups actually supported an immigration bill in the Senate that would have greatly *increased* annual immigration levels, describing it as an immigrants' rights bill while carefully avoiding any mention of its demographic implications.[12] Judging by media coverage in 2007 and 2013, reporters and commentators on immigration reform apparently felt no need to consider this legislation's impact on overall population numbers, or the impact of those numbers on the environment.

The reasons for this retreat from a concern with US population growth are complex and warrant further study. Key reasons for environmentalists' retreat, according to Kolankiewicz and Beck, included declining fertility among US citizens (leading many to conclude that "zero population growth" had been achieved), the heating up of anti-abortion politics, and a focus on women's empowerment rather than on limiting births at the international level, which in turn affected domestic efforts.[13] This last development made any talk of population *control* anathema, and any suggestion that women should have fewer children appear an intolerable interference with their right to have as many children as they wanted.[14]

Most important in this retreat, I believe, was the simple fact that immigration had replaced native fertility as the main factor driving US population growth. Immigration policy in the US links up with racial issues in ways that make progressives uncomfortable. As Kolankiewicz and Beck write, during the 1970s, "at the same time that American fertility declines were beginning to put population stabilization within reach, immigration was rising rapidly to three or four times traditional [pre-1965] levels. During the first decade [after these trends began] some groups directly advocated that immigration numbers be set at a level consistent with U.S. environmental needs." But over the next few decades that advocacy ceased. According to Kolankiewicz and Beck, environmentalists began to worry "that immigration reduction would alienate progressive allies and be seen as racially insensitive." Today, they write, "some environmental leaders express fear that if they are perceived as anti-immigrant, a backlash against environmentalists could develop among immigrants and their US-born descendants."[15] Given current demographic trends, these leaders worry that their groups will lose members and influence over time, if newly numerous groups think of them as bigoted or unconcerned with their interests.

Long-time Sierra Club executive director Carl Pope had lobbied in the 1970s for reducing immigration into the United States. But in 1998 when members placed an initiative on the ballot to reinstate a commitment to immigration reduction, he led the charge against the initiative, which was defeated. Pope said that "he used to agree . . . that immigration should be cut for environmental reasons. But he changed his mind because he didn't believe it possible to conduct a public discussion about immigration cuts without stirring up racial passions." In a statement to the membership, Pope wrote:

> While it is theoretically possible to have a non-racial debate about immigration, it is not practically possible for an open organization like the Sierra Club to do so . . . the desire for rational debate does not yield a rational debate in the public arena of America today . . . [Recent history in California has] caused me to change my view of whether it is possible for the Sierra Club to deal with the immigration issue in a way which would not implicate us in ethnic or racial polarization.[16]

Left unaddressed was whether environmentalists' political goals could actually be achieved in a context of continued domestic population growth, or whether club members washing their hands of the issue would lead to a less racially charged discussion of immigration policy in the United States.

ENVIRONMENTALISTS' OBJECTIONS TO ADDRESSING IMMIGRATION

In researching this book, I interviewed several dozen Sierra Club leaders active at the state and local levels, many of whom participated in the immigration debate in 1998 or in subsequent discussions. I also conducted additional interviews with environmentalists from several other organizations. These interviews confirmed my initial sense that it is above all the racial aspects of the debate that tend to drive environmentalists away from domestic population matters. Some of my interview subjects supported the Sierra Club's retreat from immigration politics (these interviews were conducted before the Club's recent re-entry into immigration debates in favor of *more* immigration), while others thought it had been a mistake. But almost all of them exhibited some degree of discomfort with the issue.

"The debate gets so cantankerous and aggressive," noted one Club activist.[17] "It became very ugly," remembered another, about the 1998 discussions, "and I'm a social worker! I'm about as far from a racist as you can get. It was very uncomfortable and is not an area of my expertise."[18] To call a person or their policy proposal "racist" is a sure conversation stopper in progressive political circles. Noted another participant: "A lot of times, these debates devolve into accusations of racism." According to him, many people simply opted out of the 1998 debate because "they didn't want to deal with the possibility of being called racists."[19]

Another concern that I often heard invoked in my interviews was the apparent selfishness of limiting immigration. One long-time Club activist, who stated that "we ought to be rigorous in enforcing our immigration laws that restrict immigration," nevertheless remarked: "The fact that I was fortunate enough, I believe, to have been born on the north side [of the US/Mexico border, and] other people were unfortunate enough to have been born on the south side, strikes me as unfair, just a stroke of luck."[20] Another said, "My great-grandparents and a grandmother were immigrants and I feel hypocritical saying to other people, 'you shouldn't be here.'" [21]

Some interviewees who voiced these concerns nevertheless believed that American environmentalists still had to press on and take a stand for reducing immigration. They felt that population growth was too important and too powerful in undermining key environmental goals not to do so. Others, however, as orthodox progressives, simply could not accept the idea of limiting opportunities for poor people trying to better their lot. Some argued directly on this basis for an expansive immigration policy, while others took refuge in the position that environmentalists should steer clear of advocating any particular immigration policies.

These worries regarding racism and selfishness are important ones, which I propose to treat at length in chapter 10 ("Objections"), focused specifically on the moral objections to limiting immigration. Progressives are right that a fair and racially impartial immigration policy is absolutely essential; however, I think that is most likely to be achieved through free and open debate. Avoiding the issue won't help, and in fact represents an abdication of our responsibility as citizens. I believe Americans can craft an immigration policy that is fair to all concerned, but not one that will make everyone happy, because a commitment to fairness does not magically nullify limits to growth or banish hard choices regarding how to divide up limited resources. In the end, I argue that a reasonable reduction in immigration can be accomplished in ways that are fair toward would-be immigrants, while excessive immigration represents an injustice toward poorer Americans, toward other species, and toward future generations here and abroad.

For now, though, let's return to the interviews I conducted with environmentalists and consider some specifically *environmental* reasons that my respondents gave for supporting or at least tolerating continued high levels of immigration into the United States. Because these counterarguments recur regularly in discussions about whether or not to limit immigration for environmental reasons, they deserve our attention.

CONSUMPTION, NOT POPULATION

One commonly heard argument says that we should focus on excessive consumption, not overpopulation, as the root cause of our environmental problems. As Michael Kellett, the executive director of the small, scrappy group RESTORE: The North Woods put it in an interview, "Obviously, population has an impact" on the environment: the more people, the greater the impact. "But it is not really population *per se*, it's wasteful and exorbitant use of natural resources." Kellett, whose work focuses on protecting forests in Maine, noted that a lot of trees harvested in the northeastern United States "go to make catalogues" that flood people's mailboxes. "It's just waste," he said, "that has nothing to do with population, really."[22]

I heard such arguments repeatedly in my interviews, coupled with the suggestion that environmentalists redouble our efforts to get Americans to cut their consumption of goods and services. These arguments are appealing because they seem to put the responsibility for change where it belongs, not on poor immigrants but on average Americans, who in fact do consume too much, and who in many cases could consume less without harming their quality of life. But as we saw in the previous chapter, it is Americans' *overall* consumption that determines our environmental impact. Overall consumption equals *per capita* consumption multiplied by population. So if high consumption levels are a problem, then population growth must necessarily be one, too.[23] Just because we need to consume less does not mean that more people will not consume more. In fact, we know that more people *will* consume more, all else being equal.

In a variation on this theme, it is sometimes asserted that immigrants, or recent immigrants, consume less than the average American. One problem with this argument is that there are apparently no good figures comparing immigrants' and native-born Americans' consumption patterns. But the main problem is that it focuses on a moment in time, rather than thinking through the full, long-term effects of immigration-driven population growth.

Immigrants' lower consumption levels, if they exist, are presumably a function of their relative poverty. Indeed, immigrant doctors and software engineers who can afford to buy big houses and fancy cars tend to do so, just like wealthy native-born Americans. However, immigrants are not coming to America to live in poverty, but rather to consume like Americans: to achieve "the American dream" and pass greater opportunities on to their children and grandchildren. Two million more immigrants this year may mean ten million more Americans one hundred years from now, and if history is any guide, those ten million Americans will live pretty much like other Americans. The descendants of last century's Jewish and Italian immigrants do not consume less than the average American today; there is no obvious reason to think that the descendants of today's Mexican and Chinese immigrants will consume less than the average American one hundred years from now.

The key point is that if American consumption levels are too high, the problem is only made worse by population growth. Since both overpopulation and overconsumption drive our environmental problems and since neither of these problems appears likely to solve itself, focusing exclusively on one or the other dooms our efforts to failure.

Another argument made by many American environmentalists is that overpopulation is important, but it is a global rather than a national issue, that can be solved only through international action. The world's population increased by about 83 million people in 2010 and 95% of that increase occurred in the developing world.[24] Rather than cutting immigration to keep our own population from growing, they argue, we should fund family planning programs overseas. We should advocate for more education for girls and increased rights and economic opportunities for women—steps that have proven successful in driving down fertility rates in many countries around the globe. If we do these things, we will act humanely and help both poor people and the environment.

Before analyzing this argument, we should pause for a moment to appreciate its oddity. No one argues: "Deforestation is a global problem, therefore we should not worry about deforestation in our own country, or on the local landscape." Or: "Species loss is a global problem, therefore we should fund species protection efforts everywhere but where we live." On the contrary, those who care about deforestation or species extinction often work especially hard to prevent them in the places they know best and are applauded for doing so. Besides, "global" efforts to halt deforestation and species loss are largely a summing up of local and national efforts focused on particular forests and species. This is how environmentalism works, when it works. Advocates for an exclusively global approach to overpopulation owe us an explanation for why this one issue should, or could, play out differently, while still leading to environmentally acceptable results.

Comforting as it is, the globalist argument fails, partly because it mischaracterizes overpopulation, which in fact can occur at various scales. It makes sense to say: "The world is overpopulated: we do not know whether essential global ecosystem services can be sustained at these numbers over the long haul." But it also makes sense to say: "Tokyo is overpopulated: its sidewalks, streets, and trains are so crowded that there is no room to move." Or: "Nigeria is overpopulated: its population is so large and growing so fast that it has trouble providing jobs for its young adults, or building sufficient water and sewer facilities for its cities." And just as Tokyo's citizens may try to alleviate local air pollution and Nigeria's citizens may try to protect their remnant forests, so they may try to address local or national overpopulation. After all, they will have to live directly with their failure to do so and they cannot wait for the world to solve all its problems before they act to solve their own.

Returning to the United States, the third most populous country in the world, a strong case can be made that we are overpopulated right now. Signs of stressed ecosystems and lost biodiversity abound. Certainly we have not yet found a way to bring air and water pollution within limits acceptable to human health. Nor have we stemmed the loss of productive farmlands and wildlife habitat. Nor have we succeeded in shrinking the dead zone at the mouth of the Mississippi River, now the size of New Jersey and growing. Nor have we recovered more than a handful of the many hundreds of species we have endangered. And as we will see when considering global climate change in the next chapter, a large and growing population also makes it much harder for Americans to live up to our environmental responsibilities as global citizens. It is hard to reduce your global ecological footprint with ever more feet.[25]

Let me be clear: I believe advocates for international action are correct that wealthy countries should help poor countries stabilize or reduce their populations, provided the citizens of those countries want to do so. Rapid population growth remains a terrible problem in many developing countries. Increasing financial and logistical support for family planning is an effective form of foreign aid that can bring great environmental and social benefits to poor people around the world.

However, "think globally, *don't* act locally" is terrible advice, and hypocritical to boot. Americans do have significant international environmental obligations, but our primary responsibility (and best opportunity to actually meet our international obligations) is to create a sustainable society right here in the United States. In any case, it is possible and necessary to work on multiple levels at once. We can make more generous contributions to the United Nations Population Fund *and* cut back on US immigration levels *and* limit local building permits. Successful efforts at one level and in one place strengthen efforts at other levels and in other places. *Failures* at one level or in one place undermine efforts at other levels and in other places.[26] Meanwhile population growth is a problem in America right now. If you live in the United States, the chances are good that your community is threatened by environmentally damaging development that is being caused (or justified, in the planning stages) by population growth.

IMMIGRATION JUST MOVES PEOPLE AROUND

In a third argument, some environmentalists assert that immigration "just moves people around," so it is, or may be, environmentally neutral. As a reader of an early paper I wrote on this topic commented, "Efforts to reduce overpopulation in New York or the United States do not help alleviate overpopulation worldwide, because people who aren't let in have to go someplace else." Added another reader, "Ecological damage may be worse if people remain in their home countries rather than immigrating to the US. Immigration restrictions seem to privilege the USA's wild places over other, perhaps more biodiverse, places around the world."

Now, I have to plead guilty to a special concern for America's wildlife and wildlands. But I do not apologize for it. Environmentalism necessarily involves love, connection, and efforts to protect particular places. Progressives should think long and hard before advocating anything that weakens this local focus, because a passionate connection to places that are near and dear to us is how environmentalism works, in Boston or Beijing. This does not involve believing American (or Chinese) landscapes are more intrinsically valuable than others, but acting *as if* they are the most important landscapes in the world and using our most accessible political levers to protect them. Again and again, my interviews with environmental leaders confirmed the importance of local environmental connections in motivating their activism. For all these people's sophisticated understanding of national and international environmental policy issues, for all their efforts to think globally, a personal connection to nature typically emerged as the basis for their activism. And such personal connection is almost always particular and local.

However, cosmopolitan readers who reject my parochial concern for American landscapes should still support proposals to reduce immigration into the United States, since doing so would also benefit the rest of the world.[27] This is because moving people to America, far from being environmentally neutral, greatly increases overall global resource consumption, pollution, and habitat loss. This in turn threatens to compromise the already-stressed global ecosystem services that all people depend upon,

Table 7-2 Average ecological footprint of citizens of the United States and its ten largest immigration source countries, in global hectares per person.

	% of US immigrants, 2000–2010	Cropland and grazing land footprint	Forest use footprint	Carbon footprint	Total ecological footprint
United States	. . .	1.22	1.09	5.57	8.0
Mexico	29.3	1.03	0.19	1.18	2.6
China and Taiwan	5.4	0.64	0.15	1.21	2.2
India	4.5	0.39	0.12	0.33	0.9
The Philippines	4.4	0.50	0.09	0.32	1.3
Vietnam	3.1	0.53	0.17	0.45	1.4
El Salvador	3.0	0.77	0.41	0.64	2.0
Cuba	2.8	0.77	0.11	0.76	1.9
South Korea	2.6	0.83	0.26	3.17	4.9
Dominican Republic	2.2	0.55	0.11	0.72	1.5
Guatemala	2.1	0.55	0.56	0.49	1.8

Source: Demographic information from Steven Camarota, "A Record-Setting Decade of Immigration: 2000–2010," table 7; footprint calculations from Global Footprint Network, "National Footprint Accounts." Note that several more categories are included in calculating total ecological footprints, so rows in the table do not add up.

with the world's poorest people facing the greatest danger from possible ecological failures.

Consider Table 7-2, comparing the average American's "ecological footprint" with the averages from our ten largest immigration source countries.

On average, immigrating from nine of these ten countries greatly increases an individual's ecological footprint and the ecological footprints of his or her descendants. In the case of Mexico, which accounts for nearly a third of all immigration into America, immigration increases individuals' consumption and pollution by about 200%. These tens of millions of people use *a lot* more water, *a lot* more fossil fuels, and *a lot* more other resources than they would have had they stayed in their countries of origin. There might be cases where immigrants consume more but do less ecological damage than they would have had they remained at home (slash-and-burn agriculturalists inhabiting biologically rich forests, perhaps) but if such cases exist, ecological footprint calculations strongly suggest that they are the exceptions. More Americans is bad news for America's native flora and fauna. But given global climate change it is also bad news for poor people living in the Sahel or in the Bhramaputra

Delta. Given declining ocean fish stocks it is bad news for Indonesians, Vietnamese, or Filipinos, whose limited protein intake is heavily dependent on ocean fish. Every nation on Earth would benefit ecologically from a smaller US population.

If emigration helped America's source countries get their own demographic houses in order, or opened up an ecological space that they used to create more sustainable or just societies, a case might be made for continuing to allow mass immigration into the United States. But it isn't. Instead, America's permissive immigration policies appear to enable demographic and ecological irresponsibility and continuing social injustice in these countries. As an example, consider Guatemala, where currently about 10% of the adult population lives and works in the United States and a recent poll showed that a *majority* of young Guatemalans hope to do so in the future. Guatemalan women's fertility rates averaged 4.15 children between 2005 and 2010, driving an annual population growth rate of 2.5% per year.[28] The Guatemalan government outlaws abortion except when a mother's life is at risk and does little to encourage contraception. Guatemala has high deforestation rates and an unjust, highly inequitable distribution of wealth. But there is little effort to change any of this, perhaps because the negative effects of local overpopulation are lessened through immigration and counterbalanced, for many individuals, by the positive incentives of having more remittances from family members in the United States.

Similar remarks hold true for Mexico, where corruption and gross economic inequality greatly limit many people's hopes for building a decent life. Mexico's ruling elites have resisted more fairly sharing their country's wealth, preferring instead to send their fellow countrymen and countrywomen north.[29] The many millions of industrious, hard-working Mexicans who fled to the United States over the past four decades could have been powerful advocates for justice and fairness within Mexico. Instead of picking lettuce, cutting lawns, and making beds in America, these strivers might have fought for opportunities and rewards within their own country. They could have helped to make it a better place: one where wealthy Mexicans treated their fellow citizens with dignity and respect, and where fewer inhabitants wanted to leave. I am not saying such reforms would have been easy or assured, and we'll never know what might have been, because for so many people it was easier to leave. Numerous individual

Mexicans benefited by abandoning their country, but it seems likely that Mexico as a whole was harmed.

A final rebuttal to the argument that immigration is environmentally neutral is that in many cases "just moving people around" appears to *increase* overall population growth. The clearest example again involves Mexico, whose government, starting in the 1980s, instituted relatively effective family planning programs that significantly reduced birthrates. The average number of children born to Mexican women decreased from more than five in the 1950s to 2.4 children today.[30] Surprisingly though, mass immigration has helped undermine this achievement: studies have found that Mexican immigrants in the United States have averaged 3.5 children per woman in recent years, *much higher than in their home country*.[31] Perhaps immigrants' greater wealth in the United States releases them from economic constraints that are helping bring down fertility rates in Mexico. Whatever the explanation, in this case, which covers almost one-third of all immigration into the United States, mass immigration greatly increases both per capita consumption and the total number of persons in North America as a whole.

In the end, we cannot really decouple global population and environmental issues from exclusively American ones. They are interconnected and American citizens have responsibilities regarding both. The question is how to understand the linkages between the two and how to best respond to all our responsibilities. My contention is that current US immigration policies are bad both for the United States and for the world as a whole. Whether we are thinking as inhabitants of our local towns or watersheds, as patriotic eco-nationalists, or as cosmopolitan citizens of the world, more Americans is an environmental disaster.

EFFICIENCY, NOT POPULATION

A final environmental argument against reducing mass immigration is that with greater efficiency in energy use, resource use, and land use, the United States could accommodate further population growth and still improve our environmental stewardship. Readers who are active environmentalists probably will have heard versions of this argument in other contexts. "We do not need to cut back on farm, industrial, or residential water use; instead, better irrigation practices, more efficient management, and innovative water sharing agreements will allow us to increase all these uses, at least for now." "We do not need to drive less or use fewer electric appliances to curb global climate change; instead, more fuel-efficient cars and smarter appliances will allow us to decrease emissions even as our consumption of goods and services increases." Perhaps the highest development of this approach is found in the books of the *New York Times'* Thomas Friedman, who can rhapsodize for many pages over smart appliances, smart resource management, and various other technological and managerial innovations, but who has never, to my knowledge, stopped to ask whether it is smart to keep increasing human numbers and per capita resource demands while trusting to new technologies and organizational improvements to keep our ever-more-complex life-support systems humming smoothly.

The appeal of this approach is no mystery. It allows people to display environmental concern while continuing to overconsume or maximize profits. In place of hard choices among various resource users, it promises "win/win solutions" that improve everyone's well-being, while patting us all on the back for being so clever. When I asked Gary Lindstrom, a Sierra Club member and former county commissioner in rural Colorado, whether the United States could continue to grow economically and demographically and still create a sustainable society, he responded with an emphatic: "Yes! And the way we do that is we become more creative, more innovative." "The amount of knowledge we have is growing by leaps and bounds," he told me. "We'll have cars that get one thousand miles to the gallon. Technology is going to be our savior."[32] Optimism is an attractive trait, but taken too far it shades over into irresponsibility.

While Friedman and Lindstrom seem to advocate efficiency and better management in order to prop up the pro-growth status quo, including high levels of consumption, other environmentalists whom I interviewed expressed disdain for American consumerism and made this an integral part of their arguments for continued mass immigration.[33] Americans consume so much, they argued, that there is room to cut back and accommodate more people, while still reducing overall consumption and keeping everything within sustainable limits. Progressives who make this sort of efficiency argument, not to justify continued high levels of consumption but to accommodate poor people from other countries, perhaps strike a higher moral tone.

Here, though, a little realism is in order, whether we are cornucopians or moralists. It is unlikely that environmentalists can convince our fellow Americans to cut back drastically on their consumption for *any* reason, much less in order to cram tens of millions more foreigners into the United States (incremental decreases in consumption for clear and specific benefits are another matter). We also need to acknowledge that it is working-class Americans, not "the one percent," whose incomes are being reduced by mass immigration. In this way high immigration levels cut consumption by the poor while increasing consumption by the rich, who as we saw earlier benefit the most from reduced costs for goods and services. These are hardly the kind of consumption changes sought by most progressives. Realistically, too, there is great uncertainty about what levels of population and consumption really are sustainable over the long term. As already noted, some scientists who have looked into these matters believe we are much too populous and consume and pollute far too much already for our own safety.[34]

Finally, we need to recognize the way efficiency improvements tend to be swallowed up by growth, leaving environmentalists empty-handed and other species simply out of luck. River conservationist Tim Palmer recently discussed an example from his own career in California that is worth considering.

"After thousands of dams had been built through the 1960s, people began to realize the tremendous detrimental effects on rivers, fish, and whole landscapes, and a movement grew to protect the best rivers that remained," Palmer writes:

A powerful political alliance was driven away from the old pork barrel politics and spending on dams. The demand for water was still enormous and expanding with no end in sight, but rather than make more water available via new dams or take it from other people, a strategy was pursued to make improved use of the water we already had. These efficiency efforts paid off and use of water, *per capita*, declined by 20 percent nationally between 1980 and 1995. In California, per capita use was halved over 40 years.

But here's the catch: population growth has rendered the savings almost meaningless. In the same fifteen-year period, the national population increased by 16 percent, and in California's last 40 years the population nearly doubled. Water shortages have increased and they require unpopular adjustments by farmers and consumers, while still spelling ruin to whole ecosystems from the Sacramento Delta to Apalachicola Bay.

Even though much of the low-hanging water-saving fruit has been picked, we can probably cut the current use in half once again. But by the time we do that the population is likely to double for a second time. With the numbers of people outstripping the amounts of water saved, we'll be back in the same place where we started, except with less potential for further conservation and with a lot more people waiting in line for water. In the end, we will not have protected wild rivers, spared endangered species, or saved public money as we had intended, but will have principally served to make more population growth possible. Then, the momentum to grow will be even greater. . . . The point here is that many people sought to do something good in conserving water, something of lasting value. But nothing can truly be protected if the source of the threat continues to grow.[35]

Palmer is not arguing against efficiency improvements; he has pushed hard for them throughout a distinguished environmental career. His point is that efficiency improvements must be combined with limits to what we demand from nature if we hope to achieve real, lasting environmental protection. By themselves they will not lead to sustainability, or a fair sharing of resources with other species. The story is similar when we turn from water use and river conservation to energy use and climate change, or land use and urban sprawl. Efficiency without an "enough" somewhere only facilitates more growth, uses up any margin of error, and locks in a belief in the possibility and goodness of perpetual growth. All this makes it harder, not easier, to create genuinely sustainable societies.

Efficiency arguments for continuing mass immigration into the United States are perhaps best seen as the progressive counterpart to conservative arguments for continuing to push for increased consumption, profits, and wealth under the endless growth economy. Progressives may feel more comfortable, or nobler, making the immigration argument, but they are just as unrealistic in their failure to confront limits to growth. Indeed, if climate change denial is the prime example of conservatives' inability to confront limits, the denial of the environmental harms of immigration-driven population growth may be the prime example on the progressive side.[36]

*

At this point, a caveat is in order. We do not want to overreact and imagine population is the sole determinant of ecological sustainability; that would be just as mistaken as dismissing its importance altogether. Effective environmentalism must rein in consumption *and* population growth, in the fast-growing United States *and* in fast-growing developing nations. It must achieve efficiency improvements *and* set reasonable limits to demographic and economic growth. All this is a mighty tall order, but only such an inclusive strategy has any hope of achieving lasting success.

Working through the ecological objections considered above should confirm that we need an honest reckoning with limits if we hope to achieve progressive environmental goals.[37] A lot of these objections—what the heck, let's call them excuses—equivocate or try to finesse growth issues. That will not work. We need to accept limits to growth in order to create sustainable societies. And like charity, such acceptance begins at home.

Of course, Americans should do what we can to help other countries move toward sustainability and justice, whether that means increasing funds for green development projects, or shutting off the safety valve that allows political elites to postpone economic reforms. But I am convinced that our primary moral responsibility is to create a sustainable and just society right here in the United States. Not just because we have special responsibilities and opportunities to act in our own country (although we do), but because proper action at home is the main way we may further our responsibilities as global citizens. Perhaps most significant would be the powerful example of the world's wealthiest nation rejecting the path of endless growth and embracing sustainability and economic fairness instead. Limiting immigration into the United States and stabilizing our population would send a powerful message around the world that the time to create just and sustainable societies is now.

CAN WE TALK?

As we have seen, many environmentalists are leery of talking about immigration or about population matters more generally. I noted earlier Carl Pope's view that the Sierra Club could not have a "non-racial debate" about immigration matters, or discuss them without furthering racial polarization. Weighing in on the controversy at the time, the head of ZPG, Peter Kostmayer, made a similar point. Speaking to members in West Virginia in 1998, Kostmayer answered a question about immigration this way: "Let me be frank. You are a wealthy, middle-class community, and if you concentrate on the issue of immigration as a way of controlling population, you won't come off well. It just doesn't work."[38]

Pope and Kostmayer were no doubt correct, on one level. Anyone who argues for reducing immigration into the United States opens up himself or herself to charges of racism and selfishness. In the same way, anyone who argues for protecting wildlands throws himself open to the charge of being an elitist who cares more about animals than people. Anyone who argues for stronger environmental regulation of business or a more equitable distribution of wealth risks being called a "commie." So be it. One hundred years ago even the most conservative labor leaders were often termed "reds," while progressive reformers who took on the urban political machines of their day were derisively labeled "goo-goos," because they were proponents of good government.

In the past, environmentalists' answer was not to throw in the towel in the face of such charges, but to redouble their efforts to end population growth and protect the environment. To run from name-calling is to court irrelevance. Besides, there seems something pernicious in the assumption that certain policy debates are off-limits to American citizens, simply because they cannot discuss them without accusations of racism, or worse, having the debate hijacked by actual racists. Such self-censorship hits at a core value of environmental groups, which are an integral part of contemporary American democracy. There can be little doubt that in the past racial concerns played an excessive role in American immigration debates. The right response to this would seem to be to consciously downplay the racial aspects of the topic and debate immigration policies on their merits, including their ecological merits. I think public-spirited environmentalists and other progressives are fully capable of doing so (that's why I wrote this book!). If we want to de-racialize discussions of immigration and not just wash our own hands of the issue, these are the very people we need to hear from.

Of course, debating immigration policy and overpopulation is contentious and difficult. But that just confirms that getting to sustainability will be difficult, a fact that serious environmentalists already knew. I think we need more discussion of such difficult issues, not less, because we have hard choices to make and because the path toward true sustainability is not fully clear. We need to find ways to promote justice and value racial diversity, while also respecting ecological limits. Hard work, no doubt, but it's our work. Whether or not we are comfortable doing so, American environmentalists need to discuss immigration.

eight

DEFUSING AMERICA'S POPULATION
BOMB—OR COOKING THE EARTH

After decades of debate, the facts regarding global climate change have come into clearer focus, thanks largely to the work of many thousands of the world's scientists. According to the Intergovernmental Panel on Climate Change's Fifth Assessment Report, published in 2013 and 2014, we now know the following:

- The Earth grew roughly 1.35°F hotter on average over the past century, with greater warming at the poles, and this warming trend is accelerating.
- Recent global warming has been caused primarily by human activities—not natural climate cycles, sunspots, God's righteous anger, or anything else the deniers would have us believe. About 75% of human contributions have come through increased greenhouse gas emissions and about 25% have come through land use changes, particularly deforestation and soil erosion. Atmospheric concentrations of the three most important greenhouse gases (carbon dioxide, methane, and nitrous oxide) are higher than they have been for the past 800,000 years or more.
- If emissions continue to increase we can expect even higher temperatures and more chaotic weather in the years ahead. The greater the emissions, the greater the likely temperature increases and the more

extreme and unpredictable the weather. If instead we drastically cut greenhouse gas emissions, leave the world's remaining primary forests standing, and significantly improve bad land use practices, we can avoid much of the climate change that would occur under "business as usual."

- "Global warming" involves a lot more than higher average worldwide temperatures. Climate change is also leading to rising sea levels, more frequent and severe storms in many parts of the world, the mass extinction of many species of plants and animals, increased ocean acidification, and numerous other problems. And climate change will likely provide significant surprises in coming centuries, many of them unpleasant. For all these reasons, a better term than global climate *change* might be global climate *destabilization* or global climate *degradation*.[1]

How worried should we be about all this? Very worried. According to the IPCC, climate change threatens the well-being and even the survival of hundreds of millions of people, through increased risk of malnutrition and starvation, and increased frequency of deadly weather events. An earlier report predicted that in Africa, "by 2020, between 75 million and 250 million are projected to be exposed to an increase in water stress due to climate change. . . . In some countries, yields from rain-fed agriculture could be reduced by up to 50%. Agricultural production, including access to food, in many African countries is projected to be severely compromised. This would further adversely affect food security and exacerbate malnutrition." Meanwhile in Asia, "coastal regions, especially heavily-populated mega-deltas in South, East, and Southeast Asia, will be at greatest risk due to increased flooding. . . . By the 2050s, freshwater availability in Central, South, East and South-East Asia, particularly in large river basins, is projected to decrease."[2] Those most threatened by climate change tend to be among the Earth's poorest people, whose poverty leaves them with insufficient protection against potential climate ills and who bear little to no responsibility for causing the problem.

Grave as these threats are to people, the dangers to other species from climate change are even greater, since beyond harms to individual organisms they threaten to extinguish whole species on a mass scale. Again according to the IPCC, "by midcentury, increases in temperature and associated decreases in soil water are projected to lead to gradual replacement of tropical forest by savanna in eastern Amazonia. . . . There is a risk of significant biodiversity loss through species extinction in many areas of tropical Latin America." Halfway around the world, in Australia, "significant biodiversity loss is projected to occur by 2020 in some ecologically rich sites, including the Great Barrier Reef."[3] By threatening the greatest reservoirs of natural diversity on land (tropical forests) and in the ocean (coral reefs), climate change bids fair to accelerate the sixth great mass extinction in the 700-million-year history of complex life on Earth. Recent scientific assessments confirm that climate change and other anthropogenic ecological stressors have the potential to extinguish half or more of Earth's species during the lifetimes of children living today.[4]

Nothing mortifies American environmentalists more than our country's failure to do its part to limit global climate change. The United States is the world's historically largest greenhouse gas emitter, responsible for about 30% of total world carbon emissions between 1750 and 2010. Today, with less than one-twentieth of the world's population, we contribute nearly one-fifth of its annual greenhouse gas emissions, the second most in the world after China. We thus bear a large responsibility for causing the problem.[5] With the world's biggest and most innovative economy, however, we could also be a big part of the solution.

Instead, America has led the world ever deeper into an uncertain and possibly catastrophic environmental future. This has been a bipartisan failure. Both Democratic and Republican leaders have done little to reduce America's energy consumption or greenhouse gas emissions. In its place they have worked to keep gasoline prices low and open up new areas for oil and natural gas drilling. Even worse, the United States has actively impeded other countries' efforts to act more decisively. Under George H. W. Bush and again during his son's two administrations, US negotiators worked to prevent international agreements that included binding national commitments to decrease carbon emissions. President Obama has continued this diplomatic policy, most recently in climate negotiations in Warsaw in 2013, substituting concerned platitudes for significant action to address the problem. The Obama administration has also vigorously opposed European Union plans to reduce greenhouse gas emissions in aviation by taxing airplane flights, signing legislation prohibiting American airlines from paying the tax.[6]

Along with misguided energy and transportation policies, US population policies have played an important role in this failure. In recent decades, Congresses led by both parties have repeatedly increased annual immigration levels, committing the United States to continued rapid population growth. This in turn has pushed US carbon emissions higher. Between 1990 and 2003, US *per capita* CO_2 emissions increased 3.2% while *total* US CO_2 emissions increased 20.2%.[7] Why the discrepancy? Simple. During this same period, America's population increased 16.1%, primarily due to immigration.[8] More people drove more cars, built more houses, took more vacations, and did more of the many things that emit carbon. Population growth accounted for about four-fifths of increased CO_2 emissions during this period, while individual consumption growth accounted for only one-fifth.

Policy analysts around the world are beginning to wake up to the importance of ending population growth in order to deal successfully with climate change. A study several years ago from the London School of Economics entitled "Fewer Emitters, Lower Emissions, Less Cost" found that reducing global population growth, through improving women's educational opportunities and providing inexpensive contraception, was cheaper than most other climate mitigation alternatives currently under consideration. These population reduction efforts also increase the freedom and opportunities available to women and couples, while decreasing the whole range of human demands on the environment—truly a win/win scenario.[9]

Such studies have tended to focus on the developing world, where most population growth now occurs. But because the rapidly growing United States has the third largest population in the world and our consumption levels are very high, curbing US population growth turns out to be especially important to worldwide emissions reduction efforts. Another study, published in 2008, concluded that "the impact of immigration to the United States on global [greenhouse gas] emissions is equal to approximately 5 percent of the increase in annual world-wide CO_2 emissions since 1980." Note, immigration-driven US population growth caused 5% of *total worldwide* CO_2 emissions increases during this period, not 5% of *American* CO_2 emissions increases.[10] As a contributing factor to climate change, American population growth is on a par with deforestation in the Brazilian Amazon and first car purchases in China.

I believe that justice demands vigorous action from this current generation of Americans to prevent potentially catastrophic climate change.[11] For ourselves and our children, for the sake of the world's poorest people, for future generations, and for the sake of other species, we need to act now.[12] And beyond questions of justice, it's in Americans' common interest that we come together on this issue. After all, there is only one atmosphere that we all share: you, me, Al Gore, and Rush Limbaugh. Republicans and Democrats will both suffer if recent megastorms like Katrina and Sandy multiply and increase in intensity, or if large parts of Florida and Louisiana sink beneath the waves. We also remain part of a larger world where benefits and harms routinely cross borders, and disasters visited on one country tend to radiate outward and affect the well-being of their neighbors.

The case for action seems overwhelming. Yet American efforts have come up short; largely, I believe, because both progressives and conservatives have been reluctant to embrace limits to growth. Progressives have a greater willingness than conservatives to discipline individual economic behavior and limit corporate profits in service to the common good, so they have been somewhat more disposed to consider measures to combat climate change that might slow economic growth. Few progressive politicians, however, are prepared to stray far from the orthodox position that fostering economic growth should be the primary goal of government policy. And when it comes to population growth, the other primary driver of increased carbon emissions, progressives appear less willing than conservatives to consider alternatives to continued growth. Yet as we will see, if Americans are serious about meeting our global environmental responsibilities, the multiplier effect of population growth is simply too important to ignore.

REDUCING EMISSIONS SUFFICIENTLY WHILE DOUBLING OUR POPULATION: IMPOSSIBLE, OR JUST EXTREMELY UNLIKELY?

In order to avoid the worst harms threatened by climate disruption, participants in the United Nations Framework Convention on Climate Change, including the United States, have formally committed to work to prevent average global temperatures from rising more than 3.6°F above twentieth century baseline temperatures. In order for the United States to do our part to achieve this goal, plausible analyses suggest that we will need to reduce annual greenhouse gas emissions to approximately one-fifth of current levels over the next five decades.[13] That is a huge decrease, although credible pathways for reaching it have been sketched out using existing technologies.[14] Meeting such an ambitious goal or even more modest ones, however, will prove more difficult the more America's population continues to grow.

Consider the numbers. United States' greenhouse gas emissions were approximately 6700 million metric tons (CO_2-equivalent) in 2011.[15] With a population of 315 million people in 2011, that averages out to 21.3 tons of emissions per person per year. By hypothesis the United States needs to decrease our annual emissions by four-fifths by 2063, to 1340 million metric tons. How much of a per capita decrease would that involve?

At a population of 315 million people we would have to decrease annual emissions to 4.3 tons per person per year. But remember, even with no further immigration, the US population is set to increase to 357 million people by 2063. So we would have to decrease per capita annual emissions to 3.75 tons to bring overall US emissions down to that acceptable total of 1340 million metric tons. Instead of an 80% decrease in per capita emissions we will need an 82.5% per capita decrease.

That would be with no further immigration. Now recall that the United States takes in far more immigrants than any other country in the world. At current levels of immigration our population will increase much more, to 444 million people by 2063. Factoring in current immigration, we would have to decrease per capita annual emissions to 3.0 tons to bring overall US emissions down to our acceptable total: an 86% decrease in per capita emissions.

That would be at current immigration levels. But recent reform legislation, which passed the Senate in 2013 and has a real chance of becoming law as I write these words, would increase immigration to about 2.25 million immigrants per year. In that case, the US population would be projected to increase to 513 million people by 2063 and we would have to decrease per capita annual emissions to 2.6 tons. Rather than the 80% reductions needed with a stable population, we would be faced with achieving an 88% decrease in per capita emissions in order to bring annual US emissions down to our target of 1340 million metric tons.

Now let's ask: how much harder might immigration-driven population growth make reducing total US greenhouse gas emissions the necessary four-fifths over the next fifty years? Our current immigration path would necessitate 20% lower per capita emissions than under zero net immigration (3.0 tons per capita versus 3.75 tons), while increasing immigration along the lines of the Senate's 2013 bill would require 31% lower per capita emissions (2.6 tons versus 3.75 tons). As a first approximation, then, we might say that at current immigration levels population growth will make it 20% more difficult for Americans to do our part to sufficiently mitigate global climate change, while a more expansive immigration regime could make it 31% more difficult to do so. Arguably, these figures should provide reason enough for progressives concerned about climate change to support reducing immigration into the United States. However, our analysis so far probably significantly understates the impediments to success caused by immigration-driven population growth, for several reasons.

The problem of achieving sufficient emissions reductions is compounded by the fact that at any particular time, each successive "slice" of reductions is more costly, assuming that we rank-order our important emissions reduction choices and implement the cheapest ones first. Measures to decrease current greenhouse gas emissions 10% would likely *save* American consumers money, due to efficiency gains and pollution reduction benefits. But the next 10% would likely cost a significant amount, the next 10% reduction would cost much more, the following 10% much, *much* more, etc. At some point, further reductions may be technically impossible. Before that point is reached they would likely have become prohibitively expensive.

Similarly, each succeeding slice of reductions is likely to demand more in the way of behavioral changes from Americans. The first 10% or 20% in emissions reductions might require little change beyond a willingness to pay a small amount for various efficiency improvements. But at some point, if we want to reduce emissions far enough, we will have to demand real sacrifices from people: either forcing them to spend big money for the efficiency improvements they need to continue behaving as they have, or forcing them to behave differently (drive smaller cars or take public transportation, eat less meat or forgo unnecessary plane flights, etc.). Again, at some point further behavioral-based reductions may not be possible, and long before then they would probably have become impossible to achieve politically.

The key point is that beyond some relatively easy initial steps, the deeper the emissions cuts, the more sacrifice they will entail. So the figures of 20% and 31% probably significantly underestimate how much more demanding immigration-driven population growth will make the emissions reductions desired by US environmentalists. Such population growth could easily make it two or three times more difficult to achieve our emissions reduction goals, in terms of the monetary costs or lifestyle changes demanded. Immigration-driven population growth thus makes it much less likely that Americans will achieve those goals. After all, we already have ample evidence of our fellow citizens' unwillingness to make significant behavioral changes or sacrifice financially in order to address climate change.

It is even possible that continued population growth could make it physically impossible to adequately reduce US greenhouse gas emissions, even if Americans were to suddenly wake up to our moral responsibilities and try very hard to meet them. The maximum number of people that can be sustained over the long term in modern, industrialized societies requiring high levels of energy use to sustain a high standard of living for their members is simply unknown. There is considerable evidence that even current population numbers around the world are much too high, if people hope to sustain themselves in safety and comfort without resorting to levels and kinds of energy use that are toxic to the environment.[16]

*

"Aha!" a progressive critic might respond at this point. "Now you have shown your true colors. You are willing to sacrifice nature, poor immigrants, or both, in order to sustain "the American way of life." But it is precisely this wasteful and thoughtless way of life, in America and around the world, which has caused the problem in the first place. We can and should cut US energy use and carbon emissions drastically over the next five decades. The technologies exist and America is wealthy enough to meet our moral obligation to address climate change. Above all, the problem is Americans' hoggish overconsumption."

Point taken. I agree that limiting consumption must play a major role in reducing US greenhouse gas emissions.[17] American progressives should work to enact policies that reduce excessive consumption as much as possible. Such policies should include increased taxes on fossil fuels, redirecting transportation funding away from highway construction to mass transit, heavy subsidies for wind and solar power, big increases in auto fuel standards (thankfully recently enacted by the Obama administration), improved building codes that reduce the energy needed for heating and cooling, and more.

However, re-engineering the world's largest economy and changing the consumption patterns of hundreds of millions of people are immense undertakings that will be difficult, expensive, and (we may assume) only partly successful. Even if such efforts succeed beyond our fondest hopes, change will take time. For example, we cannot just snap our fingers and create hundreds of thousands of wind turbines, millions of solar panels, and the additional power lines necessary to carry their electricity hundreds of miles to our cities. Can we decrease Americans' greenhouse gas emissions 86% or 88% per capita over the next fifty years? In theory, maybe, but in practice, probably not. In practice, there are bitter fights over doing anything of substance to deal with the problem.

Whether environmentalists win large or small per capita reductions in greenhouse gas emissions over the next five decades, those reductions would accomplish more if we could stabilize our population, or cut back significantly on its growth. If Al Gore is right that global climate change is "the moral challenge of our time,"[18] shouldn't we be doing everything within reason to help meet it — including halting our population growth? Instead, at current immigration levels our population will grow 41% between 2013 and 2063. We will need to run fast just to stay in place. Clearly, continued population growth ratchets up the likelihood that the United States will fail to do our part to sufficiently mitigate global climate change.

Please note that I do not claim that by itself, stabilizing America's population will meet our responsibilities in this area, any more than I think it will stop sprawl, end air and water pollution, or solve our other environmental problems. Americans must reduce our per capita energy consumption in order to meet the climate change challenge. On the other hand, the evidence clearly shows that recent population growth has increased Americans' total energy consumption and amplified the impacts of our gluttony. Addressing both excessive consumption *and* overpopulation are necessary, if we hope to create a sustainable society and do our part to create a sustainable world. However, developing a sane view of growth and implementing it politically are a lot easier said than done, for reasons that are worth exploring.

GRAPPLING WITH GROWTH

There is a curious disconnect in climate change discourse between explanations of its causes and discussions of possible solutions. On the one hand, it is widely acknowledged that the primary causes of global climate change are unremitting economic and demographic growth. As the IPCC's Fourth Assessment Report succinctly put it: "[increased] GDP/per capita and population growth were the main drivers of the increase in global emissions during the last three decades of the twentieth century. . . . At the global scale, declining carbon and energy intensities have been unable to offset income effects and population growth and, consequently, carbon emissions have risen."[19] On the other hand, most proposals for climate change mitigation take growth for granted and focus on technical efforts to ameliorate its negative effects.

Climate scientists speak more formally of the "Kaya Identity" (developed by Japanese energy economist Yoichi Kaya): the four primary factors that determine overall greenhouse gas emissions. They are economic growth per capita, total population, energy used to generate each unit of GDP, and greenhouse gases generated per unit of energy. In recent decades improvements in energy and carbon efficiency have been overwhelmed by increases in population and wealth. Here are the numbers, again according to the IPCC: "The global average growth rate of CO_2 emissions between 1970 and 2004 of 1.9% per year is the result of the following annual growth rates:

population +1.6%,
GDP/per capita +1.8%,
energy-intensity (total primary energy supply [TPES] per unit of GDP)
    −1.2%,
and carbon-intensity (CO_2 emissions per unit of TPES) −0.2%."[20]

Crucially, the IPCC's projections for the next several decades see a continuation of these trends. More people living more affluently mean that under "business as usual," greenhouse gas emissions will probably double sometime during the next half century, *despite expected technical efficiency improvements.*[21] If we allow this to occur, it will almost surely lock in global temperature increases of more than 3.6°F over pre-industrial levels, exceeding the threshold beyond which scientists speak of potentially catastrophic climate change.

A reasonable person reading the scientific literature on climate change would likely conclude that humanity is bumping up against physical and ecological limits right now. Given the possible dangers, a prudent response might be: "Wow, this is going to be hard! We need to start working on this problem with all the tools at our disposal. Increasing energy and carbon efficiency, to be sure. But also decreasing consumption, reining in the pursuit of affluence, and reducing human populations now, slowly and humanely, before nature culls our numbers abruptly and harshly. Maybe in the future we can grow like gangbusters again. But for now people need to make fewer demands on nature. After all, our situation is unprecedented—over 7 billion people, most living or aspiring to live in modern, industrialized economies—and there is good evidence that we are already in overshoot mode." Such convictions would only be strengthened by considering further evidence of global ecological degradation from the *Millennium Ecosystem Assessment*, including the depletion of important ocean fisheries, accelerating soil erosion, ongoing species extinctions throughout the world, the growth of immense "dead zones" at the mouths of many great rivers, and more. According to the MEA, humanity is currently degrading or utilizing unsustainably fifteen of twenty-four key ecosystem services.[22]

However, climate change and our other global environmental problems have been slow to spur a widespread re-evaluation of the goodness of growth.[23] A few old-line environmentalists have continued to insist that limits to growth are essential to an intelligent environmentalism.[24] In a hopeful sign, in recent years they have been joined by a small but growing group of "ecological economists" who believe that creating ecologically sustainable economies depends on accepting limits to wealth, human numbers, and material throughput within human economies, and that such economic reforms can be implemented in ways that actually improve people's quality of life.[25] But for now, such challenges to growth are little more than stirrings among the intelligentsia, at least in the United States. The broader political debate regarding climate change has focused on techno-fixes and efficiency solutions: among politicians, scientists, and even environmentalists, who really should know better. The reasons are not hard to discern.

Humanity has created a dynamic world economy with unprecedented powers of wealth creation, and people want that ever-increasing wealth. Our political discourse now centers on economic growth: in America, as in many other countries, the major political parties vie with one another concerning which one can ratchet it up most quickly. Growth is seen as an unalloyed good, inevitable, or both, and policy discussions take place within that framework. Most Americans literally cannot conceive of any alternative to prioritizing growth. In any case, big money dominates the political process in the United States, and big money wants continued, rapid economic growth.

Conversations about limiting *population* growth, meanwhile, push buttons on both the left and the right. Significant numbers of conservatives oppose legalized abortion, increased funding for contraception or family planning, and sex education in public schools, all of which have been proven to decrease unplanned and unwanted pregnancies. Among progressives, proposals to reduce immigration have become toxic for reasons we explored in the previous chapter. Immigration expansionists have not been shy about playing the race card, leading to a relatively uninformative debate about immigration matters among progressives and hence to a weak, unbalanced immigration debate among Americans generally. Population-related issues tend to be discussed in isolation and with little understanding of how they add up to a de facto US population policy: one which will make a profound difference to how many people live in the United States fifty and one hundred years from now. In turn, this limits any discussion about how overall numbers might constrain Americans' options as we respond to social and environmental challenges like climate change, and prevents Americans from considering how population policy might further the common good.

*

In the face of this political reality, environmentalists have generally been careful to frame their calls for climate action in ways that emphasize that the challenge can be met without slowing growth or lowering standards of living. In fact, they often claim, global warming is chock full of economic opportunities! On the website for Al Gore's earlier initiative Wecansolveit.org, the section proposing "Solutions" for a "Clean Energy Economy" exclaimed: "Thousands of new companies, millions of new jobs, and billions in revenue generated by solutions to the climate crisis — this is the clean energy economy we can adopt with today's technologies, resources, know-how, and leadership from our elected officials." It continued: "A recent report showed that investment in a clean and efficient economy would lead to over 3 million new green-collar jobs, stimulate $1.4 trillion in new GDP, add billions in personal income and retail sales, produce $284 billion in net energy savings, all while generating sufficient returns to the US treasury to pay for itself over ten years." Note the politician's traditional promise of something for nothing; no need for sacrifice here. The website concluded: "This is the opportunity of our generation — to lead the transformation to an economy that is robust without causing environmental harm."[26]

Or consider the rhetoric of another climate action champion, former Colorado Governor Bill Ritter. "Global warming is our generation's greatest environmental challenge," Ritter stated in his introduction to the *Colorado Climate Action Plan* released in 2007. "Can Coloradans really make a difference? I believe we can, and that we have a moral obligation to try." But again, he assures us that meeting this moral obligation will not involve excessive costs, or personal sacrifice. "[Our] success depends on everyone doing his or her part. We can reduce global warming and keep our economy strong and vibrant. This is an exciting time for Colorado as we look toward an expanded New Energy Economy with new jobs, new businesses and new investments."[27]

There are often good practical reasons to emphasize self-interest and economic benefits in talking to our fellow citizens. If Americans think the only way to do our part to stop climate disruption is to give up our cars, or keep our houses heated to 55°F during the winter, we probably will not make the effort. If enough people believe they will benefit economically from greatly ramping up our use of renewable energy, we may be able to make that new energy economy a reality. Al Gore alerted tens of millions of people around the world to the need to rein in climate change, while Bill Ritter helped Colorado usher in some of the most far-reaching alternative energy mandates in the United States. Those were real accomplishments. Score two points for the power of positive thinking.

However, an *exclusive* reliance on such tactics engenders two worries. First, they probably do not support all the measures needed to adequately address our environmental problems. What happens when mitigating global climate change doesn't save people money or contribute to growth, but instead costs them money or inhibits growth? Second and more fundamentally, this approach's boosterism seems likely to solidify the economic paradigm that is causing climate change and our other environmental problems in the first place, and further entrench the economic mindset which makes it so difficult to solve them. Can we really "expand" our economies and keep them "vibrant and strong" (i.e., growing even more) while also "reducing global warming"? Can an economy really be "robust [that is, rapidly growing] without causing environmental harm"? The evidence suggests not, starting with, well, *global climate change,* which the IPCC tells us has been caused primarily by rapid population growth and a swiftly growing world economy. According to the US Department of Energy, "Economic growth is the most significant factor underlying the projections for growth in energy related carbon dioxide emissions in the mid-term, as the world continues to rely on fossil fuels for most of its energy use."[28]

Pushing the "green and growing" mantra postpones a necessary conversation for Americans, in which we reconsider and perhaps redefine "growth." The United States is a mature country. The frontier was settled long ago. We can continue to grow in all sorts of ways: morally, intellectually, spiritually, creatively. It would be great if we grew in our understanding and appreciation for nature and in our willingness to share the Earth with other species. But piling up more possessions or cramming ever more people onto the American landscape do not appear compatible with these kinds of moral and intellectual growth. Whatever we might say about previous historical periods, focusing on increasing our wealth or our numbers no longer makes sense in the United States. Such growth has clearly become toxic to the ecosystems that, despite all our technological achievements, we remain dependent on for our survival and flourishing.

Why resist the most important economic lesson global climate disruption has to teach us? The endless growth economy is unsustainable and must be replaced by a fundamentally different alternative. I know that's a scary thought. But it also could prove a liberating one, if the next few generations take creating a truly sustainable economy as the twenty-first century's great challenge and opportunity.

Mainstream economists insist that economic growth itself need not increase greenhouse gas emissions, habitat loss, species extinctions, or other environmental harms. But an economy that continued to grow yet which did not increase resource demands or pollution would be a fundamentally different economy from the one we have today. Whether or not such a growing yet environmentally benign economy is possible, the evidence strongly suggests that conventional economic growth, the kind that is actually on offer today, is ecologically toxic. Creating a truly sustainable society in the United States is incompatible with continuing to try to maximize such growth.

Mainstream economists also rightly remind us that economic growth need not depend on population growth. Countries can combine stable or even slowly declining populations with significant economic growth, a combination we see today in Germany, the fifth largest economy in the world, and elsewhere. But in practice, the desire to maximize economic growth has been used to justify pro-natalist policies in many parts of the world where people are freely choosing to have fewer children. An unwillingness among business interests to accept slower economic growth appears to lie behind many countries' attempts to reverse stable or declining population trends, as documented in a recent proliferation of stories in the business press.[29] In the United States and elsewhere, the desire to increase economic growth is often explicitly cited in support of expanding mass immigration.[30]

Americans need to shift out of the endless growth economic paradigm, if we hope to avoid the worst of global climate change and meet our other social and environmental challenges. I am an optimist: I believe we can do this while creating a more just and flourishing society.[31] But the political path forward, focused less on economic growth and increased consumption, and more on creating stronger communities and increasing human well-being, is not yet obvious. This makes it even more important to tackle the other key aspect of growth—population growth—that would be much easier to end.

Here I challenge a common assumption among American environmentalists, that ending population growth would be much harder than convincing people to consume less. But think about it: while most Americans today would probably reject any effort to end the full-bore pursuit of economic growth, an overwhelming majority think that the United States has a sufficiently large population right now. If you don't believe me, ask the next ten people you meet whether they think their city or town would be a better place to live in with twice as many people. Shifting from an immigration-fueled, endless-growth demographic model to a stable population could be achieved simply by reducing immigration levels and continuing legal access to birth control and abortion, all measures that are supported by a majority of Americans. With a fertility rate below replacement rate (2.05 at last measurement), the United States is poised to enter a period of demographic stabilization—if our politicians follow their constituents' lead, revise immigration policy, and allow us to do so.

Ending US population growth would also remove an important incentive for maximizing economic growth: the need to create jobs for an ever-growing number of people. Combined with a stronger social safety net, stabilizing our population could set up a "virtuous circle" in which Americans evolved beyond our current materialistic concentration on increased wealth and consumption. We could instead focus on building better communities and on growing morally and intellectually, in our relationships with one another, and in our understanding and appreciation of the world around us. Isn't that the kind of growth we really want?

A COMPREHENSIVE SOLUTION

Effective US action to combat global climate change must attack the problem with all the means at our disposal. We should develop and implement technological innovations to increase efficiency, make serious efforts to cut unnecessary consumption, and stabilize our population as quickly as possible. Paul Ehrlich and John Holdren had it right over forty years ago: Impact = Population × Affluence × Technology. Failure to attend to any one of these three causative factors undermines actions focused on the other two.

Consider automobiles, which contribute roughly one-quarter of current US greenhouse gas emissions. If we support the wrong technologies, as we did for much of the 1980s and 1990s when Americans purchased vast fleets of gas-hogging SUVs, then our greenhouse gas emissions will soar. Yet if we keep increasing the number of miles we drive (increased *per capita* consumption), then technological improvements in fuel efficiency will be negated. Finally, if we increase our population by hundreds of millions more people over the next century, as we are on track to do, then even if Americans drive hybrid cars fewer miles per person, the savings will be swallowed up by more people driving more cars.

So, we will need a comprehensive approach. On the technological side, we will need cars and trucks that get more miles per gallon, and more-energy-efficient buildings and appliances. We will need to replace hundreds of coal-fired power plants with solar, wind, geothermal, and natural gas-generated electricity. We will need to deploy new tillage and forestry practices that better sequester carbon in soils and trees. And more. On the consumption side, we will need to drive and fly less often. We will need to use less water and less paper, spray fewer chemicals on our lawns, and put fewer plastic doo-dads in our children's Christmas stockings. And more. Finally on the population side, we will need to continue to have small families, fund family planning services, and keep abortion safe and legal. And we will need to reduce excessive immigration rates. This will allow us to stabilize or reduce our population while encouraging other countries to do the same.

The temptation will continue to be to focus exclusively on technological fixes. We should avoid this temptation! Remember: $I = P \times A \times T$.

Drastically limiting greenhouse gas emissions relatively quickly, in ways that will cost people money and perhaps significantly impact their lifestyles, will be a lot to ask of Americans, who have not been asked to sacrifice much for the common good in recent years. I believe we are up to the challenge. But it's hard to imagine sustaining a significant society-wide commitment to combating climate change if we continue policies that encourage rapid population growth.

How can environmentalists ask our fellow citizens to drive their cars fewer miles, or pay significantly more for gasoline as part of a nationwide effort to decrease total miles driven, if *at the same time*, we import tens of millions of people to drive more cars? How can we ask them to scale back their air travel, or pay significantly more for a flight as part of a nationwide effort to decrease total miles flown, if *at the same time*, we encourage more air travel by importing tens of millions of potential flyers? How can we ask them to pay more for electricity, or for food or wood products that are grown in ways that better sequester carbon, if *at the same time*, we increase demand for electricity, food, and wood products by greatly increasing the American population? Under these circumstances, requesting Americans to significantly decrease their own energy use borders on the absurd.

Eventually Americans will have to end population growth if we hope to keep total US greenhouse gas emissions within reasonable limits. This follows as a matter of simple math, once we accept the fact that there is no way to get to zero per capita emissions. In a similar way, there is no way to get to zero per capita water use, zero per capita wildlife displacement, or zero per capita for any other important human impacts on the landscape. We can work to lessen these per capita impacts and a lot of good environmental work consists in precisely such efforts. But the bottom line is that Americans cannot get our environmental house in order with an endlessly growing population. Why wait until later, then, to deal with population matters? Better that serious environmentalists bite the bullet now and advocate for domestic population stabilization as part of a broad effort to limit climate change and deal with our other environmental problems. Like climate change itself, the longer we put off dealing with population matters, the more difficult they become and the worse our choices.

*

Put this way, most environmentalists tend to agree. "Of course," my green friends say, "we cannot reduce personal environmental impacts to zero. Eventually, more and more people will destroy everything we care about and wind up creating a barely habitable planet for these immense crowds of people." And yet when I look at how environmentalists actually discuss issues and spend resources, there appears to be little recognition of these facts.

Sprawl is bad, the big environmental groups tell their members, worthy of million dollar anti-sprawl campaigns. But they accept the number one cause of sprawl by far, population growth, and agree to work around it. Water pollution is bad, whether it comes from farms, factories, electricity plants, or new oil and gas wells. But there's no mention that a bigger economic infrastructure will be necessary if we have to accommodate lots more people, and that it's bound to generate some pollution. The Keystone XL oil pipeline, proposed to run from the Alberta tar sands to the Gulf of Mexico, is very, very bad, repeated "action alerts" from the Sierra Club inform us. But there's no recognition that tens of millions more Americans will need to get oil from *somewhere* to run our cars, even if many of us switch to hybrids. (Meanwhile the Club curries favor with Hispanic advocacy groups by backing an immigration reform bill that would increase America's population even more, in the process joining forces with corporate America in support of faster growth and the continued exploitation of low-income workers.)

When it comes to domestic population growth, American environmentalists have gone AWOL. Meanwhile successive Congresses and Presidential administrations have pursued immigration policies leading directly to continued rapid population increase in the United States. These policies are set and implemented without any consideration of their ecological impacts. We are in the curious position of needing multimillion-dollar environmental impact statements to decide whether to build a single dam or add another lane to a particular highway in the United States, but not for choosing population policies that will determine whether *hundreds* of new dams and highways will be needed in the future.[32] What sense does that make?

CONCLUSION

Environmentalism encompasses a myriad of concerns, from air and water pollution to transportation and zoning policies, from parks and wildlands protection to the preservation of endangered species. But at its core it can be summed up by the phrase "generous sustainability" and defined in terms of two overarching goals: creating societies that leave sufficient natural resources for future human generations to live good lives; and sharing the landscape generously with nonhuman beings.[33] Environmental protection thus conceived is no mere amenity, but an essential part of the progressive vision, because it is crucial to securing the conditions necessary for the happiness and flourishing of future generations.[34] A strong environmentalism, with a realistic view of limits, can help us create ecologically sustainable societies and achieve our progressive political goals. But we cannot do so within a context of endless population growth. It simply will not work.

I am an environmentalist. So I lobby politicians on particular issues and walk door to door to help elect the good ones. I write checks to environmental groups and opinion pieces for the local newspapers, analyze dry technical documents and send in comments to the Forest Service and the Corps of Engineers. I do these things in hope that they will help create a sustainable society and conserve the landscapes that I have come to love. In particular, I want to protect the Cache la Poudre River, the same river along which I have bird-watched and skipped stones with my sons on so many mornings. If my neighbors and I can save our river, if we succeed in building a community along its banks that lives in harmony with its wildlife, and if in 30 years I can walk with my wife along its banks and point out ospreys and river otters to my grandchildren, then I will be ready to die a contented man. That will be enough.

Creating such communities, preserving what is most precious today, and providing opportunities for future generations are the ultimate goals of environmentalism. It's about so much more than just finding a way to cram as many people as possible onto the landscape without everything collapsing. Managing ever-larger herds of people in dull, completely artificial environments will not secure a decent future for people, let alone all the other beautiful and interesting creatures with whom we currently share the planet.[35]

So let's turn over a new leaf, and build societies where our children and grandchildren can live well with nature and with each other. Let's create communities along the banks of the Cache la Poudre and the Oconee Rivers, the Connecticut and the Colorado, the Yangtze and the Irrawaddy, that achieve real sustainability and justice. Ending human population growth is one key to doing so. In the United States, that means significantly reducing immigration.

nine

SOLUTIONS

Mass immigration no longer makes economic or ecological sense for the United States. The question is how best to reform immigration policy so as to further the common good, while treating everyone involved fairly.

Clearly the overall number of immigrants into the United States needs to be reduced—but by how much? Currently immigrants enter the country under a number of different programs and quotas—should some of these be eliminated and the system simplified? Under any plausible immigration regime, immigration laws will need to be enforced more effectively—but how can this be done while still respecting people's rights and without creating onerous bureaucracies? Finally, what should be done about undocumented immigrants—some of whom have been in the United States for decades or have children who are American citizens? These are some of the questions that need to be answered if our consideration of immigration reform is to be truly comprehensive.

MY PROPOSAL

If you have read this far you probably will not be surprised that I believe immigration should be reformed in ways that increase wages for poorer Americans, reduce economic inequality throughout society, and help make possible ecological sustainability. That means, above all, reducing the number of immigrants allowed into the United States. In line with these goals, I propose the following seven steps to reform United States immigration policy:

1) Initiate a temporary moratorium on all non-emergency immigration, to last until unemployment falls below 5% nationally and remains there for three consecutive years.

2) Cut legal immigration permanently, from 1.1 million to 300,000 per year (the approximate rate in 1965, when Congress began significantly increasing immigration levels).

3) Reduce illegal immigration by mandating a national employee verification program and strictly enforcing criminal sanctions against employers who hire undocumented workers.

4) Pass carefully targeted amnesties to regularize the status of long-time illegal residents, particularly children whose parents brought them to this country at an early age.

5) End birthright citizenship for the children of foreigners living in or passing through the United States.

6) Rework trade agreements and increase well-targeted development aid, to help poor people around the world live better lives in their own countries.

7) Revisit immigration policies periodically and revise them so as to further the common good, in line with progressive principles of justice and sustainability.

These policy changes would allow many of the benefits of immigration to continue, such as providing asylum for genuine political refugees, accommodating family reunification while ending chain migration, and allowing small influxes of workers with special skills. At the same time, they would help the United States move in a more progressive direction politically, particularly if they were combined with the right economic policies. By pointing the way toward a more just and sustainable human presence on Earth, these immigration policies would be good for America and good for the rest of the world. In what follows, I elaborate on these seven steps and consider some possible objections and alternative proposals.

GOAL 1: TIME OUT

As I write these words, the official (U-3) unemployment rate stands at 7.0% nationally. The true unemployment rate is much higher: the current U-6 unemployment rate, which includes workers who have been unemployed long-term, those who have given up looking for work, and those working part-time who would like full-time work, is 13.2%.[1] Millions more Americans are working temporary jobs, or jobs far below their qualifications. Meanwhile the forecast is for relatively "jobless" economic growth in the coming years, meaning that the numbers of unemployed workers are likely to come down only slowly, at best.[2] Tens of millions of Americans will probably still be vainly searching for adequate work two years from now, as they are today.

In such a situation it makes no sense to continue to import a million new workers annually. Yet that is what the United States did in 2008, 2009, and 2010, in the midst of the most severe economic downturn since the Great Depression. It is what we are poised to do in 2015, 2016, and indefinitely into the future, under the status quo. Despite persistent unemployment in recent years, successive American administrations and Congresses, both Republican and Democratic, have encouraged millions of job-seekers to come to our country and fill jobs needed by American citizens. That's just plain wrong.

There can be legitimate disagreement over where to set immigration levels in normal years; legitimate disagreement over how to weigh wage increases versus economic growth, or the labor needs of growing businesses versus the ecological needs of ecosystems. But I cannot see how Americans can support the mass importation of labor at a time when so many of our fellow citizens are hurting economically. Our neighbors are not only losing their jobs, but often their homes, their marriages, and their families, due to financial reverses. Millions of Americans desperately need work. Given how slow the economy has been to create jobs, we should take all possible steps to ensure that what jobs this country has to offer go to citizens and legal residents, including the millions of previous immigrants who are also looking for work.

For this reason, we need an immediate moratorium on all non-emergency immigration (with exceptions made for legitimate political refugees and asylum seekers), or at least a moratorium on all non-emergency immigration by immigrants of working age. How long such a moratorium should last is open to debate. Economists typically view some level of unemployment as normal in a complex, evolving economy; they sometimes speak of 4% to 5% unemployment as "acceptable." (Acceptable to whom is a fair question: it is likely that most economists define acceptability more from the perspective of the rich than the poor, employers rather than employees. But let's assume that 5% unemployment is acceptable.) Progressives should propose that all non-essential immigration be frozen until the official unemployment rate falls to 5% nationally and remains there for three consecutive years.

Of course, when you read these words, economic conditions will be different than when I wrote them. Things may have improved and the sense of urgency to create jobs may have abated. On the other hand, the situation may be even worse and people may be even more desperate. Simply put, my proposal is that *the unemployment rate should make a difference to immigration levels*. Our government should consider whether conditions are better or worse for American job-seekers and set immigration levels accordingly. In fact, there have been various proposals to consider economic conditions when setting immigration quotas, as part of recent immigration reform plans; depending on the details, such proposals may have merit. Here I merely suggest that in particularly grave situations, where poorer Americans are suffering economically, non-essential immigration should be temporarily halted.

Some progressives may reject this proposal on the grounds that it will harm potential immigrants. After all, in a global recession, poor people in Mexico or the Philippines may be even more desperate for work than poor Americans. They and their children may be even more exposed to hardship, because of greater poverty or weaker government safety nets. But here, I think, Americans may be faced with a tough choice. We can set immigration policy to help our fellow citizens, or the citizens of other countries. If we cannot help both groups find jobs in the United States, then I believe we have a moral obligation to help US citizens first (see the following chapter for a more extensive defense of this position). If we want to help people from Mexico or the Philippines (as we should), then we need to help them in ways that do not harm the poorest Americans in the process.

If America were such an economic dynamo that it could create jobs for the whole world (including our own citizens) and *if* the resultant population increase caused no grave ecological problems, then I think mass immigration into the United States might well be justified. But these conditions do not hold. The ability of the US economy to create jobs is limited and continued population increase will make achieving ecological sustainability in the United States impossible. In our finite world, every nation must limit its population in order to have a reasonable hope of taking care of its own citizens and not becoming a burden on the rest of the international community. American elites should not attempt to solve the world's unemployment problem while profiting at the expense of their fellow citizens. It's wrong, and it won't work.

Furthermore, when Vietnamese citizens decide how many children to have, or people from El Salvador debate whether contraception or abortion should be legal in their country, I believe they should do so with a full understanding of the consequences and a willingness to bear those consequences themselves. One-tenth of adult Mexicans now live in the United States, while about 12% of Filipinos live and work abroad. Arguably mass emigration from these countries encourages their citizens to engage in irresponsible procreation decisions and allows their governments to support unsustainable population policies. In the long term, this is bad for them, bad for us, and bad for the world as a whole. It would be better if Americans set an example of a country willing to grapple sensibly with limits: one that can preserve economic opportunities for its citizens while fashioning a genuinely sustainable economy. It would be better if our immigration policies increased other countries' incentives to do these things, too.

The idea of a moratorium on immigration until conditions improve in the United States could be pushed considerably further. For example, if our main concern is the welfare of poorer American workers, we might prohibit immigration of less-skilled workers until such time as labor markets tighten sufficiently to increase wages for the lowest quintile of workers by 20% or 30%. If our main concern is growing inequality in the United States and we know current immigration policies further inequality, we might prohibit immigration until such time as we have successfully reduced income inequality to the levels seen in the 1960s or 1970s, or to the current levels in the European Union or Japan. If our main concern is ecological sustainability, we might prohibit immigration until such time as the United States was demonstrably living within our environmental means: not degrading essential ecosystem resources or driving other species to extinction.

I believe these longer, more expansive moratoriums might be justified. However, they would shift the status quo so much that they would probably be rejected by most Americans. In contrast, I have found that the idea of a short pause in immigration, until unemployment declines sufficiently so that poor Americans can find jobs and support their families, meets with widespread approval. It is simply a matter of helping fellow citizens and legal residents who are already here, and that is an attainable goal with broad appeal across the political spectrum.

GOAL 2: REDUCE LEGAL IMMIGRATION

Assuming decent economic conditions and relatively low unemployment, how many immigrants should we let into the United States annually? From the perspective of poor American workers, the optimum number of immigrants is probably zero. That is the number that would do the most to tighten up labor markets in the short term, raising their wages. It is also the number that would spur society to educate and train their children to take up more highly paid jobs in the future. From the perspective of other species, the optimum number of immigrants likewise would be zero. That is the number that would best limit further human appropriation of landscapes and resources that other species need for their own survival. From the perspective of general sustainability, the optimum number of immigrants would also appear to be zero. Both human and nonhuman flourishing depends, long-term, on Americans creating a genuinely sustainable society and it is not clear that we have the will to do so even at our current population.

On the other hand, there are some important benefits to immigration that need to be considered. Immigration can reunite family members (after previous immigration has split them apart). It can help create new families, when people of different nationalities decide to marry. Immigration can provide a safe haven for political refugees who cannot return to their own countries. In these ways immigration benefits individuals. In addition, immigration benefits our nation as a whole, by bringing in new energy and new perspectives. As the proponents of mass immigration often remind us, immigration is an important part of our country's history and our national identity. All this argues for allowing a reasonable amount of immigration to continue.

I propose that we cut legal immigration from the current 1.1 million per year to 300,000 per year. This would still be 50% above the average level allowed during the four decades prior to 1965. I further recommend that we reserve most of these slots for those who most need them: binational couples who want to marry and settle in this country; refugees who cannot return home safely; and spouses, parents, and young children who want or need to be reunited. This will allow us to meet some of the most important interests involved without undermining our country's economic and ecological well-being. It will allow us to continue to offer significant opportunities to poor people from around the world, without doing so at the expense of poor American citizens and previous immigrants. It will allow for some "new blood" while also helping rein in unsustainable population growth.

From 1.1 million to 300,000 annually is a steep cut, but I think the case for it is clear. Less sweeping changes are possible. We could, for example, cut immigration in half, as recommended in 1997 by the US Commission on Immigration Reform (commonly called the Jordan Commission after its chairman, liberal icon Barbara Jordan),[3] or by even smaller amounts. Such measures would slow growing inequality and rapid population growth and would to that extent be improvements over current policy. But as progressives, we should be committed to *reversing* these trends, not just slowing them down. Accomplishing that will require firmer action.

How would such cuts look in detail? As previously discussed, legal immigrants enter the United States under a complicated system of quotas and programs, with annual immigration numbers over the past three years breaking down approximately as follows[4]:

Family-sponsored	710,000
Refugees and asylum seekers	160,000
Employment-based	145,000
Diversity programs	50,000
Other minor categories	25,000
Total legal immigration:	1,090,000

I suggest changing these numbers along these lines:

Family-sponsored	100,000
Refugees and asylum seekers	150,000
Employment-based	50,000
Diversity programs	0
Other minor categories	0
Total legal immigration:	300,000

Let me say a few words about the specific changes proposed, with the understanding that they are made within a framework that recognizes the need to significantly decrease overall numbers.

For a start, I would keep *refugee resettlement* numbers at their current levels. Doing so will help us continue to fulfill our moral obligation to aid legitimate political refugees. This is also a legal obligation under international law. The United States is an original signatory to the UN Universal Declaration of Human Rights, whose article 14 states: "Everyone has the right to seek and to enjoy in other countries asylum from persecution." Although this right can often be secured through temporary asylum, conditions in refugees' countries of origin sometimes demand longer or even permanent stays. Rather than create large numbers of "long-term temporary" residents, it is often better to grant such asylum seekers citizenship and help them start new lives in the United States.

Note that the argument above pertains only to legitimate political refugees: those who face persecution in their countries of origin. In recent years, there have been numerous proposals to grant refugee status to economic migrants and to those said to be displaced by climate change. In effect, this would create a legal right for half the world to immigrate into the United States, while encouraging developing nations to ignore overpopulation. I believe such proposals are largely without merit and discuss them more fully in the following chapter. The current level of approximately 150,000 annual slots for refugees and asylum seekers seems adequate to fulfill our valid responsibilities in this area.

On the other hand, *family sponsorship* programs, which currently bring in more legal immigrants than all other categories put together, have ballooned far beyond what is reasonable or ever intended by Congress. These programs allow individuals to sponsor brothers, sisters, parents, and adult children for permanent residency, with no limit on the annual numbers. As currently constituted these programs encourage endless chain migration. For example, an immigrant woman might marry a man who is a US citizen. They can then sponsor her brothers and sisters for citizenship, who can bring over *their* spouses and children, etc. The current approach unfairly skews US immigration toward immigration from a few favored countries, particularly Mexico, and toward less-skilled, less-educated immigrants. Combined with periodic amnesties, the system also rewards people who break US immigration laws, rather than those who play by the rules and wait their turn. Many undocumented immigrants have sponsored relatives once they themselves were granted amnesty.

To fix this broken system, we should restrict sponsorship to spouses and minor children. We should also count all those brought in under these programs toward the total number of immigrants allowed in annually. These changes would focus the programs' benefits on the people for whom they were originally intended: international couples who want to get married, and younger children who need to be with their parents for their safety and well-being. By restricting it to these cases, we could cut back significantly on the total numbers allowed under this category, while still allowing legitimate "family reunification."

The third main category to consider is *employment-based* immigration. This includes those acquiring permanent citizenship and those granted "temporary" permission to work in the United States under a dozen or so special visas or sector-specific programs ("temporary" is in ironic quotation marks, because most of these workers wind up staying in the United States permanently, whether or not they eventually apply for citizenship). I would cut this category by roughly two-thirds, to 50,000 slots maximum. For each slot filled, I would tax employee sponsors $25,000, with the proceeds earmarked for education and job training for current US citizens.

I believe that employment-driven immigration is largely unnecessary in the United States in the twenty-first century. Currently, with 22 million Americans unemployed or underemployed, we have more than enough workers for the work that is available. Happier economic days may be on the way, when there will be a robust demand for more workers overall and perhaps an acute need for more workers in particular sectors of the economy. When and if those days ever come, however, progressives do not want that demand met too quickly. We want it to generate higher wages for American workers. We want difficult or unpleasant jobs—collecting garbage or butchering hogs, for instance—to generate a premium for American workers. We want industry's need to fill high-tech jobs in computer programming and engineering to mean that 55-year-old programmers and engineers already here in the US can get a call back when they apply for them. If businesses instead want younger workers for such jobs, then we want them to pay to create science and technology magnet schools in our inner cities, where hundreds of thousands of creative, intelligent children of color languish for lack of resources and encouragement; and we want them to pay for scholarships to send these high school graduates on to the nation's universities.

At the other end of the economy, we would like the need for more people to pick cabbages to drive up hourly wages for cabbage-pickers, or spur mechanization that makes such jobs superfluous, or convince farmers to leave more of their fields fallow. For in the end not every need of "the economy" is a need that should be met. Higher wages will inevitably mean that some jobs disappear, and there is nothing wrong with that. Remember that from an ecological perspective we need less economic activity, not more. Not only *can* we leave some economic needs unmet, we *must* do so in order to solve our ecological problems. So to the argument that importing workers with special skills in key areas of the economy will help our economy grow more quickly, or that bringing in more entrepreneurs from abroad will do so ("what, reduce immigration and keep out the next Sergey Brin?"), I respond that we do not need a more rapidly growing economy. Rather, we need to transition to a genuinely sustainable economy and move beyond a fixation on growth.

Some immigration reform advocates argue for shifting the mix of immigrants from poorly educated, low-skilled applicants to well-educated, higher-skilled ones. Skilled immigrants are more economically productive and less likely to cost taxpayers money in social services. Several other nations with high immigration rates, such as Canada, have taken this road: more visas for computer programmers and engineers and fewer visas for waiters and roofers. If our goals for immigration policy were purely selfish and continued rapid economic growth was our main goal, then I think this approach might make sense. But rejecting pure selfishness and the goal of maximizing economic growth, I reject this approach to immigration reform.

Taking young, well-educated, highly skilled citizens from poor countries, "skimming the cream" in this way, is arguably bad for poorer countries. The resulting brain drain has been extensively documented.[5] In addition, it's more generous to give less-favored immigrants a chance. Emma Lazarus' poem says, "Give me your tired, your poor, your huddled masses yearning to breathe free," not "give me your engineers, your computer programmers, your nurses and doctors, yearning to triple their salaries." In the end, with limited immigration places to distribute, we must make a choice: more spots for family reunification and political refugees, or more spots for more highly trained, economically valuable migrants. Since we have to choose, we should make the more generous choice and let poor countries keep the benefits accruing from their own highly skilled citizens.

In any case, the American economy is immense and remarkably adaptive. It can adjust to more or fewer workers, and to their being paid higher or lower wages. It will not grind to a halt if wages increase; after all, historically the economy has not stopped growing during eras of rising wages. Nor will it fail to provide us with the necessities of life that will always remain in demand. Cutting immigration will not produce empty shelves in American supermarkets or rationing at the gas pump.

The final main immigration category, *diversity programs*, can be dealt with briefly. This category is dominated by a "diversity lottery" which brings in 50,000 immigrants per year, selected from countries that are underrepresented in the total immigrant pool. I believe the diversity lottery should be discontinued and this category zeroed out. With the curtailment of excessive family-sponsored immigration, the overrepresentation of Latin American countries, which drove the creation of this program, would be alleviated. The program gives false hope to too many would-be emigrants around the world (the 2013 lottery received nearly 8 million applications for the 50,000 slots available). Most simply, the program presupposes continued mass immigration, which needs to end.

*

The cuts outlined above would allow us to reduce legal immigration into the United States to 300,000 people a year. This is the heart of my proposal, but I suspect some progressives may find the proposal itself heartless and recoil from significantly reducing overall immigration numbers. I do not deny that reducing immigration in this way will prevent many individual immigrants from bettering their lives, but I repeat—any immigration policy will necessitate hard choices and trade-offs. If we refuse to reduce immigration, then we must accept the economic, demographic, and environmental consequences of continued mass immigration, which together ensure the failure of the progressive political agenda in the United States.

GOAL 3: REDUCE ILLEGAL IMMIGRATION

For progressives, one of the hardest aspects of this whole issue involves what to do about undocumented immigrants. On the one hand it is clear that no coherent policy, even one more expansive than the current one, is possible without enforcing immigration laws. That means telling some people that they cannot settle in the United States and finding and expelling those who refuse to take "no" for an answer. On the other hand our hearts go out to individual illegal immigrants, who in most cases have snuck into the United States in order to make better lives for themselves and their families, not to cause anyone trouble. We may know that our neighbor is in the country illegally, or suspect some of the crew who cut the neighbor's grass. But we wish them well and do not blow the whistle on them. I know I don't.

So, we have some hard choices to make. If you are a progressive and you are unconvinced by the body of this book, then you may see no pressing need to enforce US immigration laws. You may support an "open borders" policy, or at least acquiesce in the lax enforcement we have seen during the past forty years. Perhaps, like the editorial board of the *New York Times*, you will indignantly reject the "open borders" tag while labeling every attempt to reduce immigration as racist and unjust.[6] However, if you do see a need to reduce overall immigration, even by less than I have proposed, then you are committed to finding some way to fairly and efficiently enforce US immigration laws and reduce illegal immigration. Fortunately, doing so need not involve elaborate high-tech efforts to secure our southern border, or futilely trying to track the travels of tens of millions of visitors. Instead, we need to dry up the key resource bringing most undocumented immigrants to America: illegally held jobs.

Jobs are the immigration magnet. Make these unavailable and most illegal immigration will disappear, without elaborate expense or intrusive policing. This can be done, provided we take two steps. First, mandate use of a national employment verification database for all new hires, where employers can quickly and easily verify US citizenship or certification to work. Second, strictly enforce existing civil and criminal sanctions against *employers* who hire illegal workers, meting out penalties sufficient to deter employers who break the law. For all the Sturm und Drang over immigration in recent decades, neither of these common sense policies have yet been tried, perhaps because the elites who set government policy are afraid they might work.

Regarding the first measure, over the past ten years the federal government has spent several hundred million dollars to create the computerized E-Verify database to check work eligibility. According to US Citizenship and Immigration Services, as of November 2012, "More than 409,000 employers, large and small, across the United States use[d] E-Verify to check the employment eligibility of their employees, with about 1,300 new businesses signing up each week."[7] In fiscal year 2011, the program ran more than 17.4 million individual employment queries.[8] E-Verify has steadily improved in recent years; it now effectively catches most unjustified applications and deters many more, while quickly waiving through more than 99% of lawful job applicants. It appears ready to deploy as a mandatory national system, which can be further improved for accuracy and ease of use in coming years. Nothing stands in the way of requiring E-Verify nationally for all new hires right now, except the unwillingness of Congress and the Obama administration to require it.

The second measure, serious civil and criminal penalties for employers who break the law, also remains to be tried. In response to growing public opposition to illegal immigration, the potential penalties for employers who hire illegal workers are now impressive, including fines that can total in the hundreds of thousands of dollars for major offenders and jail time for company executives who encourage immigration fraud. However, in their sporadic efforts at workplace enforcement, successive Democratic and Republican administrations have failed to seek jail time for employers, even those who have been found to have repeatedly and systematically broken the law. Meanwhile, the fines meted out have represented a small fraction of the profits these businesses have earned by breaking the law. Under these circumstances highly publicized workplace raids, including several netting thousands of illegal immigrants, have failed to effectively deter further lawbreaking by employers. All this could change quickly though, should an administration come to power with a real commitment to deterring illegal immigration.

With these two complementary steps in place, we could ratchet back efforts to police the US-Mexican border with fences or elaborate electronic surveillance and return to the traditional, semiporous border that has always existed. If some illegal immigrants get across, that will be okay, because they will not find jobs. This should avoid pushing people out into the desert, where, at the mercy of the elements and unscrupulous criminals, hundreds have died in recent years. It would also take a big chunk of money away from Mexican crime syndicates running undocumented immigrants into the United States; allow important wildlife corridors and migration routes to remain open, while cutting back on damage done to remote natural areas on both sides of the border; and save the American people a tremendous amount of money. In a similar manner, deploying effective job screening would allow us to streamline our system for monitoring visitors who enter the country via our airports and seaports, and avoid futile, expensive efforts to track them throughout their stay in the United States. Such a system is another boondoggle like the border fence, but one that is still in the planning stages and thus able to be headed off before it wastes any more funds from US taxpayers.

A focus on employment and employers will also allow us to avoid any hint of racial profiling; an objection that has been made, for example, against Arizona's controversial law S.B. 1070. *Every* new hire would have to be run through E-Verify, minimizing the potential for differential treatment or profiling. All Americans, including wealthy business owners and corporate executives, would have to follow the rules. In this way Americans could have an efficient, fair, and relatively inexpensive system for enforcing our immigration laws without the taint of racism.

GOAL 4: TARGETED AMNESTIES

Serious efforts to enforce our immigration laws would, in time, create a culture where lawfulness was expected and law breaking was condemned in the immigration sphere. If we hope to create such an environment, we will need to avoid the kinds of mass amnesties for undocumented immigrants that Congress passed in 1986 and 1990. Such amnesties were sold to the public as part of larger efforts to reduce illegal immigration, but instead they clearly encouraged more. When the 1986 amnesty passed, granting permanent residency to 3 million illegal immigrants, there were an estimated five to six million in the country. Today that number has grown to ten to twelve million, spurred in part by the belief among the undocumented that if they get jobs, establish residency, have children, or simply hang on long enough, another amnesty is coming.

Common sense tells us that we cannot incentivize illegal behavior and expect it to diminish. Amnesty proponents have responded by replacing the word *amnesty* with the words *earned legalization* or similar euphemisms. "No one is proposing that anyone be given an *amnesty*," they indignantly assert. "These people will have to pay a fine! They will have to go all the way to the back of the line and wait years to receive citizenship!" This is disingenuous. The big prize here is permanent residency with the entitlement to work. A fine of a few hundred or even a few thousand dollars is well worth paying for a privilege that will be worth hundreds of thousands of dollars over the average immigrant's lifetime. No great harm is done by postponing official citizenship, as long as he or she can stay in the United States and work. Indeed, many immigrants with permanent resident status never bother to apply for US citizenship.

So, we must avoid blanket amnesties, and this brings up some hard cases. What about children brought illegally into the United States by their parents? Parents here illegally whose deportation would separate them from their children? What about illegal residents who have lived in the United States for many years, paying taxes all the while and otherwise following our laws? Here I think some humanitarian leniency is in order, even though it means rewarding illegal behavior and makes the creation of a culture of lawfulness around immigration that much harder.

In this regard, I favor targeted amnesties that legalize children who were brought to the United States by their parents at a young age and who may know no other home. I also support legalizing parents whose young children are US citizens, in order to avoid breaking apart these families. This would acknowledge important family ties and improve a vulnerable population's security and well-being. However, I would call these actions what they are: amnesties, or formal pardons for breaking the law. In order to weaken the incentive for further illegal behavior, I would prohibit these new citizens from bringing any more relatives into the United States.

I would also explicitly rule out amnesties for other classes of illegal residents, including some who have lived in the United States for many years. I say this despite my belief that a reasonable argument can be made for amnesty for long-term undocumented residents, given long-standing US policies that have winked at the breaking of our immigration laws. My reason is that a culture of legality must begin somewhere and too many exceptions will undermine attempts to create it. Blanket amnesties, such as that contained in the Senate's recent immigration reform bill, would clearly weaken future efforts to enforce US immigration laws and should be rejected for that reason. Amnesties for one to two million undocumented immigrants are justified, on grounds of justice and practicality, while amnesties for ten or twelve million must be rejected for the same reasons.

GOAL 5: END BIRTHRIGHT CITIZENSHIP

In line with the goal of creating an immigration regime based on following the law, it is time to end "birthright citizenship" for the children of people living illegally in the United States. Between 300,000 and 400,000 children are born to undocumented immigrants in the United States each year, while tens of thousands more are born to foreigners just passing through the country, whether as tourists, students, or diplomats.[9] All these children automatically receive US citizenship under current law. This both adds significantly to US population growth and incentivizes illegal behavior, since having children can often forestall deportation when parents are caught in the country illegally.

Most countries around the world restrict birth citizenship to the children of current citizens or legal residents. Today the United States and Canada stand alone as the only developed nations that continue the outmoded policy of granting citizenship to all children born within their borders, a policy that made sense in the age of sail, but not in an age of jet airplanes and massive illegal immigration. According to one study comparing policies around the world:

> In recent years, the international trend has been to end universal birthright citizenship. Countries that have ended universal birthright citizenship include the United Kingdom, which ended the practice in 1983, Australia (1986), India (1987), Malta (1989), Ireland, which ended the practice through a national referendum in 2004, New Zealand (2006), and the Dominican Republic, which ended the practice in January 2010. The reasons countries have ended automatic birthright citizenship are diverse, but have resulted from concerns not all that different from the concerns of many in the United States. Increased illegal immigration is the main motivating factor in most countries. Birth tourism was one of the reasons Ireland ended automatic birthright citizenship in 2004. If the United States were to stop granting automatic citizenship to children of illegal immigrants, it would be following an international trend.[10]

Of course, children born to foreign parents in these countries are not rendered stateless. Instead, they become citizens of their parents' countries.

Most cases of birthright citizenship in the United States involve a single country, Mexico, whose citizens have gotten used to jumping in line in front of potential immigrants from other countries. Ending birthright citizenship would help end an immigration status quo that is bad for both countries, as I argue in the following chapter. In concert with my other proposals, ending birthright citizenship would help reduce illegal immigration and create a culture of legality, while costing taxpayers less money than we currently spend on fruitless and inept shows of law enforcement. It would also go a long way toward restoring fairness and workability to our immigration system as a whole.[11]

GOAL 6: ADDRESS THE PUSH FACTORS DRIVING IMMIGRATION

Still, what about those aunts and uncles who will no longer be able to move to the United States once we reform our current, flawed "family reunification" policies? What about the waitresses and roofers, vegetable pickers and slaughterhouse workers and nurses, who will no longer get to emigrate in search of a better economic future? These would-be immigrants will have to make a better life for themselves in their home countries. This always has been the only option for the overwhelming majority of the world's poor. With several billion people around the world living in poverty and the world's population growing by almost 80 million a year, mostly in developing countries, allowing one or two million annual immigrants into the United States was never a plausible route to ending global poverty.

Still, by no means should we turn our backs on the world's poor. The United States remains a wealthy and powerful country. There is a lot we can do, individually and collectively, to help people better conditions for themselves in their home countries, and a number of counterproductive policies we can end that will also improve matters.

In the first place, the United States could negotiate new trade agreements and rework old ones so that they improve economic conditions for poor workers in our trading partners' countries, *even if this means slowing rather than increasing the growth of trade.* Too often, US trade agreements have sought to maximize the volume of trade regardless of all other considerations. Exhibit A is the North American Free Trade Agreement. By opening up Mexican markets to cheap US corn and produce, NAFTA tossed over a million Mexican farmers off the land in just a few years.[12] Many of these farmers wound up emigrating north in search of work. Proponents assert that such "creative destruction" is necessary to get the full benefits of free trade, but in countries with large numbers of small farmers and large cohorts of young adults already looking for work, policies that facilitate "rapid modernization of the agricultural sector" may be unwise. We live in a world where increased productivity often contributes less to human happiness and well-being than continued job availability and equitable access to basic resources. By ignoring this, US trade policy often harms people in poor countries, giving them increased motivation to emigrate.

Second, we could increase and better target development aid to help poor people around the world enhance their lives in their own countries. Although the United States ranks first globally in total foreign aid disbursed, we consistently rank last among the major donor nations in foreign aid as a percentage of gross national income.[13] Worse, too much US foreign aid comes in the form of military aid—guns, bombs, or military training—which often causes more harm than good. Why waste $50 million sending Egypt or Colombia a new fighter plane or a few old bombers, when that same $50 million could support five thousand more elementary school teachers, or provide one thousand scholarships to train new doctors in those countries? Wasteful aid funding also goes to ecologically harmful mega-projects like new dams and highways, and to subsidize the purchase of US agricultural surpluses, harming foreign farmers.

Only a small percentage of American foreign aid appears likely to improve conditions for poor people in the developing world, making them less likely to emigrate. Yet in many conversations I've had while researching this book, immigrants have told me that they would have preferred to stay in their home countries, surrounded by friends and family. Some have said they would have been willing to forego considerably higher wages in the US in exchange for living decent lives at home.[14] Perhaps some foreign aid could be specifically targeted at countries from which large numbers of people are emigrating, in programs that are designed to improve the lives of just those groups or age cohorts who are choosing to leave. Perhaps our agricultural aid, which now focuses on hastening agricultural industrialization around the world, should instead focus on helping small farmers stay on the land and farm efficiently and sustainably. Certainly US aid for family planning and reproductive health, which has declined over the past two decades, should instead be greatly increased, perhaps funded by cuts in military aid.[15]

Third, US foreign policy should be refocused on upholding human rights and helping poor people around the world live better lives. Too often, particularly during the Cold War, we intervened politically on the side of right-wing dictatorships that tyrannized their own poor citizens. In some cases, such as El Salvador and Guatemala, American support for repressive regimes led directly to large exoduses of political refugees into the United States. In other cases, our support for corrupt governments that denied workers' rights may also have helped spur emigration; at a minimum, our actions did nothing to create conditions that would have made emigration from those countries unnecessary. Studies have shown that government corruption is an important factor retarding economic growth in many developing countries[16]; my interviews with immigrants from Latin America confirm their sense of crooked systems that are stacked against them. This provides a strong incentive for many men and women to emigrate, and I can't blame them. By supporting the rights and interests of poor people overseas and encouraging their governments to reduce corruption and embrace democracy, we can help create a world where fewer people will find it necessary to go into exile in order to live decent lives.

In all these ways, the US government could help improve conditions in poor countries. In addition, Americans with a particular concern for poor people abroad have many private aid organizations that they can support. Religious and secular charities help to build schools, staff and fund hospitals, monitor elections, and otherwise improve lives and opportunities in the developing world. Such efforts do much good and deserve our support. Crucially, we may support these programs without harming our poor fellow-citizens at home.

GOAL 7: REVISIT AND REVISE

Although this book is highly critical of mass immigration into the United States today, it is focused on our current choices. Nothing I have said necessarily implies negative judgments regarding mass immigration in past eras, when economic and social conditions were very different and ecological challenges poorly understood. Similarly, conditions may be vastly different in the future. Though it is hard to imagine the trends moving in ways that would justify a resumption of mass immigration, it could happen. Perhaps our country's fertility rate will drop precipitously (as has recently happened in Japan and much of southern Europe) and stay low for decades. In that case we might want to ratchet immigration back up. On the other hand, economic or ecological deterioration might lead us to limit immigration even more sharply.

For these reasons, it is only prudent to periodically revisit immigration policy and revise it to further the common good, in line with our guiding principles of justice and sustainability. We should debate immigration policy freely, making sure that special interests do not hijack policy making, as they have so often in the past.

IMMIGRATION REFORM AND A
COMPREHENSIVE PROGRESSIVE VISION

At the start of this book, I defined the core political goals of progressivism as a relatively equal distribution of wealth across society, economic security for workers and their families, environmental protection, an end to racial prejudice, and maximizing the political power of common citizens while limiting the influence of large corporations. Of course, immigration reform is only one part of a full progressive agenda. But when we spell out such an agenda more fully it becomes clearer how the right immigration policy can help further it.

Consider first progressivism's main economic goals: higher incomes, more economic security for workers, and greater economic equality across society. In pursuit of these goals progressives support strong labor unions, increases in the legal minimum wage, universal health care, bankruptcy laws that favor poor debtors rather than their wealthy creditors, and steeper progressive taxation. We defend social programs that benefit the working class and middle class, such as Social Security, Medicare, and Medicaid, while calling for an end to tax loopholes for the wealthy, unnecessary wars, and wasteful, excessive military spending. If revenues must be increased to close budget deficits, progressives argue that taxes should be raised on the rich.

Reducing immigration will help this progressive economic agenda in several ways. Most important, as we have seen, it will tighten labor markets and thus raise wages and decrease unemployment, benefiting workers across the board but especially poorer workers. It will strengthen labor unions by making it harder for companies to "divide and conquer" transient workers who may have little in common with one another, or may not speak the same language. It will also make it harder to replace workers who go out on strike, or who bargain individually for better wages or working conditions.

Reducing immigration will also ensure that over time a greater percentage of poor US residents are actually citizens. I believe this would make a big difference in defending and extending the panoply of pro-worker policies detailed above. With citizenship comes the vote. Politicians will be more likely to support economic policies that favor the poor, when the poor have something to give them in exchange. Because they do not have much money, it's imperative that politicians covet their votes. Currently the average salary of US residents is significantly lower than the average salary of eligible voters, skewing policy-making even further toward benefiting the wealthy.

When large percentages of poorer workers are noncitizens, this undermines progressive policy initiatives in further ways. During recent debates over universal health care, for example, the argument was often made that many of the uninsured were in the United States illegally and so did not deserve coverage. This was used to disparage the whole initiative. In a similar way, arguments to raise the minimum wage are sometimes rejected on the grounds that they would primarily benefit immigrants, who, while poorly paid by American standards, are doing much better than they would have in their countries of origin. These examples show how mass immigration can undermine solidarity among different classes and lead to greater acceptance of economic inequality. When I tell students in my ethics classes that waiters and waitresses in Denmark and Germany get four to six weeks of paid vacation a year, they find it amazing. Often they seem to find it *disturbing*: out of the natural order of things. It seems likely that mass immigration plays a role in reinforcing their belief that many menial jobs should not command good benefits or middle-class wages, just as the fact that Danes and Germans more often see their fellow citizens working in these jobs probably plays a role in their belief that these workers *are* entitled to good wages and benefits. In all these ways, reducing immigration will enable a progressive economic agenda.

Next, consider progressivism's main environmental goals. These include limiting air and water pollution, using resources sustainably, creating pleasant, green towns with bicycle lanes and livable, uncrowded cities with good mass transit. They also include preserving other species by securing wildlife habitat in parks, refuges, and wilderness areas. As we have seen, increasing human numbers makes all these goals harder to achieve. More people lead to more pollution and crowding, more concrete and asphalt. More people reduce the habitat available for other species and the space available for those seeking solitude. More people mean fewer natural resources to share per person. Crucially, mass immigration means more people: a *lot* more people. That's why American environmentalists should support immigration reduction.

I know that talking about immigration makes many environmentalists uncomfortable. But we need to remember that we are not winning the battle for nature, and the stakes are high. A massive *Millennium Ecosystem Assessment*, sponsored by the United Nations and involving over 1,300 experts, stated in 2005: "At the heart of this assessment is a stark warning. Human activity is putting such strain on the natural functions of the earth that the ability of the planet's ecosystems to sustain future generations can no longer be taken for granted."[17] Given mounting evidence that human beings are stressing Earth's ecosystems to the breaking point and given the central role the United States will play in creating or failing to create an ecologically sustainable world, environmentalism in the United States must succeed. It makes little sense to create even longer odds for ourselves by remaining silent about excessive immigration.

The progressive political agenda also includes a strong commitment to racial equality. That means an end to all race-based discrimination through active enforcement of anti-discrimination laws. It means ensuring that economic and educational opportunities are open to all, regardless of race or ethnic background. For much of the past century, it has meant a special concern among progressives for improving conditions for African Americans. It should disturb us when any racial or ethnic group is doing much worse than society as a whole.

Progressives need not compromise our anti-racist commitments when it comes to immigration policy. Efforts to reduce illegal immigration should avoid tactics that could lead to racial profiling, such as mass sweeps through immigrant-heavy neighborhoods. Instead we should mandate the use of an effective employee verification system for all new job hires, regardless of the race or ethnicity of potential employees, and monitor the compliance of employers, again *universally*, without regard to race or ethnicity. Similarly, we should avoid favoring particular racial or ethnic groups when allocating legal immigration slots, as current family reunification policies favor Hispanic immigrants at the expense of candidates from the rest of the world. Instead, we should dispense such places solely on the basis of demonstrated need or potential contributions to society.

If we want to avoid racial profiling and other heavy-handed law enforcement, the key is to dry up the jobs that are encouraging illegal immigration through mandatory, universal, nondiscriminatory employment verification. No neighborhood sweeps, no asking random people off the street or in their cars to "see their papers." If immigrant advocates still object to this proposal, we can reasonably conclude that what they really object to is enforcing our immigration laws. Indeed, defenders often portray undocumented immigrants as victims of racial discrimination solely on the basis of their being charged with violating immigration law, and call those who want the laws enforced racists.[18] Instead of ratcheting up the invective and inflaming racial tensions in this way, I think people of good will should look for solutions that dial such rhetoric back. Instead of creating a new class of racial victims, we would probably all be better off trying to create a society that moves beyond racial animosities to the degree that we can and that treats everyone fairly and equally, while still enforcing necessary laws.

I believe my immigration proposals would do just that. In addition, reducing immigration would help improve conditions for African Americans, a cause for which many progressives feel a special responsibility, given our country's shameful history of slavery and segregation. In recent decades, growing numbers of African Americans have taken advantage of new opportunities to join the middle class, pursuing careers in business and the professions that were largely unavailable to earlier generations. Meanwhile many others have remained poor, kept down partly by the structural economic trends we discussed in previous chapters. It is this group that could be greatly helped by reduced immigration, as economists Vernon Briggs, George Borjas, and Steven Shulman have shown.[19] As markets for unskilled labor tightened up, the labor of low-income people of color would be in greater demand, leading to more job opportunities and higher wages. As markets for skilled labor tightened up, incentives would increase for society to better educate African American children. Given that our country's willingness to use government power to help poor people seems to have waned in recent decades, we have all the more reason to reduce immigration and get labor markets working to reduce poverty.

Instead, before Americans have dealt fairly with our oldest and most impoverished underclass, we seem bent on creating another, Hispanic one: relatively poor, relatively poorly educated, and apparently less upwardly mobile than some other ethnic groups.[20] Beyond its contributions to economic inequality, this path also seems likely to heighten ethnic and racial tensions unnecessarily. Rather than continue to build a poor Latin

American underclass, our country would probably do better to reduce immigration, the better to economically assimilate the tens of millions of new Hispanic citizens we have added over the past forty years.[21] Moving as many recent immigrants and their children as possible into the middle class could help us achieve a less racially polarized future.

Here we come to the last key element in the progressive vision: empowering common citizens and revitalizing our democracy. We must limit the power of corporations and the power of money, corporate and individual, to decide elections and to corrupt government decision-making. This includes decisions regarding immigration policy. As a first step to reining in corporations, we should take the power of chartering them away from the states, with their race to the bottom in terms of social accountability, and instead require federal registration governed by uniform federal laws. These should set high standards regarding transparency, legality, and ecological sustainability—and make explicit that these are legitimate corporate goals that are not trumped by profit making.

Such changes to corporate governance, while crucial to reforming our corrupt politics, are not directly tied to immigration policy. However, enacting them would probably help in reforming that policy, because while most Americans favor reducing immigration or keeping it at current levels, corporations have repeatedly and successfully lobbied to expand it.[22] Interestingly, there seems to be a "corporate consensus" on this issue. Whether they are progressive or reactionary on other issues, corporate leaders tend to favor immigration policies that generate more consumers and cheaper labor. In recent decades, corporate interests have consistently won out over the interests of citizens in setting immigration levels.

The flip side of decreasing the power of corporations is increasing political opportunities for citizens. Another important way that mass immigration arguably undermines citizen power is demographically, as population growth makes each individual citizen less important. In 1800, members of the House of Representatives represented on average 33,000 constituents. Today each Congressman or Congresswoman represents about 710,000 constituents—over twenty-one times as many. Clearly the value of any one individual's vote declined during this time. The chances that the average person might meet his or her Congressman, much less influence their vote, declined as well.

In response some might say, "That ship has sailed," and it's true that we are not going back to the time when a Congressman might stand by the ballot box in his home town in Virginia or New Hampshire and personally thank a small but significant percentage of the voters who elected him to Congress. Yet perhaps we do not want that ship to sail ever further in the same direction, because numbers still make a difference. Consider an example.

Here in Fort Collins, I know my state representative and state senator personally. We have discussed forest management issues, state funding for education, immigration policy, and other matters numerous times. Whether this has ever swayed one of their votes, I cannot say with certainty. But I've appreciated the opportunity to bend their ears, just as they seem to have appreciated my willingness to introduce them to some of my neighbors, so they could ask for their votes. Such small-scale democracy is a lot more possible today in Colorado than in California, because each Colorado state representative represents 66,000 people on average, while each California state representative represents about 423,000 people. It is even more possible in Vermont, with only 4000 constituents per state representative.[23] I'm reasonably sure that Colorado is not going to turn into Vermont, but I do not want to see it "Californicated" either. Unfortunately, at current rates of growth Colorado's population may reach California's present population by the time my grandchildren are old enough to vote.

The more people, the more we will have to be governed, rather than *self*-governed. The more people, the more money talks, rather than the people themselves. Would my state representative have valued my walking him around my neighborhood, if he had to chase ten or twenty times as many voters in order to get elected? He might have preferred instead to work the phones calling wealthy donors in search of cash to pay for repetitive but more efficient media buys. I do not want to exaggerate: reducing immigration and stabilizing our population are not panaceas for the inevitable limitations of living in an immense representative democracy. But given the fact that population growth magnifies these limitations, we need to ask whether the time has finally arrived to end such growth. Especially since, as I have repeatedly emphasized, population growth is not inevitable, but a choice.

CONCLUSION

The recommendations outlined in this chapter provide a fair and workable framework for a twenty-first-century immigration system focused on furthering the common good. Immigration policy should be made with the interests of all Americans in mind, but especially poor Americans, young Americans, and future Americans. Not just the wealthy few, who already are coddled by both Democrats and Republicans. We don't need to further empower our corporate class, who have had great success driving down wages for workers in recent decades and do not need any more help from our politicians. Done right, immigration reform could help create a significantly more egalitarian and just America.

ten

OBJECTIONS

Having detailed my recommendations for reforming United States immigration policy in the previous chapter, this one considers some of the most important remaining objections to my proposals. I've already considered the main economic objections to reducing immigration into the United States (see chapters 4 and 5), as well as many of the objections environmentalists tend to raise against limiting immigration to promote ecological sustainability (see especially chapter 7). But I suspect that even if they agree that the economic and environmental objections have been fully met, many progressives will still feel uncomfortable with significantly reducing immigration into the United States. Reducing immigration, even limiting immigration at all, just does not strike many progressives as fair or compassionate.

As I wrote the first draft of this chapter in spring 2013, the US Congress was considering the first fundamental changes to federal immigration policy in twenty years. Political progressives, for the most part, pushed for greatly *increased* immigration, and their remarks on the topic suggested that many of them saw most limitations on immigration as fundamentally unjust. For example, like me, my congressional representative Jared Polis, a liberal Democrat, sees the presence of ten to twelve million undocumented immigrants in the United States as a problem. But for Representative Polis, the problem is not a past failure to enforce immigration laws, or the resultant downward pressure on working-class wages; instead, it is that enforcing immigration laws cruelly breaks apart families and foolishly keeps businesses from hiring all the workers they need. He believes this problem can best be rectified by legalizing almost all illegal immigrants currently in the United States and greatly expanding legal immigration, so individuals and businesses are not "forced to break the law" in pursuit of their goals.[1] As I found when I visited his Washington office, he and his chief immigration staffer honestly believe that this constitutes the moral approach to immigration reform, in contrast to what they see as selfish, immoral proposals to deport undocumented immigrants, or keep out of the country people who just want to better their lives and the lives of their families.[2]

Such beliefs are widely shared among political progressives; hence it remains to consider the main moral arguments against reducing immigration into the United States. I do not have the space to consider all possible moral objections. But in what follows, I hope to provide plausible responses to the most common and important ones, and to establish a general moral justification for limiting immigration from one country into another. As with previous discussions of economic and environmental objections, considering the moral objections to immigration reduction can help clarify the necessary moral commitments and practical goals of a progressive politics. As before, this increased clarity will come largely from more fully and honestly considering the role that limits must play in guiding our policy decisions.

Note once again that I do not claim that my plan would do away with the need for hard choices or trade-offs between conflicting goods. No immigration policy can do that. And bear in mind that plausible objections to some of my specific recommendations do not, by themselves, constitute compelling arguments for their alternatives. There is a particularly misleading way of discussing immigration policy, in which speakers throw up objection after objection to proposals to limit immigration: noting difficulties in implementation, pointing out negative consequences for one interest group or another, hoping that any objection, no matter how weak, will "stick" and thus carry the argument with listeners. But in the end, any immigration policy will benefit some people at the expense of others. We have to pick numbers, specify categories for admission, decide which immigration laws to pass and how seriously we want them enforced. I am convinced that readers who consider the policy alternatives with a view to which ones are most likely to further progressive political goals, will come back to my proposal with a greater willingness to consider ways that it might be modified to meet their objections.

With those caveats in mind, let's consider the most substantive moral objections to my proposal. That proposal can be summarized as follows: cut legal immigration to 300,000 per year; reduce illegal immigration by enacting a universal, mandatory, secure employee identification program for all new hires and aggressively pursuing employers who hire people to work illegally; and help would-be immigrants live better lives in their own countries through smart, sustainable trade policies and generous, well-tailored foreign aid programs.

MORAL OBJECTIONS: RIGHTS

Perhaps the most important objections raised against restrictive immigration policies are that they are unjust, because they are unfair to potential immigrants. One concise way of stating this is to say that would-be immigrants have a *right* to live and work in the United States. While some immigrants' rights proponents argue for abolishing national borders altogether, most assert a general human right to freely move and settle without regard to national borders, subject to reasonable government restrictions to keep out criminals and prevent gross harms to receiving societies. For example, philosopher Manuel Velasquez affirms such a right in his article "Immigration: Is Exclusion Just?" He argues that in a globalized world, "national borders have become an obstacle to serving the pressing needs—arising out of economic destitution and political persecution—that afflict inhabitants of less developed countries. These needs can be alleviated by opening our borders. We have no moral right to maintain a closed system of national borders in the face of such need."[3]

This is indeed a radical proposal, since a general right to immigrate does not exist currently in American law. The Constitution names no right to immigrate and the Supreme Court has consistently upheld the federal government's right to regulate and limit immigration into the country. Neither does such a right exist in international law. The UN Universal Declaration of Human Rights does not assert a general human right to immigrate into the country of one's choice, nor do other major framework international rights treaties.[4] Article 13 of the UN Declaration asserts: "Everyone has the right to freedom of movement and residence *within the borders of each state*" (emphasis added). Here the right of movement and residence is clearly limited to a citizen's home country. Article 14 asserts: "Everyone has the right to seek and to enjoy in other countries asylum from persecution." But this is a right to temporary refuge, not permanent settlement, and in any case most immigrants to the United States are not fleeing persecution but trying to better their lives economically. Hence the right of asylum does not come close to justifying their right to immigrate into the United States.

Proponents of a general right to immigrate, then, claim first and primarily the existence of a *moral* right to immigrate freely across borders. Second, they claim that national laws should be amended accordingly to better harmonize with the legitimate claims of morality: that a *legal* right to immigrate should be affirmed. Let's focus on the primary claim and ask: what arguments do proponents provide for their assertion of a moral right to immigrate freely (or relatively freely) across national borders?

Political philosopher Chandran Kukathas gives what he calls a "liberal egalitarian" argument for open borders. From a proper universalistic moral point of view, Kukathas maintains, citizens of rich countries have no special claims to the resources and opportunities into which they have been born. "Egalitarianism demands that the earth's resources be distributed as equally as possible," he writes, "and one particularly effective mechanism for facilitating this is freedom of movement." Egalitarians want to equalize not just resources, but opportunities. Allowing people to migrate from poor, overcrowded countries with high unemployment and little chance for economic advancement to wealthier, less crowded countries equalizes opportunities. "Our starting point," Kukathas suggests, "should be a recognition of our common humanity and the idea that both the resources of the earth and the cooperation of our fellows are things to which no one has any privileged entitlement." For these reasons, "the movement of peoples should be free."[5]

This is a powerful argument for many progressives, since it rests on egalitarian values that we tend to share. It also relies on the common thought: "what right do I have to shut the door on people who are just as good as I am and who, through no fault of their own, have been born into less happy circumstances?" Kukathas' argument may speak particularly strongly to political moderates who feel some sympathy with egalitarianism, but not enough to do anything about it personally. For it says to relatively wealthy Americans, "You do not have to give up anything yourself to help poor foreigners live better lives. You can fulfill any moral obligations you may have toward them by allowing them to come here and cut your grass, cook your food, and diaper your children."

Nevertheless, there are good reasons to reject the liberal egalitarian argument for open borders. Because rights help allocate scarce goods, any rights claim must be tested against its effects on all interested parties — not just the parties pressing the claim. Even widely accepted, fundamental human rights must be balanced against other rights and other important interests when it comes to their implementation. Such considerations count heavily against open borders.[6]

As we have seen, current levels of immigration into the United States are leading to a larger population, which makes it much harder to share the landscape generously with nonhuman beings. Allowing a general right to immigrate into the United States would greatly accelerate this process. With open borders the interests of nonhuman nature would be sacrificed *completely* to the interests of people. The economic interests of would-be immigrants would trump the very existence of many nonhuman organisms, endangered species, and wild places in the United States.

Like many immigrants' rights advocates, Kukathas can accept this trade-off; he may not even be aware of it. As the previous quotes illustrate, he sees nature essentially as "the earth's resources." The only question to ask about them is how people may divide them up fairly and efficiently. In seeking to make sense of Australian environmentalists' arguments for limiting immigration, for example, Kukathas speaks about their worries that "parks and sewerage services" will be degraded, a revealingly soulless locution.[7] His approach sees no value to the Earth beyond what humans can take from it.

But those of us who reject this anthropocentric perspective must consider the interests of the nonhuman beings who would be displaced by an ever-increasing human presence. I myself believe that the human appropriation of natural landscapes has progressed so far in the United States that any further appropriation is unjust toward other species; if anything, Americans should scale back our overall ecological footprint and leave more habitat and essential resources for other species.[8] Some readers may find this position extreme. But if so, I ask: how many other species must we drive extinct, before you will agree that we have taken too much?

There is room for disagreement here. However, it is important to realize that accepting a general right to immigrate leaves *no* room to take other species' continued existences seriously, in the United States or elsewhere, since it ensures that the human appropriation of nature will continue to increase. The logical end point of this is a country filled to bursting with people and our economic life-support systems (farms, factories, roads, reservoirs, channelized "rivers" turned on and off like taps) and whatever other species can survive in our tamed and "working" landscapes (lots of squirrels and cockroaches, perhaps three or four warbler species rather than the dozens existing today, no wolves or bears, etc.). For this reason alone, this right should be rejected.

Similarly, allowing a general right to immigrate would conflict with the rights of poorer Americans to a fair share of the wealth generated each year in the United States and violate their reasonable expectation that the US government should work for their economic well-being. The argument for this was fully developed in chapters 3 through 5. While highly educated, well-trained Americans might still do fine under an "open borders" scenario, at least for a few years, exposing less-favored Americans to direct competition from hundreds of millions of poorly educated, low-skilled workers from around the globe would be disastrous, swamping any efforts to bargain for or legislate higher wages and setting off a race to the bottom among businesses focused primarily on increased profits.

A general right to immigrate also would conflict with American citizens' right to self-government. Immigration can change the character of a society, for better or worse; large-scale immigration can change a society quickly, radically, and irrevocably. Since self-government is a fundamental and well-established human right, the citizens of particular nations arguably should retain, through their elected officials, significant control over immigration policies. As Michael Walzer puts it in an influential discussion on immigration: "Admission and exclusion are at the core of communal independence. They suggest the deepest meaning of self-determination. Without them, there could not be communities of [a specific] character, historically stable, ongoing associations of men and women with some special commitment to one another and some special sense of their common life."[9]

The citizens of a nation may work hard to create particular kinds of societies: societies that are sustainable, for example, or that limit inequalities of wealth, or that treat women and men as equals. They typically develop feelings of affiliation and social commitments that have great value in themselves and that enable communal projects that create further value. It seems wrong to suggest that these achievements, which may provide meaning, secure justice, or contribute substantially to people's quality of life, must be compromised because people in other countries are having too many children, or have failed to create decent societies themselves. It is unjust to create a new right that undermines the self-government of others. Instead, would-be immigrants need to take up responsibilities for self-government that they and their leaders have neglected in their own countries.[10]

Environmentalists also worry that increasing human numbers will rob future generations of their right to enjoy a healthy environment with its full complement of native species. Over the past dozen years, as I've watched increasing numbers of people displace wildlife along Colorado's Front Range, I have often recalled this rueful passage from Henry Thoreau's journal, as he reflected on his own Massachusetts landscape:

> When I consider that the nobler animals have been exterminated here, I cannot but feel as if I lived in a tamed, and, as it were, emasculated country . . . I take infinite pains to know the phenomena of the spring, thinking that I have here the entire poem, and then, to my chagrin, I hear that it is but an imperfect copy that I possess and have read, that my ancestors have torn out many of the first leaves and grandest passages, and mutilated it in many places.[11]

I believe that like Thoreau, my descendants will "wish to know an entire heaven and an entire earth." Since a growing population undermines the right of future Americans to enjoy a safe, clean environment and to know and explore wild nature, we must reject a general right to freely immigrate into the United States.

To summarize: for American progressives, the rights of our fellow citizens, the interests of nonhuman nature, the responsibility of self-government, and our concern for future generations all come together in efforts to create a just and sustainable society. Because we take these efforts seriously and because they cannot succeed without limiting immigration, we must reject a general right to immigrate into the United States.

This discussion does not deny the importance of human rights. Rather, it presupposes their importance. Rights allow us to protect important human interests and create egalitarian societies that maximize opportunities for people to flourish. I believe rights are justified ultimately because they contribute to such human flourishing.[12] But not all rights claims are justified. When such claims are pressed so far that their recognition would undermine human or nonhuman flourishing, we should reject them.[13]

Note, too, that I do not deny the right of legitimate refugees to asylum from persecution, both as a matter of morality and of binding international law. The United States, like all states that are members of the United Nations and signatories to the Universal Declaration of Human Rights, is obligated to provide such refuge. My immigration reform proposal takes this commitment into account. However, the refuge provided may often be temporary, and in any case, only about 10% of annual immigrants into the United States are asylum seekers or refugees.

MORAL OBJECTIONS: WELFARE

The considerations above suggest that there is no general right to immigrate into the United States (or anywhere else). Still, even if no such general right exists, there might still be good moral reasons for continuing the permissive mass immigration status quo, or even enlarging it. Consider the following welfare-based argument.[14]

Over a million people immigrate into the United States each year and clearly the majority believe they will improve their own or their families' welfare by doing so. Otherwise they wouldn't come. Immigrants may find educational, vocational, or other personal opportunities in the United States that they would otherwise be denied. Immigrants coming from some countries may significantly improve their own or their families' health and longevity. All else being equal, the potential improvements in would-be immigrants' welfare seem to make a powerful argument for continuing to allow mass immigration.

The problem, as I have already shown, is that all else is *not* equal.[15] Whatever may once have been the case, today mass immigration drives down the wages of working-class Americans and increases economic inequality in the United States. It threatens the very existence of many nonhuman species and compromises future generations' right to a decent environment, both here and abroad. It makes it easier for wealthy elites in other countries to ignore the conditions that are driving so many people to emigrate in the first place. For all these reasons, the welfare argument does not make a convincing case for continuing high levels of immigration. Indeed, I believe current immigration levels are so harmful to the welfare of nonhuman beings and poor Americans that our immigration policy is unjust toward those two groups.[16]

Still, immigration's benefits *to new immigrants* remain substantial, and welfare arguments of the sort we are considering cannot be ignored by good progressives. While they do not justify continued mass immigration, they do make the case for some immigration, provided it can be accommodated with justice toward all concerned and without undermining ecological sustainability. I have tried to make just such a place for a reduced immigration in my proposal.

Such welfare arguments also point to a responsibility, not to immigrants per se, but to people around the globe who live in poverty, insecurity, and injustice. Even the most generous immigration policies will not help most of them, since only a small percentage can conceivably emigrate from their home countries and the worst off rarely have the resources to do so. The wealthy people of the world—including not just citizens of "the West," but hundreds of millions of people in the developing world itself—owe the world's poor people something. I'm not speaking here of just the lucky few millions who manage to emigrate to the West, but of the *billions* who will have to sink or swim where they are. Just what do we owe them?

In *One World: The Ethics of Globalization*, Peter Singer argues that the developed nations can and should increase and better target foreign aid to improve conditions for poor people overseas. I find Singer's arguments convincing and have included such a component in my own proposal for reforming immigration policy. Less valuable is Singer's silence, typical among progressives, regarding what wealthy people within the developing nations themselves owe the poor: a fairer distribution of wealth and political power, and greater opportunities for economic advancement. Too often, these elites instead give their fellow citizens a strong shove toward the exits. In response, I propose that encouraging economic equality and opportunity in other lands be made a cornerstone of US foreign policy, replacing our current emphasis on increasing the volume of international trade. There are limits to what the United States can accomplish in these areas: the primary responsibility to create economically just and flourishing nations rests with the citizens of those nations themselves.[17] But what we can do, through diplomacy and foreign aid, we indeed have an obligation to do. And where our actions or policies actually serve to undermine those efforts, as with the immigration status quo, we should change them.

Views about the proper scope of our global obligations, the best ways to fulfill them, and how to balance them with our obligations to our fellow citizens, are likely to vary widely. However, most progressives tend to agree with me that wealthy people, West and East, have a prima facie duty to share some of our wealth and help the world's poor people live better lives. Rather than try to justify this duty, I conclude this section with three brief comments on its proper scope and pursuit.

First, mass immigration is neither a sufficient nor an efficient means of meeting it. Inviting the world's poor to America to become our servants is no substitute for helping them create safe, just, flourishing societies where they live. Even taking the most positive view possible of its effects on immigrants, mass immigration does little for the vast majority of the world's poor. One caveat is that remittances from workers in the United States can be an important source of income for immigrants' families back home. But these economic benefits must be weighed against the dispersal and breakup of families through immigration, which is an important social cost. They also must be weighed against the cost of enabling these sender countries' continued failure to create just and sustainable societies. Remember, the 1% don't just live in America, but in China, India, and Mexico, too.

Second, serious progressives will not allow efforts to help poor people overseas run roughshod over our commitments to ecological sustainability or to economic justice for our fellow citizens. It is true that the serious and immediate needs of asylum seekers may sometimes overrule our prima facie duties to protect nature or to further a more egalitarian distribution of wealth in our own society. But committed progressives cannot interpret our duties to foreigners in ways that make our duties to our fellow citizens impossible to fulfill. This rules out immigration as a cheap form of foreign aid.

Third, fortunately, our prima facie duty to help the world's poor may be pursued in ways that do not undermine efforts to meet our prima facie environmental and social duties. The United States government should be much more generous and intelligent with development aid to poor countries (as we have seen, America ranks at the bottom among Western democracies in per capita foreign aid and much of this comes as military aid that actually harms poor people). It should fully fund international family planning efforts, which help both poor people and the environment. It should set trade policies to benefit workers and protect nature, rather than to maximize trade. The United States should pressure foreign governments to respect their citizens' rights, as mandated by international law, and change any US policies that undermine other countries' efforts to create more just or sustainable societies. Individual Americans should support charities with effective international aid programs, such as Oxfam and the United Nations Children's Fund. We should cultivate personal and professional friendships across borders, in an effort to understand and appreciate our fellow human beings from every nation.

All these efforts and more may be taken up without embracing mass immigration. Mass immigration is no substitute for such efforts. Most important, endless population growth and flooded labor markets are incompatible with creating just, sustainable, flourishing societies here in the United States and around the world.

ARE BORDERS BAD?

There is a visceral sense among many progressives that borders are bad. Borders limit people, keeping them from going where and doing what they want. They separate people, interfering with personal plans and the development of international understanding. They seem to emphasize possessiveness—this country is *mine*—which is a quality that progressives tend to dislike, often equating it with selfishness. As Michael Kellett, the forest activist from Massachusetts, put it: "If we don't allow immigrants into the US, then we are walling ourselves off and floating above the increasing morass of humanity everywhere else. . . . Walling ourselves off is not a solution."[18]

Still, borders have their uses. Many homeowners have a fence around the yard, and I guess that few people reading this book allow strangers to come and go as they please through their homes. The obvious reason is that private households provide us with important benefits. Beyond the various material possessions they allow us to enjoy, there is the control of key living spaces, which helps us live the kinds of lives we want to live, and the space and time necessary to focus on our most important relationships. All these good things would be devalued or made impossible by an "open door" policy—although a judicious hospitality enhances our enjoyment of them. Even Michael Kellett, when pressed, had to admit that while he was not comfortable "walling people out" of the United States, he did want to wall off sections of the Maine woods from development ("That's survival of the planet itself," he told me).[19]

Are there certain national "possessions" that would be threatened by an open borders policy, or by a too generous hospitality? I believe there are and that truly appreciating, enjoying, and protecting these things is, perhaps regrettably, inseparable from limiting access to them. These possessions include:

- A material prosperity that is widely shared, where no one who is willing to work for a living falls below a basic living standard.
- A political system with opportunities for power and influence at a number of levels, where an individual's efforts can occasionally make a difference.
- Comradeship and concern for our fellow citizens, which is both good in itself and necessary for the better working of society. This includes the willingness to tax ourselves to provide for the common good and to support people who cannot adequately support themselves.
- Natural areas that can become ecologically degraded if forced to accommodate too many visitors, and wildlife that can become rare or extinct if its habitat is destroyed to accommodate more people. Aldo Leopold called these America's "Great Possessions," which was one of his working titles for *A Sand County Almanac*.

A relatively egalitarian society. Self-government. Social solidarity. Access to wild nature. These are indeed great possessions that we would do well to safeguard as we design immigration policy. These goods are social achievements that each generation may sustain and build on, or allow to diminish and decay. Feeling possessive about them is part of an intelligent citizenship. Far from selfishness, working to protect our descendants' access to such possessions actually manifests our altruism. Those who would diminish future generations' access to these goods in an attempt to help poor people from other lands should at least acknowledge what they are asking Americans to give up.

Still, there remains a nagging sense among many progressives that borders are morally irrelevant. In an article titled "Patriotism and Cosmopolitanism," Martha Nussbaum accuses patriotic nationalists of substituting "a colorful idol for the substantive universal values of justice and right." All human beings, simply as human beings, have equal moral value, she asserts. Morality involves recognizing this universal value and acting upon it, often in the face of surface differences or particular loyalties that obscure it. The boundaries of a nation are "morally arbitrary." "Why should we think of people from China as our fellows the minute they dwell in a certain place, namely the United States, but not when they dwell in a certain other place, namely China?" Nussbaum asks. "What is it about the national boundary that magically converts people toward whom we are both incurious and indifferent into people to whom we have duties of mutual respect?"[20]

These are important questions, if a bit tendentiously stated. I answer, first, that American patriots should not be incurious or indifferent toward foreigners; that is a straw man argument. As Stephen Nathanson notes, "Exclusive concern for one's own country is not a necessary part of patriotism."[21] We may care more about our fellow citizens, while still showing reasonable concern for people living in other countries. Second, Chinese people who legally immigrate to the United States become our fellow citizens, for whom we have special responsibilities by virtue of that tie. Such responsibilities include ensuring they have equal protection under our laws, taxing ourselves to provide them with access to health care when they are sick, etc. In return, foreign-born Americans agree to take on those same civic responsibilities when they become citizens. Third, such responsible citizenship does not appear "magically." It must be cultivated;

its absence has deleterious consequences, for society as a whole but particularly for its less fortunate members; and for that reason, we should think twice before undermining it, even unintentionally. Fourth, dividing the world up into smaller units called nations is one way to facilitate real, effective citizenship and mutual responsibility for one another in an immense world of over seven billion people. Similarly, knowledge and devotion to particular landscapes makes environmentalism possible. We are rightly admonished to "think globally and act locally."

The hard truths behind Nussbaum's jibe at "morally arbitrary" boundaries are that they do lead to differential concern and action on behalf of others, and they do perpetuate differential access to resources. Borders can lock in place the failures of societies, and often the sins of the fathers are visited on their sons (and even more on their daughters). *But borders also help lock in societies' successes.*[22] They help preserve genuine human diversity in a world that has been shrunken and homogenized by modern technology. "Arbitrary" or artificial boundaries may be out of favor with the jet-setting global intelligentsia. Yet they make self-government possible, and self-government is a key human capability and a fundamental human right.[23]

All this is not to argue against more wide-ranging moral concerns and commitments. My immigration proposal builds in the right to asylum from persecution affirmed by article 14 of the Universal Declaration of Human Rights. It also includes serious commitments to address the "push factors" currently causing people to emigrate from their homelands. We are not allowed to treat people unjustly simply because they live outside our borders; we should not remain indifferent to their struggles to live better lives. But we may support universal human rights and increased development aid for the world's poor, while also recognizing the legitimacy—indeed, the necessity—of meeting our responsibilities as neighbors, community members, and citizens. Borders remain morally relevant, because we have different and stronger responsibilities to our fellow citizens than we have to the rest of humanity. Limiting immigration recognizes our responsibilities to poor people within our borders and to our descendants to create a more egalitarian and sustainable society. Acknowledging boundaries helps people make sense of their duties and responsibilities as citizens, which is part of creating a more just and sustainable world.

Of course, political borders do limit people's freedom and can interfere with their individual pursuit of happiness. That might be a good argument for keeping them somewhat permeable. But limitations on individual freedom are sometimes necessary to further the common good. Ultimately this justifies the making and securing of borders.[24] It would be best to honestly acknowledge all this.

Instead, many progressives appear to believe, in the words of a recent conservative commentator, that: "immigration controls by rich countries are mean. They close out the poor and vulnerable who only want the chance to make a better life. They are characterised by arbitrary rules whose effects can be inhumane—breaking up families, locking up children, deporting good people to uncertain futures in godforsaken countries, etc. . . . [But the reality is that] liberals need immigration controls for their cherished welfare state to function. They're just happy to let the conservatives take the rap [for them]." The anonymous author of these reflections continues:

> One cannot build such a welfare state in which everyone in our society has the right to health care, education, unemployment protection, disability support, pensions, etc., without building a wall to keep some people out . . . The viability, legitimacy, and decency of any welfare state depends upon controlling membership to the society it is created to serve. That's what a real social contract looks like. Liberals are always criticising the racist motivations for and practical inhumanity of the immigration controls demanded by conservatives, but their objections are superficial.[25]

He or she concludes that reliable conservative support for limiting immigration "allows liberals to get away with the hypocrisy of depending on immigration controls while pretending that they are against them." In this rare case, I actually agree with the conservative critique (although not with the need for a physical wall at the border, as I explained in the previous chapter). It would be better for progressives to acknowledge frankly the need to limit immigration and help design humane immigration policies that truly further the common good.

THE LIMITS OF COSMOPOLITANISM

We can perhaps better understand the value of borders by considering another argument for doing away with them in order to facilitate increased immigration.[26] In an article titled "The Morality of Immigration," Mathias Risse, a professor at Harvard's Kennedy School of Government, states that he "wish[es] to make a plea for the relevance of moral considerations in debates about immigration. Too often, immigration debates are conducted solely from the standpoint of 'what is good for us,' without regard for the justifiability of immigration policies to those excluded." For Risse, immigration is instead "a moral problem that must be considered in the context of global justice." He believes that "the earth belongs to humanity in common and that this matters for assessing immigration policy."[27]

Many countries around the world have higher population densities than the United States. Based on this, Risse argues that: "by global standards the population of the United States is too small relative to the amount of space to which it claims exclusive control" and "the United States is severely underusing its chunk of three-dimensional, commonly owned space." We are sitting on resources that other people, in a crowded world, could use to improve their lot. For this reason, he believes, "illegal immigrants should be naturalized and more widespread immigration should be permitted." As Risse puts it, "Germany has a population density of about 600 per square mile, as does the United Kingdom. For Japan it is 830, for the Netherlands 1,200, and for Bangladesh 2,600. In the United States overall it is 80 per square mile . . . In light of these numbers, it is amusing that in debates about immigration many Americans think that there are already too many people living in their country."[28]

Risse looks out on a world of vast economic inequalities and, like many progressives, affirms a duty that those living in rich nations help those living in poor ones. "Immigration can plausibly be regarded as one way of satisfying duties toward the global poor," he argues. "Immigration— permanent or temporary—can serve this function partly because it allows some people access to greener pastures, and partly because of the remittances sent back by immigrants to their countries of origin." In fact, "once we think of immigration in a global context, we are led to ask more fundamental questions—namely, why it would be acceptable in the first place (especially to those thus excluded) that we draw an imaginary line in the dust or adopt the course of a river and think of that *as a border.*"[29]

I believe Risse's argument illustrates the limitations of an overly abstract approach to public policy, as he applies highly general ethical principles to a particular policy issue in a specific time and place, with little apparent understanding of the effects his proposals might have on the people living in that society.[30] What might higher immigration levels mean for poorer Americans? Compared to other industrial democracies, US immigration policies already bring a higher percentage of less-skilled, less-educated immigrants into our labor markets, so low-wage workers already bear the brunt of immigration's downward pressure on earnings. As we have seen, in recent decades high immigration levels have significantly driven down wages and driven up unemployment for poorer citizens, while greatly benefiting wealthier Americans. In effect, Risse proposes a massive increase in the numbers of less-skilled, less-educated immigrants. This would accelerate income inequality in America and probably drive tens of millions of American workers into poverty.

What might higher immigration levels mean for attempts to create an ecologically sustainable society in the United States? Already, some 320 million Americans fail to live in a way that shares the landscape generously with nonhuman beings, or maintains essential ecosystem services for future generations. Increasing human numbers will inevitably increase pollution, resource consumption, habitat conversion, and species loss. Even at current immigration rates, our population is set to nearly double over the next hundred years; Risse's proposal would greatly accelerate this population growth, tripling or quadrupling our population over the same period. This would surely doom efforts to create a sustainable society in the United States. And with our gargantuan appetites for natural resources, an unsustainable America is a threat to the entire world.

"Humanity as a whole owns the earth and its resources in common," Risse asserts: "not, of course, all those things that in some sense are manmade, but the original resources of the earth. After all—and this is the intuitive argument for this standpoint—such resources are needed by all, and their existence is the accomplishment of no one."[31] He affirms that young people born in a particular nation have no greater claim to the wealth or opportunities available there than young people born elsewhere, since it is merely chance, not merit, which determines the nationality into which one is born.

This argument might have made some sense in the eighteenth and nineteenth centuries, when many immigrants came to America to farm supposedly empty lands. But in the twenty-first century, people from Honduras or Pakistan are not coming to America to take up quarter sections of farmland under the Homestead Act. They are looking for better-paying jobs provided by the American economy and fleeing countries where jobs are scarce or poorly paid. Such high-paying jobs are clearly a "man-made" resource. So are the rights and freedoms, the just institutions and efficient infrastructures, that many immigrants seek to enjoy. These good things are indeed the "accomplishments" of particular societies, whose citizens have created them through their own efforts. Similarly, the bad things that immigrants are fleeing—tyranny, insecurity, too many people chasing too few jobs—are what they and their societies have managed to accomplish. Much immigration around the world today is away from countries rich in "original" natural resources, toward countries rich in human-made economic opportunities; away from countries where fertility rates are high and labor markets are swamped, toward countries where fertility rates are low and labor is in greater demand.

On its own terms, then, Risse's argument fails to justify a general right to immigrate in the twenty-first century. Even worse, his proposal would take away people's incentives to create the kinds of societies that produce and steward the very goods that immigrants are seeking.

Creating fairer, cleaner, wealthier, more egalitarian, more tolerant, less crowded, less bigoted, or otherwise better societies involves hard work and sacrifice. People typically undertake this work in the hope that they and their descendants will be able to enjoy the fruits of success, or because they fear that they and their descendants will have to live with the consequences of failure. If they can pick up and leave a difficult situation, they are likely to do so, rather than stay and fight to improve the society they live in. We see a good example of this today in Mexico, a nation with bountiful "original resources." There a small elite monopolizes the country's wealth with impunity, partly because they can force their less fortunate fellow citizens into exile to earn the decent living that a more just society would provide at home. Given pervasive corruption, the difficulty of making ends meet, and the dangers of challenging the system, it is perfectly reasonable for poor Mexicans to focus on helping themselves and their families by emigrating. But their gain is Mexico's loss.

Members of more successful societies would have little reason to work to improve them under Risse's immigration proposal, since any social achievements would be held on a very weak tenure, always at the mercy of claims coming from members of less successful societies. High wages for less-skilled workers would have to be sacrificed as a matter of "morality" if large numbers of unskilled workers wanted to emigrate from crowded, economically depressed countries. Widespread social tolerance for gays or atheists, or support for women's equality, would have to be forfeited if enough people from more conservative societies needed to emigrate in search of a better life. Efforts to set aside land and resources for other species would have to be abandoned if potential immigrants with large families needed to use the resources of another country.

Risse suggests that these kinds of concerns, because they focus on the flourishing of our own society, are selfish, being "based on little more than self-interest."[32] And he claims to know what Americans *should* do regarding immigration, because unlike most of us, he is thinking about such issues morally. But Risse holds a fundamentally mistaken view of morality, which must be more empirically grounded and more respectful of the particular commitments that actually allow people to transcend selfishness.[33] Getting clearer about this can help us specify a truly just approach to immigration policy.

Risse's abstract conception of morality emphasizes a radical split between self-interest and moral behavior, equating morality exclusively with selflessness and sacrifice. True morality, by contrast, often extends people's innate self-concern to more fully include family, friends, neighbors, and fellow community members.[34] It realizes that most of the good that we do for others is not purely selfless, but occurs within particular roles that we find meaningful and that contribute to our own happiness, too. It is especially concerned to build up the claims of citizenship and to make them more meaningful and effective in people's lives, since it sees doing so as essential to securing human happiness as widely as possible. Think of the misery that could be alleviated around the world if more of the wealthy and powerful truly thought of their fellow citizens *as* fellow citizens.[35]

Abstract morality boldly legislates for the entire world. It readily con-templates redistributing resources on the basis of a few general ethical principles. True morality looks more carefully at the details of redistri-bution in particular places, as we have done regarding the redistributive effects of immigration in the United States, and pays equal attention to redistribution and responsibility. It insists that rich people share their wealth, as a matter of justice. But it also may demand things from the poor: asking them to have fewer children, for example, if they or their societies cannot provide for more.

Abstract morality gazes lovingly at its own principles. In a transcen-dental realm, it creates beautiful pictures of justice and happiness. Mean-while, back on Earth, true morality must pay attention to realities. On the ground, a large influx of poor people may make other poor people even poorer. An agreement to leave a little water in the river for the fish may have to be abandoned, if more people move in and need the water. Of course, in theory it is always possible to do everything: accommo-date lots more people *and* keep wages high; use water so efficiently that we free up more for fish *and* for people. But unlike some philosophers, people and fish don't live "in theory" but out in the real, physical world, in towns and rivers, cities and oceans. Our abstract moral pictures may be lovely; applied intelligently, they may provide moral guidance. But they mislead us when we use them to avoid facing the real world's limitations and trade-offs.

With abstract morality we soar, pure angels, without sin or selfishness. Real morality, though, remembering that we are all self-interested, asks bluntly: how would a particular policy proposal affect particular classes of people? College professors such as myself and Mathias Risse are highly educated, well-paid professionals, often with considerable job security. As a class we will not see our wages lowered or jobs lost through an in-flux of large numbers of poorly educated immigrants. We are, however, well placed to benefit from the mass immigration advocated by Risse, as we pay poverty wages to the workers who wash our cars or reshingle our roofs, clean our homes or diaper our children. For many of our fellow citizens who earn less and who compete for these jobs, such calculations are reversed. Mass immigration can only be regarded as a just means to satisfy "our" duties toward the global poor, if wealthy professionals are willing to accept that poor Americans should bear the main economic burden of satisfying those duties.

Invoking "morality" in the way Risse does can help remind us of our legitimate responsibilities, including potential responsibilities to would-be immigrants. But abstract morality leads us astray when it assumes that our most general moral status—human being—trumps all our particular connections, such as spouse, parent, community member, citizen, or defender of a well-loved landscape. Real morality realizes that these particular roles generate genuine moral demands that must be carefully weighed against one another when they conflict. Far from being selfish, attentiveness to the full spectrum of such claims is essential to real morality and one key to creating a just immigration policy.

In the end, I do agree with Mathias Risse, that "moral considerations should influence immigration policies much more than they currently do."[36] Were Americans to take this suggestion seriously, however, I believe we would actually reduce, rather than increase, the numbers of immigrants we allow into our country.

CONCLUSION

We have now considered the main moral objections to limiting or reducing immigration into the United States. Far from undermining my policy proposal, I believe considerations of justice in fact support that proposal. In addition, trying to answer the moral objections to such a course of action can help define a stronger, more robust progressivism.

By honestly reckoning with limits, we come to a more realistic understanding and a better appreciation of a genuine progressive *citizenship*. This concept has not become outmoded in a more economically integrated world. On the contrary, it must be reinvigorated, in the United States and across the globe, in order to achieve progressive political goals. Progressives look forward to a world of just, flourishing nations, with citizens governing themselves fairly and compassionately, countries at peace with one another, and humanity as a whole living sustainably on the planet. But there is no achieving any of this without recognition of limits and a willingness to live within them.

We came to similar conclusions when considering some common environmental and economic objections to immigration reform in earlier chapters. This strengthens the general conclusion that the "key log" that needs to shift in order for us to imagine and achieve a more progressive political order is reckoning honestly with limits. As with the environmental and economic objections to reducing immigration, the temptation in meeting these ethical objections may be to equivocate, or to try to finesse hard trade-offs. That will not work. We need to accept limits to resources and limits to growth, and grapple with them intelligently, if we hope to create a just and sustainable society. The time to do so is now.

With that affirmation, this book is drawing to a close. I have given my reasons for reducing immigration into the United States, presented a detailed proposal for reforming immigration policy, and responded to the most common and consequential objections to that proposal. In the end, I return to my primary argument. Immigration is now the main driver of American population growth and a leading contributor to growing economic inequality in the United States. Continued American population growth is incompatible with sustainability, nationally or globally. Growing economic inequality saps our strength as a nation. Therefore, progressives committed to sustainability and justice should support reducing our current, excessive levels of immigration. At a minimum, we should acknowledge that at present we are not winning the battles for ecological sustainability and against economic inequality, and that new ideas and tactics are worth considering.

eleven

CONCLUSION

Since the 1980s, most American workers' incomes have remained largely flat when adjusted for inflation. Yet significant numbers of us financed greatly increased consumption during this period, by borrowing against the value of our homes or taking on heavy credit card debt. In 2008, the bubble burst and home prices declined steeply. The country entered a recession from which it has yet to fully recover and millions of Americans were forced to declare bankruptcy.

Since the 1990s, most Americans have known that our excessive energy use is generating high levels of greenhouse gas emissions, warming the Earth and destabilizing its climate. Our response has been to use even more energy and to point fingers at the Chinese, whose emissions have been rising faster. While one major party candidate for President in 2012 expressed concern about climate change and the other mocked that concern, neither proposed sufficient steps to reduce America's greenhouse gas emissions. Meanwhile, Earth continues to warm and catastrophic storms such as Hurricanes Katrina and Sandy are increasing in number, strength, and destructiveness.

In 2001 and 2002, the 107th US Congress enacted an immense tax cut, skewed heavily to benefit the wealthy, while also voting to go to war against Afghanistan and Iraq. This was the first time in history that the United States started a war without enacting taxes to pay for it. In 2003, as the country began fighting the Iraq war, the 108th Congress passed a new Medicare prescription drug benefit costing tens of billions of dollars annually, again without levying new taxes to pay for the measure. Predictably enough, the federal debt skyrocketed.

These examples suggest a disturbing pattern in recent American politics in which the perennial human desire to get something for nothing is married to an impressive ability to suspend common sense. On the conservative side, we have the dogma that cutting taxes actually raises revenue, since it stimulates growth that more than makes up for the revenue forgone through lower tax rates. The fact that this approach was tried and failed in both the Reagan and second Bush administrations, leading to lower tax revenues and increased deficits, does not shake the faith of true believers eager to give the theory another chance.

On the progressive side, many believe that we can create a genuinely sustainable society without limiting consumption or population growth, solely through technological improvements and greater efficiency. Once again, there are economic theorists ready to justify this view: we hear of the "environmental Kuznets curve," whereby as societies become rich, both the desire and the resources to finance environmental protection increase, leading to less pollution and more nature preservation. The fact that "the curve" has been disproved for carbon emissions[1] and mass species extinction,[2] the signal environmental challenges of our time, has not shaken adherents from their belief. Like the idea that we can increase tax receipts by lowering taxes, the idea that we can protect nature by taking more from her is too appealing for some to abandon.

I think of this as the "eat cake, lose weight" philosophy of life. As someone with a bit larger girth than is good for me, I feel its sympathetic pull. Yet candor compels me to state that I am not losing weight under this regimen and neither are my fellow Americans. We are fatter than ever. Our country is more deeply in debt, too, and further from genuine sustainability.

As I warned you at the outset, this book does not take an eat cake, lose weight approach to immigration policy. If there is one thing a study of America's immigration history should teach us it is that any policy will have winners and losers, and that choosing an immigration policy involves real trade-offs between genuine goods. That does not mean that some policies are not more successful at maximizing overall benefits, or superior in helping us further the common good. Obviously, I think some immigration policies are better than others or I would not have taken the time to elaborate my own recommendations. But I am tempted to say that I would be happy if readers came to support immigration policies diametrically opposed to mine, provided they understood the implications of those policies and were willing to enact them consciously.

I am tempted . . . but in the end, I hold back. That is because I believe in progressive ideals of justice and sustainability and I am convinced that these demand a reduction in immigration levels, not an increase. That is the case I have tried to make in this book. So I have proposed that we reduce immigration into the United States, by taking the following measures:

- Cut legal immigration from 1.1 million to 300,000 per year.
- Reduce illegal immigration by mandating use of a national employment verification program for all new hires and strictly enforcing sanctions against employers who hire undocumented workers.
- Rework trade agreements and increase and better target development aid, in order to help people live better lives and rein in population growth in their own countries.

Such a policy would allow many of the benefits of immigration to continue, such as providing asylum for political refugees and allowing small influxes of workers with special skills. At the same time, it would reduce unemployment by reserving most new jobs for American workers, alleviate the downward pressure on wages caused by flooded labor markets, and reduce overall economic inequality. My proposal would also move the United States toward population stabilization, a sine qua non of sustainability. Because America's current total fertility rate of 2.05 is very close to replacement rate and because reducing immigration would likely help drive that rate even lower, such stabilization is possible—provided we are willing to limit immigration.

This proposal is solidly within the mainstream of the best thinking on environmental sustainability. As the President's Council on Sustainable Development put it in 1996: "Managing population growth, resources, and wastes is essential to ensuring that the total impact of these factors is within the bounds of sustainability. Stabilizing the population without changing consumption and waste production patterns would not be enough, but it would make an immensely challenging task more manageable. In the United States, each is necessary; neither alone is sufficient."[3] One of the Council's ten national goals for creating a sustainable society was: "Move toward stabilization of [the] U.S. population,"[4] and its Population and Consumption Task Force found that "reducing immigration levels is a necessary part of population stabilization and the drive toward sustainability."[5]

My policy proposal is designed to further the interests of poor and middle-class Americans, rather than the interests of our society's wealthier members or big corporations. It would help reduce economic inequality. And it is just, both in its goals and in its proposed methods of implementation. Of course, some progressives deny that any policy that limits immigration can be just, but they are mistaken. As the Jordan Commission on Immigration Reform put it in 1997: "The Commission decries hostility and discrimination against immigrants as antithetical to the traditions and interests of the country. At the same time, we disagree with those who would label efforts to control immigration as being inherently anti-immigrant. Rather, it is both a right and a responsibility of a democratic society to manage immigration so that it serves the national interests."[6]

Reducing immigration should be part of a comprehensive US population policy, designed first to stabilize and then to reduce human numbers, slowly and humanely, both at home and abroad. As part of this effort, in addition to reducing immigration, I believe federal and state governments should:

- Increase funding for family planning clinics and take other steps to improve easy, inexpensive access to contraception domestically.
- Preserve the right to abortion (forcing women to bear children they do not want is unjust and forcing them to have illegal abortions is dangerous).
- Limit the federal child tax credit to one or two children, to encourage smaller families.

Meanwhile in our foreign policy, the United States should:

- Increase funding for international family planning efforts to help secure safe, affordable contraception in other countries.
- Vigorously support women's health and reproductive rights, and girls' equal rights to primary and secondary education, worldwide.
- Deny foreign aid and immigration slots to nations that fail to commit to stabilizing their populations or sharing wealth fairly among their citizens.

Such policies would make a strong statement that the age of endless growth is over and that the United States will no longer act as a release valve for failed or unjust societies that cannot or will not provide decent opportunities for their own citizens. It will spread the message that people who want to create good lives for themselves and their families need to do so where they are and that those nations that fail to keep their populations from ballooning will themselves have to suffer the consequences. This approach seems best calculated to convince common people and politicians worldwide to take steps to reverse global population growth and to create societies where people want to remain.

WHAT IS *YOUR* NUMBER?

Many progressive readers instinctively reject any proposal to reduce immigration into the United States. I understand and share many of your concerns. Still, I contend that paeans to sustainability or earnest expressions of our strong environmental feelings are merely hot air, when coupled with a blithe acceptance of the doubling or tripling of America's population. Similarly it is counterproductive to advocate for tax, labor, and benefits policies designed to increase security for poorer Americans and reduce economic inequality, while at the same time advocating for immigration policies that increase economic insecurity and inequality. We need to get immigration policy working for poorer Americans, not against them as it does now.

At a minimum, readers unwilling to reduce immigration into the United States need to own up to the demographic, environmental, and economic implications of their positions. If you support the immigration status quo of about 1.25 million immigrants annually, then you also support increasing America's population to approximately 525 million people by 2100, a 66% increase over current numbers. If you support an immigration policy along the lines of the Senate's immigration reform bill of 2013, which might have increased immigration to 2.25 million annually (the numbers were kept deliberately vague), then you also support more than doubling America's population to about 670 million people by 2100. If you support the *Wall Street Journal*'s "open borders" vision then you also support *tripling*, at a minimum, the number of Americans to over 900 million people by 2100.

If you support these scenarios or anything like them, then you don't just support drastically increasing America's human population. You also support more cars, more houses, more malls, more power lines, more concrete and asphalt. You support less habitat and fewer resources for wildlife; less water in the rivers and streams for native fish; fewer forests, prairies and wetlands; fewer wild birds and wild mammals (except perhaps for house sparrows, rats, and a few other human commensals). You support replacing these other species with human beings and our economic support systems—and you are willing to wager your grandchildren's happiness that those support systems can continue to supply *a lot* more people with the goods and services they need to survive and flourish, despite signs that the demands of our current 320 million people are already overstressing them.

Similarly, if you endorse an immigration status quo bringing in 1.25 million annual immigrants, the majority of them poorly educated and relatively unskilled, you also accept the downward pressure on poor workers' wages and greater unemployment that inevitably accompanies this influx. If you endorse *increasing* these annual immigration numbers, you advocate *stronger* downward pressure on those wages and *higher* unemployment among the poor. Under these or any other scenarios where mass immigration continues, we may reasonably expect an increase in economic inequality, as poorer Americans' wages decline and wealthier Americans capture the lion's share of the economic benefits of immigration-driven economic growth. With increased mass immigration we may also expect further declines in the employment rates of African Americans and younger Americans. According to Andrew Sum and his colleagues at the Center for Labor Market Studies at Northeastern University, "A one percentage-point increase in the share of new immigrants in the state's workforce will reduce the probability of employment of young adults [ages 16–24] by 2.1 percentage points," with larger declines among young African Americans.[7]

Some progressives honestly believe that these negative economic impacts are relatively small, or that they can be counterbalanced by more progressive tax rates, increases in the minimum wage, improved government benefits, or other progressive economic policies. But we saw in earlier chapters that immigration's downward pressure on income and employment is substantial and that it falls heaviest on those least able to bear it, the working poor. We also saw that enacting progressive economic policies is itself made more difficult by mass immigration. Some progressives pin their hopes for greater economic equality on a revived labor movement. But as we saw earlier, mass immigration undermines efforts to organize workers, or to strike for improved wages and benefits. It thus undercuts attempts to revive organized labor.

After nearly half a century of steadily increasing economic inequality and three decades with little progress on our most pressing environmental problems, American progressives should be skeptical of our chances of reversing these trends while completely ignoring one of their main causes. Excessive immigration is currently the main driver of US population growth and a chief cause of sprawl, excessive resource use, stagnating wages, high unemployment, and growing economic inequality. For these reasons, progressives committed to sustainability and economic justice should support reducing immigration into the United States.

LIBERTY ENLIGHTENING THE WORLD

The Statue of Liberty was first conceived by Édouard-René Lefebvre de Laboulaye, a law professor and "prominent liberal leader who admired the United States as a model of liberty and self-government."[8] In his three-volume *History of the United States*, Laboulaye spoke of the United States signifying "the dawn of a new world," and as a beacon of light shining forth to inspire other nations across the globe.[9] Like other liberals of his time, he hoped to see political and intellectual freedom spread widely as the natural birthright of all humanity.

The statue's formal title was and remains "Liberty Enlightening the

World." As originally envisioned by the French and first received by Americans in 1886, it had nothing to do with immigration. But almost immediately the statue's meaning began to shift. Cuban revolutionary José Martí, reporting on its formal unveiling, noted perceptively: "Irishmen, Poles, Italians, Czechs, Germans freed from tyranny or want—all hail the monument of Liberty because to them it seems to incarnate their own uplifting." By 1886, the Great Wave was in full swing and New York was the premier port of entry into America. Between 1886 and 1924 approximately 16 million immigrants sailed into New York harbor, and many of them never forgot their first sight of Lady Liberty. One, Edward Steiner, wrote of that moment: "The steerage is still mute. . . . Slowly the ship glides into the harbor, and when it passes under the shadow of the Statue of Liberty, the silence is broken, and a thousand hands are outstretched in greeting to this new divinity to whose keeping they now entrust themselves."[10] Another remembered simply: "Tears of joy streamed down my face as we passed by the Statue of Liberty."[11]

Emma Lazarus' celebrated poem "The New Colossus" memorably expressed this new meaning. A young writer from a wealthy, established New York Jewish family, Lazarus had been stirred by accounts of the atrocities visited against her co-religionists in Russia and by their struggles to make new lives in the United States. Bolding renaming the statue "Mother of Exiles," she sang:

. . . From her beacon-hand
Glows world-wide welcome; her mild eyes command
The air-bridged harbor that twin cities frame.
"Keep, ancient lands, your storied pomp!" cries she
With silent lips. "Give me your tired, your poor,
Your huddled masses yearning to breathe free,
The wretched refuse of your teeming shore.
Send these, the homeless, tempest-tost to me,
I lift my lamp beside the golden door!

The poem speaks to the yearning for liberty among the oppressed. It defines the spirit of America as one of generous hospitality toward newcomers, recognized here as worthy of respect and deserving of a fair chance in life. For many Americans, the statue's primary meaning is now captured by that welcoming phrase, "Mother of Exiles."

It is perfectly fitting that the Statue of Liberty has become a symbol and a celebration of immigration into the United States. It reminds Americans of the many millions of newcomers who have found a haven from oppression here and made better lives for themselves and their families. It helps us celebrate immigrants' many contributions to our country. But today it might also be appropriate to recall some of the other meanings symbolized by the statue. I make this suggestion not as a conservative desiring a return to timeless or original truths, but in a progressive spirit that seeks to match evolving ideals to changing realities.

In 1886, four years before the western frontier was officially declared closed by the US Census Bureau, the population of the United States was 58 million. As this book goes to press at the close of 2014, it stands near 320 million: an increase of 452%. Can we realistically imagine doubling or tripling our population over the next 125 years, much less increasing it 4.5 times? It is safe to assume that Emma Lazarus never imagined holes in the ozone layer, global climate change, or worldwide species extinctions. We know they exist and that we have helped cause them. Perhaps that should make a difference to US immigration policy.

In 1886, the United States was industrializing rapidly. New factories, new mines, new railroad lines, all generated an insatiable demand for unskilled labor, which immigration helped to fill. Today's postindustrial US economy does not appear to need millions more unskilled workers, as shown by high unemployment rates among those with fewer skills. While it once may have made economic sense to import many millions of workers with only an elementary education, today good jobs for unskilled workers are scarce and our ability to guarantee that these jobs pay a living wage is under severe stress. Again, we need to ask whether these new realities should be reflected in immigration policy.

Some things have not changed since Emma Lazarus' time. In 1886, as in 2014, Americans decried foreign tyrannies. We remain grateful that we can grant political refugees asylum from persecution, or provide a new start to individuals treated unfairly in their own countries. Yet 130 years after the composition of "The New Colossus," we need to think harder and ask some difficult questions regarding that "wretched refuse" streaming out from our sender-countries' "teeming shores."

Why are these people "wretched": poor, beaten down, and discontented with their lives in their homelands? Probably because their fellow citizens have been unwilling to fairly share resources and opportunities with them. Perhaps these societies have not succeeded in creating decent political conditions for any of their members. In either case, shipping some of their most striving and adventurous citizens off to the United States seems an unlikely prescription for national improvement.

Why are these countries "teeming": filled to bursting with people? Simply put, it seems that folks in Mexico and Guatemala, the Philippines and Vietnam, are having more children than their societies can accommodate. But sending surplus members off to the United States seems likely to perpetuate economic unfairness within these countries, while increasing overpopulation and ecological degradation both in the United States and globally. Americans cannot dictate that people in other countries have fewer children, but we can at least stop encouraging their demographic excesses. That would be good for them, good for us, and good for the world as a whole.

Then and now, Americans love immigrant success stories, each one reaffirming the tremendous potential hidden within each human being. But "The New Colossus" implies that a new start in the New World is *the* answer for Earth's downtrodden masses. This it never was and certainly cannot be today in a much more crowded world, with Americans bumping up against ecological limits and having trouble providing a fair deal to our own poor citizens. Total immigration into the US has never topped 2 million a year, while the global population increases by about 78 million people annually.

So let us be clear: the answer to wretchedness and oppression is to end it where it exists—not to export surplus or troublesome inhabitants elsewhere. The world's people deserve the opportunity to live good lives in their home countries and most of them will never get the chance to live good lives anywhere else.

*

Given all this, I believe we must reinterpret the Statue of Liberty once again, in terms of its original title: "Liberty Enlightening the World." Americans must prove that we can live freely and flourish as a nation, with justice for all our citizens, in an ecologically sustainable manner. If we achieve this, I believe America can indeed serve as a beacon of hope to people around the world. But not if we fail to distinguish between liberty and license. Americans cannot so revel in our freedom that we despoil our nation's lands and waters, either through pollution or overdevelopment. Similarly, our free market economic system must be balanced by a willingness to refrain from pressing our economic advantages over our fellow citizens to unjust conclusions. Restraint in these matters is inseparably tied to accepting limits. For that reason, we cannot interpret Lady Liberty's torch as license for anyone to settle in the United States whenever he or she chooses. Freedom must be coupled with restraint and balanced by a respect for law and the common good.[12]

In the United States today, both our liberty and our ability to serve as an example to the rest of the world are threatened by gigantism, under which I include our sheer numbers, our vast appetites, and the immense corporations that threaten to overwhelm our democracy. In this context, we may recall the words of a Russian émigré, returning to Europe via steamer in 1916:

> Is that the Statue of Liberty? So tiny, lost in the noise of the harbour and framed against the soaring skyscrapers of the Wall Street banks. Was this powerless, tiny figure shrinking before the all-powerful gigantic skyscrapers, those guardians of financial deals, the Statue of Liberty we had pictured to ourselves? . . . It is these solid walls of stone, the safe refuge of the kings of American capital, which now more completely express the "spirit" that reigns over the continent of Columbus than the pitiful, shrunken, green statue that seems to be embarrassed.[13]

It is true that the force and persuasiveness of the United States as a global example depends partly on our size and power. But properly fulfilling this role does not depend on increasing our bulk, any more than it depends on building a new Statue of Liberty that is ten times larger than the current version. It depends on living up to our ideals and actually creating a nation dedicated to liberty, where freedom flowers into worthy lives, just institutions, friendship among citizens ("the noble love of comrades," as another New York poet put it), and peace and fair-dealing between our country and all others. America needs to live up to these ideals, because of our myriad impacts as a great power and because our example continues to speak powerfully to people around the world.

Citizens everywhere must take up their varied burdens in the struggle for liberty. In China and Mexico, that means fighting for political rights, against corruption, and for better opportunities for economic advancement. In the United States, it means reinvigorating our democracy, living lives that are worthy of the freedoms we already have, reducing economic inequality, and finding the means to make the world's largest and (in conventional terms) most successful economy ecologically sustainable. I hope I have shown in this book how reducing immigration into the United States has an important role to play in these efforts.

APPENDIX

Historical Sources for Progressive Arguments for Reducing US Immigration

(A) REMARKS BY SAMUEL GOMPERS ON IMMIGRATION

Samuel Gompers (1850–1924), the founder and president of the American Federation of Labor (AFL), had a long career unionizing American workers and fighting for their rights and prosperity. An immigrant himself, over time he came to support reducing immigration into the United States. Like many labor advocates in his time and ours, Gompers sought to balance concern for immigrants with consideration for the well-being of American workers. These excerpts are from The Samuel Gompers Papers, *edited by Stuart Kaufman.*

I agree with you, too, that it is hardly fair to have our people crowded out of employment by those who simply come here for the purpose of working at low wages—higher than those they may be accustomed to in their own countries—and then after a while return there. I am also free to say to you, however, that I do not see how a remedy is to be obtained without closing the ports entirely, and as to that there is considerable division of opinion. It may not be amiss to call attention to the fact that the introduction of one machine in a trade may throw more men out of employment than the "Greeks" who come here even in the manner which you describe.

(Gompers to John Watts, November 23, 1899)

At the outset, I want to say that the organized labor movement of America is not a "know-nothing" organization. It does not want to erect a wall around the borders of our country and keep everybody else out; it does not declare "America for Americans," or for those who are now within American borders. But on the other hand it is equally true that the thinking workingmen of the United States have . . . come to the conclusion that there must be some better regulation and some limitation.

(Testimony before US Congress, House Committee
on Immigration and Naturalization, February 29, 1912)

The workers of America have felt most keenly the pernicious results of the establishment of foreign standards of work, wages and conduct in American industries and commerce. Foreign standards of wages do not permit American standards of life. Foreign labor has driven American workers out of many trades, callings, and communities, and the influence of those lower standards has permeated widely. . . . The labor movement has urged the adoption of a national policy that would enable us to select as future citizens of our country those who can be assimilated and made truly American. . . . It is only a half truth to say that the literacy test would close the gates of opportunity to illiterate foreigners. As a matter of fact there is very little real opportunity for these people in our industrial centers. Usually they have been brought over here either by steamship or railroad companies and other greedy corporations, by employers, or as a result of collusion between these groups. They have been brought over here for the purpose of exploitation, and until they develop powers of resistance and determination to secure things for themselves they have little opportunity here. These same qualities would secure for them within their own countries many of the advantages that later come to them here.

(Gompers writing in the *American Federationist*, April 1916)

America must not be overwhelmed.

Every effort to enact immigration legislation must expect to meet a number of hostile forces and, in particular, two hostile forces of considerable strength.

One of these is composed of corporation employers who desire to employ physical strength (broad backs) at the lowest possible wage and who prefer a rapidly revolving labor supply at low wages to a regular supply of American wage earners at fair wages.

The other is composed of racial groups in the United States who oppose all restrictive legislation because they want the doors left open for an influx of their countrymen regardless of the menace to the people of their adopted country.

(Gompers letter to Congress, March 19, 1924)

(B) EXCERPTS FROM THE REPORTS OF THE US COMMISSION ON IMMIGRATION REFORM, 1994–1997

Congress and President George H. W. Bush created the nonpartisan US Commission on Immigration Reform as part of the Immigration Act of 1990, with a mandate to explore and recommend policy options in the national interest. It is commonly referred to as "the Jordan Commission" after its first chair, congresswoman Barbara Jordan. The Commission recommended streamlining the immigration process, enforcing laws against illegal immigration, and reducing unskilled immigration and overall immigration numbers in order to avoid harming working-class Americans. None of its major recommendations were enacted into law. A record of the Commission's work, including testimony taken and its reports to Congress, may be found at http://www.utexas.edu/lbj/uscir/.

Underlying Principles
Certain basic principles underlie the Commission's work. The Commission decries hostility and discrimination against immigrants as antithetical to the traditions and interests of the country. At the same time, we disagree with those who would label efforts to control immigration as being inherently anti-immigrant. Rather, it is both a right and a responsibility of a democratic society to manage immigration so that it serves the national interest.

(*U.S. Immigration Policy: Restoring Credibility*, Executive Summary, i)

Legal Permanent Admissions

The Commission reiterates its support for a properly regulated system for admitting lawful permanent residents. Research and analyses conducted since the issuance of the Commission's report on legal immigration support our view that a properly regulated system of legal permanent admissions serves the national interest. The Commission urges reforms in our legal immigration system to enhance the benefits accruing from the entry of newcomers while guarding against harms, particularly to the most vulnerable of U.S. residents—those who are themselves unskilled and living in poverty. . . .

Current immigration levels should be sustained for the next several years while the U.S. revamps its legal immigration system and shifts the priorities for admission away from the extended family and toward the nuclear family and away from the unskilled and toward the higher-skilled immigrant. Thereafter, modest reductions in levels of immigration—to about 550,000 per year, comparable to those of the 1980s—will result from the changed priority system. The Commission continues to believe that legal admission numbers should be authorized by Congress for a specified time (e.g., three to five years) to ensure regular, periodic review and, if needed, change by Congress. This review should consider the adequacy of admission numbers for accomplishing priorities.

(Becoming an American: Immigration and
Immigrant Policy, Executive Summary, xvi–xxii)

The Commission recommends the elimination of the admission of unskilled workers. Unless there is another compelling interest, such as in the entry of nuclear families and refugees, it is not in the national interest to admit unskilled workers. This is especially true when the U.S. economy is showing difficulty in absorbing disadvantaged workers and when efforts towards welfare reform indicate that many unskilled Americans will be entering the labor force.

(Legal Immigration: Setting Priorities, Executive Summary, xxiv)

Since its very beginnings, the United States has been a place of refuge. The Commission believes continued admission of refugees sustains our humanitarian commitment to provide safety to the persecuted, enables the U.S. to pursue foreign policy interests in promoting human rights, and encourages international efforts to resettle persons requiring rescue or durable solutions. The Commission also urges the federal government to continue to support international assistance and protection for the majority of the world's refugees for whom resettlement is neither appropriate nor practical. . . .

The Commission continues to recommend against denying benefits to legal immigrants solely because they are noncitizens. The Commission believes that the denial of safety net programs to immigrants solely because they are noncitizens is not in the national interest.

(Becoming an American: Immigration and Immigrant Policy, Executive Summary, xvi–xxii)

Curbing Unlawful Migration

In its first interim report to Congress, the Commission recommended a comprehensive strategy to curb unlawful migration into the United States through prevention and removal. . . . The Commission continues to believe that unlawful immigration can be curtailed consistent with our traditions, civil rights, and civil liberties.

The Commission reiterates its 1994 recommendations supporting a comprehensive strategy to deter illegal migration. More specifically, the Commission continues to support implementation of the following deterrence strategies:

- An effective border management policy that accomplishes the twin goals of preventing illegal entries and facilitating legal ones. . . .
- Reducing the employment magnet is the linchpin of a comprehensive strategy to deter unlawful migration. Economic opportunity and the prospect of employment remain the most important draw for illegal migration to this country. Strategies to deter unlawful entries and visa overstays require both a reliable process for verifying authorization to work and an enforcement capacity to ensure that employers adhere to all immigration-related labor standards. The Commission supports implementation of pilot programs to test what we believe is the most promising option for verifying work authorization: a computerized registry based on the social security number. . . .

An effective strategy to curb unauthorized movements includes co-operative efforts with source countries to address the push factors that cause people to seek new lives in the United States. The Commission continues to urge the United States government to give priority in its foreign policy and international economic policy to long-term reduction in the causes of unauthorized migration. . . .

A credible immigration system requires the effective and timely removal of aliens who can be determined through constitutionally sound procedures to have no right to remain in the United States. If unlawful aliens believe that they can remain indefinitely once they are within our national borders, there will be increased incentives to try to enter or remain illegally. . . . The Commission urges immediate reforms to improve management of the removal system and ensure that aliens with final orders of deportation, exclusion, or removal are indeed removed from the United States.

(Becoming an American: Immigration and
Immigrant Policy, Executive Summary, xxxiii–xxxvii)

(C) EXCERPTS FROM THE REPORTS OF THE PRESIDENT'S COUNCIL ON SUSTAINABLE DEVELOPMENT, 1996

Shortly after taking office, President Bill Clinton formed the President's Council on Sustainable Development to advise him on "bold, new approaches to achieve our economic, environmental, and equity goals." The Council found that the United States, at the time, was the only major industrialized country in the world experiencing rapid population growth. In 1996, it recommended that the United States develop comprehensive and responsible immigration and population policies leading to the eventual stabilization of the US population. This recommendation was ignored by the Clinton administration and by succeeding Presidential administrations and Congresses. The publications of the Council may be found at http://clinton2 .nara.gov/PCSD/.

Together, the size of the population and the scale of consumption impinge significantly on American society's ability to achieve sustainability. . . .

Because the United States has the world's third largest population and the largest economy, with an unparalleled scale of per capita consumption and waste generation, even slight changes in U.S. consumption patterns or population size can have a significant impact on sustainability. Annual per capita gains in reducing wastes, improving resource efficiency, and promoting economic growth must exceed 1 percent to translate into real reductions in environmental impact and real growth in the American standard of living. Thus, unless some technological change substantially reduces the scale of resources needed to maintain the current quality of life in the United States, continued population growth steadily makes more difficult the job of mitigating the environmental impact of American resource use and waste production patterns. Based on current trends, efficiency in the use of all resources would have to increase by more than 50 percent over the next four or five decades just to keep pace with population growth.

Managing population growth, resources, and wastes is essential to ensuring that the total impact of these factors is within the bounds of sustainability. Stabilizing the population without changing consumption and waste production patterns would not be enough, but it would make an immensely challenging task more manageable. In the United States, each is necessary; neither alone is sufficient.

(*Population and Consumption Task Force Report*, chapter 6)

The size of our population and the scale of our consumption are essential determinants of whether or not the United States will be able to achieve sustainability. . . . For America's future, the United States must strive to manage its resources, reduce waste products, and stabilize population so that the total impact of its activity is sustainable.

The Task Force believes that the two most important steps the United States must take toward sustainability are: 1) to stabilize U.S. population promptly; and 2) to move toward greater material and energy efficiency in all production and use of goods and services. . . . Fortunately, the United States can stabilize its population by addressing the determinants of growth with the sensitivity and forthrightness these issues deserve. . . .

Meeting Americans' reproductive health needs will go a long way toward reducing unintended pregnancies and slowing population growth towards the point of population stabilization. This significant challenge for American health care can be met through provision of education, information and voluntary reproductive health services; contraceptive research and development; by attacking poverty and promoting personal responsibility; and by addressing the remaining obstacles to women's full economic and social opportunity. . . .

Finally, one-third of U.S. population growth comes from legal and illegal immigration, now at an all-time high. This is a sensitive issue, but reducing immigration levels is a necessary part of population stabilization and the drive toward sustainability.

(*Population and Consumption Task Force Report*, Executive Summary)

Policy Recommendation #4—Immigration: The United States should develop comprehensive and responsible immigration and foreign policies that reduce illegal immigration and mitigate the factors that encourage immigration. Research on linkages between demographic change, including immigration factors, and sustainable development should also increase. . . .

Today, addressing immigration is an important aspect of the broad question of population stabilization in this country. Immigration accounts for one-third of total U.S. population growth and is a factor that must be addressed in the overall effort to stabilize population voluntarily. Because new immigrants typically have high fertility rates, immigration will be a powerful factor in future population growth.

(*Population and Consumption Task Force Report*, chapters 4 and 6)

Population growth, especially when coupled with current consumption patterns, affects sustainability. A sustainable United States is one where all Americans have access to family planning and reproductive health services, women enjoy increased opportunities for education and employment, and responsible immigration policies are fairly implemented and enforced.

(*Sustainable America: A New Consensus for Prosperity,
Opportunity, and a Healthy Environment for the Future*, chapter 6)

Goal #8 [of 10 Proposed "National Goals toward Sustainable Development"]: Population—Move toward Stabilization of U.S. Population: Indicators of Progress:

- Population Growth: Reduced rate of population growth in the United States and the world.
- Status of Women: Increased educational opportunity for women; increased income equality for equivalent work.
- Unintended Pregnancies: Decreased number of unintended pregnancies in the United States.
- Teen Pregnancies: Decreased number of teenage pregnancies in the United States.
- Immigration: Decreased number of illegal immigrants.

(Sustainable America: A New Consensus for Prosperity, Opportunity, and a Healthy Environment for the Future, chapter 1)

ACKNOWLEDGMENTS

It is a great pleasure to thank the many people who have helped me research, write, and publish this book. The notes and bibliography acknowledge my numerous debts to the scholarly and popular literatures on immigration, economics, environmental studies, ethics, public policy, and related matters. I am grateful to the dozens of Colorado workers, native-born and foreign-born, who shared their candid views on immigration with me during interviews, and to the dozens of environmentalists, many from the Rocky Mountain chapter of the Sierra Club, who did the same.

Leon Kolankiewicz, Winthrop Staples III, Ronald Sandler, Paul Cafaro, Kris Cafaro, Jerry Kammer, Mark Krikorian, and Steven Camarota reviewed the manuscript, in whole or in part, providing many valuable comments and suggestions. I have profited greatly from discussing immigration and population matters with them and with Don Weeden, Ben Zuckerman, Stuart Hurlbert, Jo Wideman, John Rohe, Joe Bish, Bill Ryerson, Leslie Blackner, Pete O'Neill, Trudy Haines, and Glen Colton. Other experts who answered my questions or offered helpful suggestions included Andrew Sum, Richard Lamm, Arthur Darbie, and Sammy Zahran.

Eight years ago, I began writing an article with Win Staples, then a graduate student in the Colorado State University Philosophy Department; it was eventually published as "The Environmental Argument for Reducing Immigration into the United States." That article and associated talks ultimately led to this book. Collaborating with Win is always thought-provoking and enjoyable. I have benefitted a lot from his intellectual friendship over the years, and readers of this book will benefit from his many constructive suggestions for its improvement.

Five years ago, Eileen Crist and I began planning the co-edited volume *Life on the Brink: Environmentalists Confront Overpopulation*, eventually published by the University of Georgia Press. Although we disagree on immigration policy, I found discussions with Eileen stimulating and very helpful for better understanding the full range of changes needed to achieve real ecological sustainability. Thanks to all the contributors to that volume; if they read this book, they are bound to find some of their own ideas recycled here.

Over the past half dozen years, the following institutions and organizations hosted talks by me on immigration policy, alternatives to growth, or related topics: Fort Lewis College, Metropolitan State University (Denver), the Institute for Public Policy at the University of Denver, the Center for Values and Social Policy at the University of Colorado at Boulder, Colorado College, the University of Colorado at Denver, the Freedom Center at the University of Arizona, the University of Georgia, Clemson University, Franklin & Marshall College, the University of East Anglia, Wageningen University, Delft University of Technology, Radboud University, Saxion University of Applied Sciences, Uppsala University, the George Wright Society, the Ecological Society of America, Progressives for Immigration Reform, the US Geological Survey, the National Press Club, the American Philosophical Association, the International Society for Environmental Ethics, and the 23rd World Congress of Philosophy. These provided invaluable opportunities for feedback, constructive discussion, and collegiality, for which I am most grateful.

Thanks are due to my home institution, Colorado State University, for generous support, including funding for a sabbatical during which much of this book was written. Thanks to colleagues across the university for stimulating discussions on many topics, and especially to Holmes Rolston III, an exemplary colleague and philosopher, and to Steven Shulman, chair of CSU's Economics Department, for his friendship and skepticism and for reviewing the manuscript, too. Thanks to various groups at CSU that invited me to speak on immigration and growth issues in recent years; in addition to my home Philosophy Department, these included the Department of Fish, Wildlife and Conservation Biology, the Center for Collaborative Conservation, the Natural Resources Ecology Laboratory, and the School of Global Environmental Sustainability.

I am grateful to everyone at the University of Chicago Press who has helped see this project through to completion. Thanks to Elizabeth Branch Dyson, my editor, for believing in the book, for helpful suggestions to tighten and improve it, and for her kindly book-side manner. Nora Devlin, her editorial assistant, put the manuscript into production and helped me redraw several figures when my creaky skills in Excel began to show. Mary Corrado provided prompt and exacting copyediting that was very much appreciated. If you are reading this book, that is quite likely due to Ryo Yamaguchi's excellent work publicizing it, or to Isaac Tobin, who designed its striking cover. My thanks as well to the Press' two anonymous readers, who made numerous valuable suggestions, large and small, most of which I have incorporated into the final book.

Last but not least, I am grateful to my family. As usual, my wife, Kris, was my best reader, reviewing the whole manuscript several times and providing numerous helpful suggestions for improvement. Thanks Krissie, for your love and friendship, and for our life together! My son Henry double-checked my math in the economics chapters, saving me from a few howlers in the process, while his brother Tom provided me with crucial energy, in a secret process known only to a few, that enabled me to finish this project. My brother Paul went over the manuscript in great detail, red pencil flashing, saving readers from considerable bloviation. I have tried to follow his suggestion to write like a human being rather than a pedant. Joe and Joanne Bronars exemplified courage, humor, and perseverance in the face of great challenges. My sincere thanks to all of them for these things, and for so much more.

This book is dedicated to my parents, Claire Cafaro and Ralph Cafaro Jr., with all my love. They first taught me to try to think honestly and hard about the important things in life. So if this book sticks in your craw, blame them! Thanks, folks. After all these years, I'm still learning from you.

NOTES

CHAPTER ONE

1 Author's interview, Javier Morales, September, 2007. All personal stories and discussions related in this book actually occurred. All quotations are reported verbatim.

2 Jorge Castañeda's *Mañana Forever? Mexico and the Mexicans* discusses the causes of this fatalism and some potential cures.

3 Author's interview, Andy Moore, August 2007.

4 Author's interview, Tom Kenney, October 2007.

5 George Borjas, *Heaven's Door: Immigration Policy and the American Economy*, 13.

6 Frederick Hollmann, Tammany Mulder, and Jeffrey Kallan, "Methodology and Assumptions for the Population Projections of the United States: 1999 to 2100."

7 Roy Beck, *The Case against Immigration: The Moral, Economic, Social, and Environmental Reasons for Reducing U.S. Immigration Back to Traditional Levels.*

8 Stephen Macedo, "The Moral Dilemma of U.S. Immigration Policy: Open Borders vs. Social Justice?"

9 US Department of State, "2008 Diversity Visa Lottery Registrations."

10 US Census Bureau, "Annual Projections of the Total Resident Population as of July 1: Middle, Lowest, Highest, and Zero International Migration Series, 1999 to 2100."

CHAPTER TWO

1 Unless otherwise specified US population and immigration data in this chapter come from US Census Bureau publications. Decadal population figures are taken from the decadal census results. Annual and decadal immigration numbers are taken from US Department of Homeland Security, *Yearbook of Immigration Statistics: 2011*, table 1: "Persons Obtaining Legal Permanent Resident Status: Fiscal Years 1820 to 2011."

2 The following review of US immigration history and immigration policy draws on numerous sources. Among the more important are Vernon Briggs, *Immigration Policy and the American Labor Force*, and Otis Graham, *Unguarded Gates: A History of America's Immigration Crisis*.

3 Samuel Gompers to Congress, March 19, 1924.

4 Graham, *Unguarded Gates*, 53.

5 Roosevelt quoted in *Pittsburgh Press*, October 30, 1936.

6 Vernon Briggs, *Mass Immigration and the National Interest: Policy Directions for the New Century*; Paul Samuelson, *Economics: An Introductory Analysis*.

7 Graham, *Unguarded Gates*, 93.

8 Office of Immigration Statistics, "Annual Flow Report, U.S. Legal Permanent Residents: 2011," table 2.

9 Jeffrey Jones, "Americans More Positive about Immigration: Sixty-Six Percent Say It's a Good Thing for the U.S., Highest since 2006."

10 Roy Beck and Steven Camarota, "Elite vs. Public Opinion: An Examination of Divergent Views on Immigration."

11 Ed Lytwak, "A Tale of Two Futures: Changing Shares of U.S. Population Growth."

12 US Census Bureau, "Midyear Population and Density."

13 Steven Camarota, "A Record-Setting Decade of Immigration: 2000–2010."

14 Steven Camarota, "Births to Immigrants in America, 1970 to 2002," 5, figure 1.

15 Lytwak, "A Tale of Two Futures."

16 CIA *World Factbook*, 2011 ed.

17 US Census Bureau, "2008 National Population Projections," table 1, "Projections of the Population and Components of Change for the United States: 2010 to 2050." More recent Census Bureau projections to 2050 are lower by several tens of millions; however, immigration reform proposals being debated as I write could boost the numbers back toward these earlier estimates.

18 Jennifer Ortman and Christine Guarneri, "United States Population Projections: 2000 to 2050."

19 Jeffrey Passel and D'Vera Cohn, *U.S. Population Projections: 2005–2050*.

20 My thanks to Mark Krikorian and Steven Camarota at the Center for Immigration Studies for permission to use this projection tool to create these population projections. For information on the methodology behind the model employed, see Steven Camarota, "Projecting Immigration's Impact on the Size and Age Structure of the 21st Century American Population"; and Stephen Tordella et al., "Evaluating the Role of Immigration in U.S. Population Projections."

21 Jeffrey Jones, "Americans More Positive about Immigration." See also Lyman

Morales, "Americans' Immigration Concerns Linger: Nearly Two-Thirds Are Dissatisfied with the Current Levels of Immigration"; and Polling Company, "The Public's View of Immigration: A Comprehensive Survey and Analysis," 4.

22 Lydia Saad, "Americans Value Both Aspects of Immigration Reform: Strengthening the Border and Dealing with Illegals Already Here Both Have Appeal"; Jeffrey Jones, "More Americans Favor than Oppose Arizona Immigration Law: Among Those Who Have Heard of Law, 51% Favor and 39% Oppose It."

23 Jeffrey Jones, "Americans More Positive about Immigration"; Lyman Morales, "Americans' Immigration Concerns Linger."

CHAPTER THREE

1 Author's interview, Steve, September 2007.

2 Giuseppe Bertola and Andrea Ichino, "Wage Inequality and Unemployment: United States vs. Europe"; Bureau of Labor Statistics, "International Comparisons of Hourly Compensation Costs in Manufacturing."

3 Centers for Disease Control and Prevention, "Trends in Health Care Coverage and Insurance for 1968–2011," table 1.

4 Department of Commerce, Bureau of Economic Analysis, "National Economic Accounts," table 1.1.5.

5 US Census Bureau, "Current Population Survey, Annual Social and Economic Supplements," Historic Income Tables—Families.

6 Arthur Kennickell, "Ponds and Streams: Wealth and Income in the U.S., 1989 to 2007"; and unpublished 2010 Survey of Consumer Finance data.

7 My reflections on this question owe a lot to David Miller, *Principles of Social Justice*; Stuart White, *The Civic Minimum: On the Rights and Obligations of Economic Citizenship*; and David Schmidtz, *Elements of Justice*.

8 But see John Rawls, *A Theory of Justice*, for an argument that the talents, capabilities, and personality traits that tend to lead to greater economic productivity are largely a matter of luck and hence do not justify differential compensation.

9 After all, such productivity gains are largely a function of technological change fueled by advances in basic and applied science. They depend on the efforts of millions of scientists and engineers, not on the machinations of bankers, stockbrokers, business executives, and their heirs, who have hogged so much of the wealth recently.

10 A point made long ago by John Stuart Mill in his *Principles of Political Economy* (1848), although Mill did not conclude from this that "equal shares" was the best method of economic distribution, preferring instead to combine desert-based and welfare-based principles in his overall scheme of justice.

11 Jonathan Gershuny, "National Utility: Measuring the Enjoyment of Activities."

12 See, for example, Ben Franklin, *Autobiography*, and his "Information to Those Who Would Remove to America" (1782). In the latter pamphlet, Franklin does not brag about the superior wealth but the superior opportunities in America. An ambitious, hard-working man of humble background and few connections

could build a decent life there, unlike in the crowded, unequal countries of Europe.

13   Representative of this position are David Autor, Lawrence Katz, and Melissa Kearney, "Trends in U.S. Wage Inequality: Revising the Revisionists"; and Paul Krugman, *The Great Unraveling: Losing Our Way in the New Century*.

14   Quoted in John Marsh, *Class Dismissed: Why We Cannot Teach or Learn Our Way Out of Inequality*, 14.

15   David Card and John DiNardo, "Skill-Biased Technological Change and Rising Wage Inequality: Some Problems and Puzzles."

16   Thomas Piketty and Emanuel Saez, "How Progressive Is the U.S. Federal Tax System? A Historical and International Perspective"; Anthony Atkinson, Thomas Piketty, and Emmanuel Saez, "Top Incomes in the Long Run of History."

17   Bruce Western and Jake Rosenfeld, "Unions, Norms, and the Rise in U.S. Wage Inequality," 513. Figures from the Bureau of Labor Statistics confirm a drop of this general magnitude in union membership in the United States during this time period.

18   Ibid., 514. Emphasis added.

19   In support of this view see also James DiNardo, Nicole Fortin, and Thomas Lemieux, "Labor Market Institutions and the Distribution of Wages, 1973–1992"; and Henry Farber, "Nonunion Wage Rates and the Threat of Unionization."

20   Paul Samuelson, *Economics*.

21   Annual immigration rates taken from US Census Bureau, *Statistical Abstract of the United States: 2003*, 15, table HS-8, "Immigration—Number and Rate: 1900 to 2001."

22   Borjas, *Heaven's Door*, 11.

23   A classic statement of this position is Borjas, *Heaven's Door*. See also the essays in Steven Shulman, *The Impact of Immigration on African Americans*; and more recent articles by Borjas et al. that extend his approach and defend his earlier conclusions, particularly the following: George Borjas, "The Labor Demand Curve *Is* Downward Sloping: Reexamining the Impact of Immigration on the Labor Market"; George Borjas, Jeffrey Grogger, and Gordon Hanson, "Immigration and the Economic Status of African-American Men"; and George Borjas, Jeffrey Grogger, and Gordon Hanson, "Substitution between Immigrants, Natives, and Skill Groups."

24   Mark Cromer, "Hey Buddy, Can You Spare a Job?"

25   Borjas, "The Economic Benefits from Immigration," 7.

26   Borjas et al., "Immigration and the Economic Status of African-American Men," 255.

27   David Card, "Immigrant Inflows, Native Outflows, and the Local Market Impacts of Higher Immigration"; David Card, "How Immigration Affects U.S. Cities"; David Card, "Immigration and Inequality."

28   Gianmarco Ottaviano and Giovanni Peri, "Immigration and National Wages: Clarifying the Theory and the Empirics"; Gianmarco Ottaviano and Giovanni Peri, "Rethinking the Effect of Immigration on Wages."

29   Steven Camarota and Karen Zeigler, "Immigrant Gains and Native Losses In the Job Market, 2000 to 2013."

30 Abdurrahman Aydemir and George Borjas, "Cross-Country Variation in the Impact of International Migration: Canada, Mexico, and the United States." See also Abdurrahman Aydemir, "Immigrant Selection and Short-Term Labour Market Outcomes by Visa Category."

31 Tyler Seuc, "The Real Unemployment."

32 Steven Camarota, "Immigration and Economic Stagnation: An Examination of Trends 2000 to 2010."

33 Camarota and Zeigler, "Immigrant Gains and Native Losses In the Job Market."

34 Steven Camarota and Karen Zeigler, "Are There Really Jobs Americans Won't Do? A Detailed Look at Immigrant and Native Employment across Occupations."

35 Camarota and Zeigler, "Immigrant Gains and Native Losses In the Job Market."

36 Paul Samuelson, "Importing Poverty."

37 Author's interview, Steve, October 2007.

38 Bureau of Labor Statistics, "Employment, Hours, and Earnings from the Current Employment Statistics Survey (National) SIC." Data extracted December 2007; figures adjusted for inflation. "Today" refers to wages in 2003.

39 A good account of the rise and decline of unionized meatpacking can be found in the essays in Shelton Stromquist and Marvin Bergman, *Unionizing the Jungles: Labor and Community in the Twentieth-Century Meat-Packing Industry.*

40 Roy Beck, *The Case against Immigration*, chapter 6.

41 Carol Andreas, *Meatpackers and Beef Barons: Company Town in a Global Economy.*

42 Peter Rachleff, *Hard-Pressed in the Heartland: The Hormel Strike and the Future of the Labor Movement.*

43 Eric Schlosser, *Fast Food Nation: The Dark Side of the All-American Meal*, chapter 8; see also Andreas, *Meatpackers and Beef Barons*, chapter 5.

44 Steven Kay, "The Nature of Turnover: Packers Attempt to Reverse a Financial Drain"; A.V. Krebs, *Heading Toward the Last Roundup: The Big Three's Prime Cut*, 51.

45 Here a brief word may be in order about "diversity." The 1965 Immigration Act Revisions are often praised for making America more racially and ethnically diverse. But as slaughterhouse workers became more diverse, they often found themselves speaking different languages, hampering basic communication and undermining worker solidarity. Workers who do not speak the same language find it harder to make common cause. Workers who do not speak English may not know their rights under US law. Workers from other countries may not have a tradition of standing up to authority, while those who are in the United States illegally—a majority in some US meatpacking plants in recent years—are not in any position to do so. Like most progressives, I value diversity. But no matter what we progressives may wish was the case, in the meatpacking industry diversity has helped management divide and conquer workers.

46 Author's interview, Steve, October 2007.

47 Author's interview, Francisco Nevares, April 2008.

48 Jerry Kammer, "The 2006 Swift Raids: Assessing the Impact of Immigration Enforcement Actions at Six Facilities," note 19.

49 Alan Greenspan, "Testimony."

CHAPTER FOUR

1   Borjas, *Heaven's Door*, 90.

2   Gwendolyn Mink, *Old Labor and New Immigrants in American Political Development: Union, Party, and State, 1875–1920*; Daryl Scott, "Immigrant Indigestion: A. Philip Randolph: Radical and Restrictionist."

3   "Immigration Raids May Affect Meat Prices," *Washington Post*, December 15, 2006; "An Immigration Raid Aids Blacks for a Time," *Pittsburgh Post-Gazette*, January 17, 2007.

4   Author's interview, Jeff Gauthier, October 2007.

5   Ibid.

6   Author's interview, Tom Kenny, October 2007.

7   Author's interview, Scott (carpenter), October 4, 2007.

8   Colorado Department of Labor and Employees, cited in "Immigration Wage Debate Rages: Pay Stagnates in Sectors Full of Foreign-born Workers," *Rocky Mountain News*, August 26, 2006.

9   Borjas, *Heaven's Door*, 91.

10 Author's interview, Anne (owner of Bayou Landscaping), October 2007.

11 Steven Camarota, "A Record-Setting Decade of Immigration: 2000 to 2010," table 7.

12 Steven Camarota, "Immigration's Impact on American Workers"; George Borjas, "Increasing the Supply of Labor through Immigration: Measuring the Impact on Native-Born Workers"; Steven Camarota, "Immigration and Economic Stagnation: An Examination of Trends 2000 to 2010."

13 George Borjas, "The Labor Market Impact of High-Skill Immigration." For a dissenting view see Giovanni Peri, "Immigration, Labor Markets, and Productivity."

14 Steven Camarota, "Immigrants in the United States—2002: A Snapshot of America's Foreign-Born Population," figure 2.

15 Gianmarco Ottaviano and Giovanni Peri, "Rethinking the Effect of Immigration on Wages."

16 George Borjas, "Increasing the Supply of Labor through Immigration: Measuring the Impact on Native-Born Workers."

17 By the way, if you think that it's inevitable that the poorest workers must shoulder the largest burdens of mass immigration, you are wrong. Canada and Australia also have high immigration levels, allowing in even more immigrants than the United States, as a percentage of their populations. But since they focus on bringing in skilled workers, wage competition has fallen primarily on wealthier Canadians and Australians (doctors and engineers, rather than construction workers) and immigration does not appear to have increased inequality as in the United States.

18 Steven Camarota and Karen Zeigler, "Are There Really Jobs Americans Won't Do? A Detailed Look at Immigrant and Native Employment across Occupations." Camarota and Zeigler also note: "A number of politically important groups tend to face very little job competition from immigrants. For example,

just 10 percent of reporters are immigrants, as are only 6 percent of lawyers and judges and 6 percent of farmers and ranchers."

19 Carol Swain, "The Congressional Black Caucus and the Impact of Immigration on African American Unemployment."

20 George Borjas, Jeffrey Grogger, and Gordon Hanson, "Immigration and the Economic Status of African-American Men."

21 Vernon Briggs, "Illegal Immigration: The Impact on Wages and Employment of Black Workers." See also Vernon Briggs, "The Economic Well-Being of Black Americans: The Overarching Influence of U.S. Immigration Policies."

22 Robert Malloy, "Cast Down Your Bucket Where You Are: Black Americans on Immigration"; Daryl Scott, "Immigrant Indigestion."

23 Gianmarco Ottaviano and Giovanni Peri, "Rethinking the Effect of Immigration on Wages."

24 Author's interview, Paul McWilliams, October 5, 2007.

25 Stephen Macedo, "The Moral Dilemma of U.S. Immigration Policy."

26 Progressives arguing that Americans are wealthy enough to give more to help poor foreigners should be especially sensitive to the plight of their poor fellow citizens. After all, the argument that "we" should do something for the world's poor is grounded in a conception of justice as fairness and in the idea that "we" are comparatively wealthy. And Americans are wealthy, *collectively*, compared to most of the world. But, of course, there are wide disparities in how "we" divide up "our" wealth.

27 Michael Greenstone and Adam Looney, "The Uncomfortable Truth About American Wages."

28 Card, "Immigration and Inequality."

29 Borjas, *Heaven's Door*, chapters 2 and 3.

30 Borjas, *Heaven's Door*, chapter 7.

31 Camarota, "Immigrants in the United States—2002," tables 18 and 19.

32 Ibid., figure 1.

33 As John Marsh shows in the preface to *Class Dismissed*, this is the bipartisan, feel-good answer to income inequality in contemporary American politics. Marsh argues convincingly that as a policy proposal for reducing economic inequality, increasing education is limited at best.

34 Rebecca Thiess, "The Future of Work: Trends and Challenges for Low-Wage Workers."

35 Along with "more education," this sums up the conventional wisdom on growing US income inequality. Paul Krugman, *The Conscience of a Liberal*, describes and defends this conventional view as well as anyone.

36 Piketty and Saez, "Income Inequality in the United States, 1913–1998." Here and elsewhere, Piketty and Saez argue convincingly that tax cuts for the wealthy have played a key role in increasing economic inequality in the United States.

37 Jenn Brookens, "Population Trends Here to Stay," *Fairmont (Minnesota) Sentinel*, February 27, 2013; Elizabeth Llorente, "Struggling with a Population Decline, Baltimore Pins Its Hopes on Immigrants," *Fox News Latino* (online), March 27, 2013.

38 Steven Camarota and Karen Ziegler, "Still No Evidence of a Jobs Shortage: Immigrant and Native Employment in the Fourth Quarter of 2013."

39 Barbara Ehrenreich, "Maid to Order: The Politics of Other Women's Work," *Harper's Magazine*, April 1, 2000; Ray Ring, "The New West's Servant Economy," *High Country News*, April 17, 1995.

40 The argument against education as a panacea for growing economic inequality is made clearly and comprehensively in Marsh, *Class Dismissed*.

41 Obama quoted in Marsh, *Class Dismissed*, 14. Marsh provides similar quotes from across the political spectrum, 13–16, demonstrating how this is indeed bipartisan conventional wisdom among the "haves" who dominate our political parties.

CHAPTER FIVE

1 As I discuss in a later section of this chapter, in the past decade this unreflective acceptance of the goodness of growth has come in for serious questioning within philosophy, psychology, economics, and political science. I think it is fair to say, however, that little of this academic questioning has filtered into mainstream political discourse in the United States, with the occasional exception of local debates about environmental matters. Other countries are further along in discussing these issues. France's former President, Nicholas Sarkozy, established a national Commission on the Measurement of Economic Performance and Social Progress to consider alternatives to conventional focus on GDP increase (see Joseph Stiglitz, Amartya Sen, and Jean-Paul Fitoussi, *Report by the Commission on the Measurement of Economic Performance and Social Progress*). In recent years, Australia's major political parties have debated whether to continue to encourage rapid population growth under a "big Australia" immigration policy. No similar national political debates have occurred in the United States.

2 US advertising expenditures: "Kantar Media Reports U.S. Advertising Expenditures Increased 0.8 Percent In 2011," accessed March 12, 2012, at Kantar Media website (kantarmediana.com). Global advertising expenditures: Nielson Newswire, "2011 Closed with 7.3 Percent Increase in Global Advertising Spend," accessed April 9, 2012, at Nielsen website (www.nielson.com).

3 Tamar Jacoby, "Immigration Nation," 55.

4 Chris Isidore, "Illegal Workers: Good for U.S. Economy." CNNMoney.com, May 1, 2006.

5 Ibid.

6 George Borjas, "Immigration and the American Worker: A Review of the Academic Literature," 19–21.

7 Bradley Schiller, *The Macro Economy Today*, 372–73.

8 Note that high-skilled immigrants contribute much more, per capita, than low-skilled ones to economic growth; see Vivek Wadhwa et al., "Skilled Immigration and Economic Growth."

9 "In Praise of Huddled Masses," *Wall Street Journal*, July 3, 1984.

10 Ibid.

11 Jacoby, "Immigration Nation," 51.

12 Ben Wattenberg, *The Birth Dearth*.

13 Schiller, *The Macro Economy Today*, 11–12.

14 "What is GDP and Why Is It So Important?" Investopedia website. Posted February 26, 2009. This website provides accurate, clear explanations of basic economic terms and concepts; see also "Macroeconomics—Limitations of GDP and Alternative Measures."

15 Critiques of GDP as a measurement of economic or societal progress have proliferated in recent years. The following four pages are particularly indebted to Peter Victor, *Managing without Growth: Slower by Design, Not Disaster*; and Stiglitz, Sen, and Fitoussi, *Report by the Commission on the Measurement of Economic Performance and Social Progress*.

16 This point is emphasized in Herman Daly, *Beyond Growth: The Economics of Sustainable Development*.

17 The development of new measures of economic and social progress, such as the Genuine Progress Indicator, and their deployment by governments such as the state of Maryland, are hopeful signs. The Maryland GPI can be accessed at www .green.maryland.gov/mdgpi. To my knowledge, this is the most in-depth attempt by a US government entity to apply a more comprehensive and plausible set of indicators than GDP in order to measure economic and social progress.

18 Janet Yellen, "Economic Inequality in the United States."

19 US Census Bureau, *Current Population Survey, Annual Social and Economic Supplements*, "Historic Income Tables—Families." Accessed May 2008 at www.cen sus.gov.

20 Secretary-General Organization for Economic Co-operation and Development, *Growing Unequal? Income Distribution and Poverty in OECD Countries*.

21 Borjas, *Heaven's Door*, 98–103.

22 US Census Bureau, "Historical Income Tables—Families," table F-11: Age of Householder—Families, All Races by Median and Mean Income: 1947 to 2005. Accessed January 2009 at www.census.gov.

23 This phenomenon is discussed searchingly in Robert Lane, *The Loss of Happiness in Market Democracies*; and Tim Kasser, *The High Price of Materialism*.

24 Paul Taylor, Cary Funk, and Peyton Craighill, "Are We Happy Yet?" 11–12.

25 This issue remains contested. For a good defense of the value of absolute wealth in increasing happiness and subjective well-being, see Betsey Stevenson and Justin Wolfers, "Economic Growth and Subjective Well-Being: Reassessing the Easterlin Paradox."

26 Ed Diener and Martin Seligman, "Beyond Money: Toward an Economy of Well-Being."

27 See Stevenson and Wolfers, "Economic Growth and Subjective Well-Being"; and Diener et al., "Wealth and Happiness across the World: Material Prosperity Predicts Life Evaluation, Whereas Psychosocial Prosperity Predicts Positive Feeling."

28 For a good overview see Tim Kasser et al., "Materialistic Values: Their Causes and Consequences."

29 For a review of the first two decades of research on the existence of a hedonic treadmill regarding the material conditions of well-being, see Shane Fredrick and George Loewenstein, "Hedonic Adaptation." Important supplemental considerations are provided in Ed Diener, Richard Lucas and Christie Scollon, "Beyond the Hedonic Treadmill: Revising the Adaptation Theory of Well-Being"; Alan Waterman, "On the Importance of Distinguishing Hedonia and Eudaimonia When Contemplating the Hedonic Treadmill"; and Daniel Mochon, Michael Norton, and Dan Ariely, "Getting Off the Hedonic Treadmill, One Step at a Time: The Impact of Regular Religious Practice and Exercise on Well-Being."

30 See Kasser, *The High Price of Materialism*; and Kasser and Kanner, *Psychology and Consumer Culture: The Struggle for a Good Life in a Materialistic World*. Of course, health and security may depend importantly on money, particularly in poor or poorly organized societies. Successful societies, however, promote the health and security of all their members.

31 Emily Solberg, Edward Diener, and Michael Robinson, "Why Are Materialists Less Satisfied?"

32 Brian Czech, *Shoveling Fuel for a Runaway Train: Errant Economists, Shameful Spenders, and a Plan to Stop Them All*, summarizes how growth drives environmental problems in general. Intergovernmental Panel on Climate Change, *Climate Change 2007: Synthesis Report*, "Summary for Policymakers," affirms that economic and demographic growth are the main drivers of global climate change.

33 For an overview see Timothy Noah, *The Great Divergence: America's Growing Inequality Crisis and What We Can Do about It*.

34 Kasser, *The High Price of Materialism*.

35 John Broder, "Emissions Fell in 2009, Showing Impact of Recession," *New York Times*, February 16, 2011. Worldwide emissions have subsequently begun to rise again, while US emissions have continued to decline, as natural gas has displaced coal and oil in electricity generation.

36 Albert Bartlett, "Thoughts on Immigration into the United States," 8.

37 Robert Pear, "Percentage of Americans Lacking Health Coverage Falls Again." Note that the Affordable Care Act of 2010 bids fair to shrink the number of uninsured considerably, but will not come anywhere near universal coverage.

38 Brian Roach, "Progressive and Regressive Taxation in the United States: Who's Really Paying (and Not Paying) Their Fair Share?" table 2: Comparison of 1966, 1970, and 2000/2001 Tax Progressivity Indices.

39 Jeremy Rifkin, *The European Dream: How Europe's Vision of the Future Is Quietly Eclipsing the American Dream*.

40 Smart young economists like Rob Dietz and Dan O'Neill are working to answer many of these questions under the rubric of "ecological economics"; see their *Enough Is Enough: Building a Sustainable Economy in a World of Finite Resources*.

41 In addition to the works cited below, my views on a sustainable economy have been greatly influenced by the work of Herman Daly, particularly Herman Daly and John Cobb Jr., *For the Common Good*; and by the ongoing work of the Center for a New American Dream.

42 Richard Heinberg, *The End of Growth: Adapting to Our New Economic Reality*.

43 American Academy of Pediatrics, Committee on Communications, "Policy Statement: Children, Adolescents, and Advertising."

44 Bill McKibben, *Deep Economy: The Wealth of Communities and the Durable Future*.

45 Jerome Segal, *Graceful Simplicity: The Philosophy and Politics of the Alternative American Dream*.

46 Amartya Sen, *Development as Freedom*.

47 Robert Lane, *The Market Experience*.

48 See Daly and Cobb, *For the Common Good*. Before Sen, Lane, and Daly and Cobb, there was E. F. Schumacher, *Small is Beautiful: A Study of Economics as if People Mattered*.

49 Two fascinating arguments that mainstream capitalist societies generally encourage moral behavior are Benjamin Friedman, *The Moral Consequences of Economic Growth*; and Deirdre McCloskey, *The Bourgeois Virtues: Ethics for an Age of Commerce*. I believe one can accept many of their positive points, while still affirming some serious moral pitfalls with "actually existing capitalism," as well as the need to tame its excesses in line with robust conceptions of individual human flourishing and the common good.

50 For Aristotle see *Nicomachean Ethics*, book 1, chapter 5, and *Politics*, book 1, chapters 2, 8–10. For the Stoics and Epicureans, see Martha Nussbaum, *The Therapy of Desire*, 103–4, 360–62, 501–2.

51 On Aristotle's distinction between *chrematistics* and *oikonomia*, see Daly and Cobb, *For the Common Good*, 138.

52 Lindsay Peterson and Chris Echegaray, "Immigrants Would Leave Big Hole," *Tampa Tribune*, April 27, 2006.

53 Author's interview, Tim Griggs, October 2007.

54 Author's interview, James Thompson, October 2007.

55 David North, "Motivation for Hiring Alien Workers? Hint: It's Not a Labor Shortage."

56 California Landscape Contractors Association, website accessed August, 2008 at www.winwithclca.org.

57 Steven Camarota, "A Jobless Recovery? Immigrant Gains and Native Losses," 5–6, table 5, "Immigrants and Natives by Occupation in 2004, Ranked by Immigrant Share of Occupation."

58 "Serving U.S. Parishes, Fathers without Borders," *New York Times*, December 28, 2008.

59 California Landscape Contractors Association website.

60 Ibid.

61 Juliet Schor, *The Overworked American: The Unexpected Decline of Leisure*.

62 "Landscaping Services," IbisWorld industry report, accessed January 2009 at www.ibisworld.com.

63 National Research Council, *Urban Pest Management: A Report*.

64 "If someone wants to work, we should let them," insisted Anne, the small landscape firm owner we met in the previous chapter. "We're a nation of immigrants; why shut the door now? Do we think we're filled? Do we think there's no space

left?" (author's interview, October 2007). Well, maybe so. The United States quadrupled its population during the twentieth century. Whether or not we are "filled up" with people, there is not any space left on the landscape that is not being used by somebody: some *body*, human or nonhuman. I believe there is a limit to the goodness of replacing nature with people and our economic support systems.

65 Author's interview, Jamie Garcia, October 2007.

66 Ibid.

67 A striking example of this appeal to growth can be found in a "White House Fact Sheet on the Economics of Immigration Reform," released March 22, 2013, by the White House Office of the Press Secretary, accessible at www.uspolicy .be/headline/white-house-fact-sheet-economics-immigration-reform. "As the United States faces the prospect of a slow-growing population," it states, "immigrants are likely to play an increasingly important role in the American economy."

68 Author's interview, Jamie Garcia, October 2007.

69 Aldo Leopold, "A Criticism of the Booster Spirit," in *The River of the Mother of God and Other Essays*. Leopold also addresses population issues in his lecture "Ecology and Politics" in the same volume, 281–86.

70 Henry David Thoreau, *Walden*, 27.

CHAPTER SIX

1 Lee Shearer, "Bear Creek a Boon So Far, But Will It Be Enough?" *Athens Banner-Herald*, September 22, 2002.

2 US Environmental Protection Agency, "Air Quality Trends."

3 Ibid.

4 American Lung Association, "State of the Air 2012."

5 South Coast Air Quality Management District, "Historic Ozone Air Quality Trends."

6 For representative improvements in a particular region, during the first two decades after passage of the Clean Water Act, see R. P. Richards and D. B. Baker, "Trends in Water Quality in LEASEQ Rivers and Streams (Northwestern Ohio), 1975–1995." For a general overview of trends in the recent decades (unfortunately not clearly summarized, but containing a wealth of information on various water quality trends), see US Geological Survey, "National Water-Quality Assessment (NAWQA) Program."

7 US Environmental Protection Agency, *Wadeable Streams Assessment: A Collaborative Assessment of the Nation's Streams*.

8 Holmes Rolston III, "Duties to Endangered Species."

9 Jeffrey McKee, *Sparing Nature: The Conflict between Human Population Growth and Earth's Biodiversity*.

10 D. S. Wilcove et al., "Quantifying Threats to Imperiled Species in the United

States: Assessing the Relative Importance of Habitat Destruction, Alien Species, Pollution, Overexploitation, and Disease."

11   Richard Cincotta and Larry Gorenflo, *Human Population: Its Influences on Biological Diversity*; Dave Foreman, *Man Swarm and the Killing of Wildlife*.

12   Natural Resources Conservation Service, "National Resources Inventory 2001, Urbanization and Development of Rural Land."

13   Roy Beck, Leon Kolankiewicz, and Steven Camarota, *Outsmarting Smart Growth: Population Growth, Immigration, and the Problem of Sprawl*, 5.

14   Ibid.

15   Ibid., 68–69.

16   Personal communication, Reagan Waskom, director, Colorado State University Water Institute, Fort Collins, December 2013.

17   US Energy Information Administration, "Energy Sources Have Changed throughout the History of the United States."

18   Richard Alexander and Richard Smith, "County-Level Estimates of Nitrogen and Phosphorus Fertilizer Use in the United States, 1945 to 1985."

19   At least ceteris paribus. But if smart growth is used to facilitate continued growth, then smart growth may be even worse than dumb growth. If dumb growth uses up resources and limits further growth, it may help alleviate more long-term damage.

20   Albert Bartlett has argued this persuasively; see his "Reflections on Sustainability and Population Growth." My thinking about population and resource matters has been deeply influenced by the work of Professor Bartlett.

21   The following projections are all based on Census Bureau projections to 2050, extrapolated out another fifty years. See chapter 2 for methodological details.

22   Indeed there are good reasons to think that 320 million Americans is already much too high. David and Marcia Pimentel suggest a US population of 40 to 100 million might be truly sustainable, given the right environmental policies and consumption levels. See "Land, Energy and Water: The Constraints Governing Ideal U.S. Population Size."

23   Dickson Despommier, *The Vertical Farm: Feeding the World in the 21st Century*.

CHAPTER SEVEN

1   Leon Bouvier, "The Impact of Immigration on United States' Population Size: 1950–2050," table 1. In reproducing Bouvier's table I have rounded off his figures to the nearest million or tenth of a million. Note that writing in 1998, Bouvier did not yet have official census results for the actual population for 2000. He used the most recent Census Bureau "middle series" projections, which turned out to be a bit low.

2   For a summary of how future population growth is used to justify current development projects, see Winthrop Staples III, "Population Growth Is a Cause of Many Projects Requiring Environmental Impact Statements."

3 This is not just a problem for American environmentalists, but for conservation-minded individuals worldwide, grappling unsuccessfully to insert conservation into an endless growth political economy that is fundamentally hostile to their goals. A specular example of this was the *Millennium Ecosystem Assessment* published in 2005. The MEA's authors included many biologists with a primary concern to preserve biodiversity. Despite this, all of the future scenarios they developed and analyzed in detail included massive biodiversity loss. The authors either could not imagine, or saw no point in developing, a scenario where economic and demographic growth was consciously limited. Hence they could not explore scenarios where the hemorrhaging of biodiversity was ended. See Walter Reid et al., *The Millennium Ecosystem Assessment: Ecosystems and Human Well-Being: Synthesis.*

4 According to the Environmental Protection Agency, annual US greenhouse gas emissions increased from 6172 million metric tons in 1990 to 6708 million metric tons in 2011: an increase of 536 million metric tons, or 1.18 trillion pounds. US Environmental Protection Agency, *Draft Inventory of U.S. Greenhouse Gas Emissions and Sinks: 1990-2011,* 2-1, "Trends in Greenhouse Gas Emissions."

5 United Nations Population Fund, *State of World Population 2010: From Crisis and Conflict to Renewal: Generations of Change*; United Nations Population Fund, *State of World Population 2012: By Choice, Not By Chance: Family Planning, Human Rights and Development*; Population Reference Bureau, *2012 World Population Data Sheet.*

6 Paul Ehrlich, *The Population Bomb.*

7 Leon Kolankiewicz and Roy Beck, "Forsaking Fundamentals: The Environmental Establishment Abandons U.S. Population Stabilization," 23. See also Celia Evans Miller and Cynthia Green, "A U.S. Population Policy: ZPG's Recommendations."

8 Sierra Club Board of Directors policy, adopted May 3-4, 1969.

9 Sierra Club Board of Directors, "U. S. Population Policy and Immigration."

10 "Sierra Club Population Report," Spring 1989.

11 In my interviews of environmental activists for this book, a number of them asked, in the words of Rich Levy, "Whatever happened to ZPG?" Levy continued, "It doesn't seem as if we've got a national ZPG movement anymore. I can't find an article, or a reference, to them." Author's interview with Rich Levy, 2010.

12 Sierra Club, "Sierra Club Supports Path to Citizenship for Undocumented Immigrants."

13 Kolankiewicz and Beck, "Forsaking Fundamentals." See also Lindsey Grant, "The Great Silence: U.S. Population Policy"; and Jerry Kammer, "Strategic Negligence: How the Sierra Club's Distortions on Border and Immigration Policy Are Undermining Its Environmental Legacy."

14 For good examples see Carmen Barroso, "Cairo: The Unfinished Revolution," in Laurie Mazur, editor, *A Pivotal Moment: Population, Justice and the Environmental Challenge,* and other essays in the same volume.

15 Kolankiewicz and Beck, "Forsaking Fundamentals."

16 Quoted in ibid.

17 Bill Myers, author's interview, 2010.

18 Myrna Poticha, author's interview, 2010.

19 Alan Apt, author's interview, 2010.

20 Will Walters, author's interview, 2010.

21 Kelly McNicholas, author's interview, 2010. At the time, McNicholas was the population issues chair of the Rocky Mountain (Colorado) chapter of the Sierra Club.

22 Michael Kellett, author's interview, 2010. Kellett founded RESTORE, which is best known for its work to establish a Maine Woods National Park and Preserve centered on Baxter State Park in central Maine.

23 Kathleene Parker, "The Day of Seven Billion and the World's Most Overpopulated Nation."

24 Population Reference Bureau, "2011 World Population Data Sheet: The World at 7 Billion."

25 Leon Kolankiewicz, "From Big to Bigger: How Mass Immigration and Population Growth Have Exacerbated America's Ecological Footprint."

26 This point has been emphasized by Garret Hardin; see *Living within Limits: Ecology, Economics, and Population Taboos.*

27 Joe Bish, "Toward a New Armada: A Globalist Argument for Stabilizing U.S. Population."

28 United Nations Population Division, "World Population Prospects, the 2010 Revisions." Country Profiles, Guatemala. Accessed March 6, 2013, at http://esa .un.org/unpd/wpp/index.htm.

29 William Clark, *The California Cauldron: Immigration and the Fortunes of Local Communities*, 29–32.

30 United Nations Population Division, "World Population Prospects, the 2010 Revisions," Country Profiles, Mexico. Accessed March 6, 2013, at http://esa.un.org /unpd/wpp/index.htm.

31 Steven Camarota, "Birth Rates among Immigrants in America: Comparing Fertility in the U.S. and Home Countries."

32 Author's interview with Gary Lindstrom, 2010. Yes, he actually said: "technology is going to be our savior."

33 Author's interview with Nicholas Komar, 2012.

34 For a good overview of the issues, if not the latest numbers, see Joel Cohen, *How Many People Can the Earth Support?*

35 Tim Palmer, "Beyond Futility," 98–100. See also Kathleene Parker, "Population, Immigration, and the Drying of the American Southwest."

36 Conservatives sometimes show their denial of limits in irrational beliefs about climate change and sometimes, more cynically, by bankrolling publicity efforts to hoodwink the general public about climate matters. In a similar fashion, progressives may irrationally deny the role of population in driving environmental problems, or more cynically, they may fund efforts to confuse the general public about the connections between immigration, population growth, and the environment. For example, in recent years, the Carnegie Corporation has bankrolled efforts to slander environmentalists who speak up about these con-

nections, in an effort to silence them. See Jerry Kammer, "The Carnegie Corporation and Immigration: How a Noble Vision Lost Its Way."

37 Bob van der Zwaan and Arthur Petersen, *Sharing the Planet: Population—Consumption—Species: Science and Ethics for a Sustainable and Equitable World*.

38 Kolankiewicz and Beck, "Forsaking Fundamentals."

CHAPTER EIGHT

1 Intergovernmental Panel on Climate Change, *Climate Change 2013: The Physical Science Basis*.

2 Intergovernmental Panel on Climate Change, *Climate Change 2007: Synthesis Report*, 48–52.

3 Ibid.

4 Secretariat of the Convention on Biological Diversity, *Global Biodiversity Outlook 3*.

5 Donald Brown et al., *White Paper on the Ethical Dimensions of Climate Change*.

6 "U.S. Fight Against E.U. Airline Emissions Plan Heats Up," *New York Times*, August 6, 2012.

7 Carbon Dioxide Information Analysis Center, "National Fossil Fuel CO_2 Emissions—All Countries."

8 US Census Bureau, International Data Base, "Country Summaries." Accessed March 15, 2013, at www.census.gov.

9 Thomas Wire, *Fewer Emitters, Lower Emissions, Less Cost: Reducing Future Carbon Emissions by Investing in Family Planning: A Cost/Benefit Analysis*. See also Philip Cafaro, "Climate Ethics & Population Policy."

10 Leon Kolankiewicz and Steven Camarota, "Immigration to the United States and World-Wide Greenhouse Gas Emissions."

11 Peter Singer, *One World: the Ethics of Globalization*, chapter 2; Donald Brown, *American Heat: Ethical Problems with the United States' Response to Global Warming*.

12 Kathleen Dean Moore and Michael Nelson, *Moral Ground: Ethical Action for a Planet in Peril*; Donald Brown et al., *White Paper on the Ethical Dimensions of Climate Change*; Stephen Gardiner, *A Perfect Moral Storm: The Ethical Tragedy of Climate Change*; Winthrop Staples III and Philip Cafaro, "For a Species Right to Exist."

13 Amy Luers, Michael Mastrandrea, Katharine Hayhoe, and Peter Frumhoff, *How to Avoid Dangerous Climate Change: A Target for U.S. Emissions Reductions*.

14 See, for example, Rachel Cleetus, Stephen Clemmer, and David Friedman, *Climate 2030: A National Blueprint for a Clean Energy Economy*.

15 US Environmental Protection Agency, *Draft Inventory of U.S. Greenhouse Gas Emissions and Sinks: 1990–2011*, Executive Summary. Carbon dioxide (CO_2) accounted for 83.6% of the warming potential of these emissions, methane (CH_4) for 8.7%, and nitrous oxide (N_2O) for 5.6%.

16 For a rare recent discussion of energy policy within the context of limits to

growth, see Tom Butler and George Wuerthner, *Energy: Overdevelopment and the Delusion of Endless Growth.*

17 Philip Cafaro, "Economic Growth or the Flourishing of Life: The Ethical Choice Global Climate Change Puts to Humanity in the 21st Century"; Philip Cafaro, "Beyond Business as Usual: Alternative Wedges to Avoid Catastrophic Climate Change and Create Sustainable Societies"; Philip Cafaro, "Reducing Consumption to Avert Catastrophic Global Climate Change: The Case of Aviation."

18 Al Gore, "Moving beyond Kyoto," *New York Times*, July 1, 2007.

19 Intergovernmental Panel on Climate Change, *Climate Change 2007: Mitigation Report,* Technical Summary, 107.

20 Ibid.

21 Intergovernmental Panel on Climate Change. *Climate Change 2013: The Physical Science Basis.*

22 Walter Reid et al., *The Millennium Ecosystem Assessment: Ecosystems and Human Well-Being: Synthesis.*

23 As noted, for example, by Brian Czech, *Shoveling Fuel for a Runaway Train*; and Gustave Speth, *The Bridge at the Edge of the World: Capitalism, the Environment, and Crossing from Crisis to Sustainability.*

24 Lester Brown, *World on the Edge: How to Prevent Environmental and Economic Collapse*; Dave Foreman, *Man Swarm and the Killing of Wildlife.*

25 D. W. O'Neill, R. Dietz, and N. Jones, *Enough Is Enough: Ideas for a Sustainable Economy in a World of Finite Resources: The Report of the Steady State Economy Conference*; Rob Dietz and Dan O'Neill, *Enough Is Enough: Building a Sustainable Economy in a World of Finite Resources.*

26 Accessed September 2007 at www.wecansolveit.org. The website has subsequently been deactivated.

27 Bill Ritter, *Colorado Climate Action Plan: A Strategy to Address Global Warming*, 2.

28 United States Energy Information Administration, "International Energy Outlook 2009," chapter 1.

29 "The Incredible Shrinking Country," *Economist*, March 25, 2014.

30 "Immigration Overhaul Would Benefit Big States the Most." *Wall Street Journal*, July 16, 2013.

31 Philip Cafaro, "Economic Consumption, Pleasure and the Good Life"; Joshua Gambrel and Philip Cafaro, "The Virtue of Simplicity."

32 Steve Kelton," Too Many New Americans: Why NEPA Should Be Applied to Immigration Policy."

33 I call this "generous sustainability" to differentiate it from narrower anthropocentric conceptions of sustainability, such as the Brundtland Commission's "development which meets the needs of current [human] generations without compromising the ability of future [human] generations to meet their own needs." Contrast Philip Cafaro and Eileen Crist, *Life on the Brink: Environmentalists Confront Overpopulation*, with World Commission on Environment and Development, *Our Common Future.* Note that even those holding narrower anthropocentric conceptions of sustainability should arguably support reducing US immigration, for the good of future generations in the United States and around

the world. Even if all you care about is people, you might think there can be too many of us.

34 Holmes Rolston III, "Values in Nature."

35 Eileen Crist and Philip Cafaro, "Human Population Growth as if the Rest of Life Mattered"; Philip Cafaro, "Wild Nature."

CHAPTER NINE

1 Figures from the US Bureau of Labor Statistics website, www.bls.gov, accessed on December 23, 2013.

2 Benjamin Friedman, "Brave New Capitalists' Paradise: The Jobs?"

3 US Commission on Immigration Reform, *Becoming an American: Immigration and Immigrant Policy.* The Jordan Commission recommended an immigration ceiling of 550,000, which is roughly half of current legal immigration into the United States.

4 US Office of Immigration Statistics, "Annual Flow Report, U.S. Legal Permanent Residents: 2011," table 2.

5 See, for example, Paul Collier, *Exodus: How Migration Is Changing Our World.*

6 Jerry Kammer, "Sulzberger's Voice: How Arthur Sulzberger Radicalized the *New York Times* Editorial Page on Immigration." See also Jerry Kammer, "All the News that Fits: Ideologically Skewed Coverage of Immigration at the *New York Times.*"

7 US Citizenship and Immigration Services, "What is E-Verify?" Accessed November 12, 2012, at www.uscis.gov (figures last updated November 1, 2012).

8 John Feere, "An Overview of E-Verify Policies at the State Level."

9 John Feere, "Birthright Citizenship in the United States: A Global Comparison"; Jeffrey Passel and Paul Taylor, "Unauthorized Immigrants and Their U.S.-Born Children."

10 Feere, "Birthright Citizenship in the United States," 14.

11 There might seem to be a contradiction between proposal 4 (targeted amnesties which include legalizing children brought to the United States illegally by their parents) and proposal 5 (ending birthright citizenship) since 4 is more permissive and 5 is more restrictive, and both deal with children. But in practice I think both should be implemented, and implementing one need not get in the way of implementing the other. I conceive of the amnesty as a one-time event (not the latest in a series of never-ending amnesties), while ending birthright citizenship would be part of a comprehensive effort to reduce incentives to break immigration laws and to tighten immigration enforcement.

12 Marceline White, Carlos Salas, and Sarah Gammage, *Trade Impact Review: Mexico Case Study—NAFTA and the FTTA: A Gender Analysis of Employment and Poverty Impacts in Agriculture,* iv. But see also Norbert Feiss and Daniel Lederman, "Trade Note 18: Mexican Corn: The Effects of NAFTA," which disputes assertions that NAFTA led to much greater agricultural unemployment than would have occurred without it.

13 Representative figures for 2003 show Norway leading the way, distributing 0.92% of its gross national income as foreign aid, followed by the Netherlands (0.8%), France (0.42%), the United Kingdom (0.32%), Germany (0.28%) and Japan (0.2%), with the United States bringing up the rear at 0.15%. Curt Tarnoff and Larry Nowels, "Foreign Aid: An Introductory Overview of U.S. Programs and Policy," 22–23.

14 Jamie Garcia, author's interview, October 4, 2007; author's group interview with three illegal Mexican immigrants (unidentified), October 22, 2007, Timnath, CO.

15 Tarnoff and Nowels, "Foreign Aid," 10–11.

16 Boris Podobnik et al., "Influence of Corruption on Economic Growth Rate and Foreign Investment."

17 Robert Watson et al., *Millennium Ecosystem Assessment: Living Beyond Our Means: Natural Assets and Human Well-Being: Statement from the Board*, 5.

18 See the websites for La Raza and Maldef (the Mexican American Legal Defense and Education Fund) for numerous examples. These and other immigrant rights groups often take the position that enforcing immigration laws violates the civil rights of illegal immigrants. Such claims are examined in chapter 10.

19 Vernon Briggs, "Illegal Immigration: The Impact on Wages and Employment of Black Workers"; George Borjas, Jeffrey Grogger and Gordon Hanson, "Immigration and African-American Employment Opportunities: The Response of Wages, Employment and Incarceration to Labor Supply Shocks"; Steven Shulman, *The Impact of Immigration on African Americans*.

20 Eileen Patten, "Statistical Portrait of the Foreign-Born Population in the United States, 2010."

21 Roy Beck discusses how "the Great Pause" in immigration from the mid-1920s to the mid-1960s helped America economically and culturally assimilate tens of millions of immigrants who had arrived in the first "Great Wave." See Beck, *The Case against Immigration*.

22 Peter Schuck, "The Disconnect between Public Attitudes and Policy Outcomes in Immigration."

23 National Conference of State Legislatures, "Constituents per state legislative districts." Accessed November 2012 at www.ncsl.org.

CHAPTER TEN

1 Jared Polis, informal discussion at a campaign event in Fort Collins, Colorado, July 2012; Jared Polis, official Congressional website, http://polis.house.gov, accessed May 8, 2013 (see "Issues: Immigration").

2 Author's interview, Conchita Cruz, Representative Polis' chief immigration aid, January 24, 2013, Washington, DC.

3 Manuel Velasquez, "Immigration: Is Exclusion Just?" See also the response from Martin Cook, "Immigration and Ethics," both accessible at www.scu.edu/ethics /publications/.

4   See, for example, the *European Convention for the Protection of Human Rights and Fundamental Freedoms* (1950) and the *International Covenant on Civil and Political Rights* (1966).

5   Chandran Kukathas, "Immigration," 571–72, 586. See Michael Dummett, "Immigration," for a somewhat different rights-based argument for more expansive immigration policies.

6   Stephen Kershnar, "There is No Right to Immigrate to the United States"; Robert Chapman, "Confessions of a Malthusian Restrictionist."

7   Kukathas, "Immigration," 574.

8   Winthrop Staples III and Philip Cafaro, "For a Species Right to Exist."

9   Michael Walzer, *Spheres of Justice: A Defense of Pluralism and Equality*, 62. Current attempts to increase immigration into the United States also run afoul of the right to self-government more directly. Polls typically show that Americans want either less immigration or the status quo, not more immigration. See Peter Schuck, "The Disconnect between Public Attitudes and Policy Outcomes in Immigration."

10 In researching this book, I asked numerous immigrants from Mexico and Central America why they came to the United States. Often they have spoken of "corruption" and the fact that a poor man or woman cannot make a good life in their countries of origin. What is the proper response to this? Surely not: "Well, then, let Mexico go to the dogs! Come to America, and bring all your relatives!" A better response, I think, would be: "Mexico needs to reform itself. You need to get to work; what can Americans do to help?" I have to admit, my respondents usually snorted with incredulity at the suggestion that their countries might be reformed. But perhaps their fatalism is part of the problem.

11 Henry Thoreau, *Journal*, volume 8, 220–21 (March 23, 1856).

12 For justification and application of a "rights grounded in flourishing" approach, see Amartya Sen, "Women's Empowerment and Human Rights: The Challenge to Policy"; and Martha Nussbaum, *Frontiers of Justice: Disability, Nationality, Species Membership*.

13 As Holmes Rolston III puts it: "Human rights are welcome where they are nonrival with the health of the [ecological] system. But human rights that claim to trump the system are doubtful rights." *Conserving Natural Value*, 233.

14 I thank Simon James, Clare Palmer, and Ron Sandler for helping me formulate this argument.

15 This theme is well developed in Mark Krikorian, *The New Case against Immigration: Both Illegal and Legal.*

16 Ryan Pevnick, Philip Cafaro, and Mathias Risse, "An Exchange: The Morality of Immigration."

17 A point emphasized in Martin Cook, "Immigration and Ethics."

18 Michael Kellett, author's interview, June 14, 2010. Like Kellett, many environmentalists I interviewed seemed to think about immigration in all-or-nothing terms—letting everyone in or keeping everyone out—rather than as involving a spectrum of possible immigration levels. For example, Bill Myers, a Sierra Club activist from Denver, responded to the question "What should US immigration policy be?" as follows: "Do you want to be the shining beacon on a hill, accept-

ing anyone who wants to come here, or do you want to shut the doors and post restrictions on who can and can't be coming to America? . . . If you've made up your mind to limit immigration into the US, what is your moral obligation as the leader of the entire world to make the conditions in home countries acceptable enough so that the people in those countries do not have an incentive to migrate into this country?" (author's interview, June 2010). This response shows how an all-or-nothing view of limiting immigration slides over into the grandiose position that the solution to immigration-driven US population growth is for Americans to make things so good everywhere else that no one will want to emigrate.

19 Michael Kellett, author's interview, June 14, 2010.

20 Martha Nussbaum, *For Love of Country: Debating the Limits of Patriotism*, 5, 14.

21 Stephen Nathanson, "In Defense of Moderate Patriotism," 538.

22 Michael Walzer, "Spheres of Affection," in Martha Nussbaum, *For Love of Country*.

23 David Miller, *On Nationality*. For more on this topic see Philip Cafaro, "Patriotism as an Environmental Virtue."

24 Another "border objection" focuses on the negative environmental impacts of building or strengthening Mexican border fences (see, for example, Aaron Flesch et al., "Potential Effects of the United States–Mexico Border Fence on Wildlife"). I share the worry that these fences may limit wildlife migrations and fragment desert ecosystems. That is one reason my immigration reform proposals focus on limiting illegal employment, rather than on preventing border crossings. If we have an effective system to combat illegal employment, we can go easy on border enforcement. This is a superior approach environmentally, economically, and morally.

25 Anonymous, "Liberalism requires immigration controls," at *The Philosopher's Beard* (http://www.philosophersbeard.org/2011/08/liberalism-requires-immigration.html).

26 Mathias Risse, "On the Morality of Immigration." See also Ryan Pevnick, Philip Cafaro, and Mathias Risse, "An Exchange: The Morality of Immigration."

27 Mathias Risse, "On the Morality of Immigration," 25.

28 Ibid., 25, 30.

29 Ibid., 26.

30 The following critique of Risse's argument builds on Pevnick, Cafaro, and Risse, "An Exchange: The Morality of Immigration."

31 Risse, "On the Morality of Immigration," 27.

32 Ibid., 32.

33 Kwame Anthony Appiah, *Experiments in Ethics*; John Cottingham, "Partiality and the Virtues."

34 Numerous helpful explorations of this theme may be found in Ellen Frankel Paul, Fred Miller, and Jeffrey Paul, *Self-Interest*; particularly valuable are Kelley Rogers, "Beyond Self and Other" (1–20); and David Schmidtz, "Self-Interest: What's in It for Me?" (107–21).

35 John Rawls, *Justice as Fairness: A Restatement*.

36 Risse, "On the Morality of Immigration," 32.

CHAPTER ELEVEN

1   Jie He and Patrick Richard, "Environmental Kuznets Curve for CO_2 in Canada"; Mouez Fodha and Oussama Zaghdoud, "Economic Growth and Pollutant Emissions in Tunisia: An Empirical Analysis of the Environmental Kuznets Curve."

2   Simon Dietz and W. Neil Adger, "Economic Growth, Biodiversity Loss and Conservation Effort"; Julianne Mills and Thomas Waite, "Economic Prosperity, Biodiversity Conservation, and the Environmental Kuznets Curve."

3   President's Council on Sustainable Development, *Sustainable America: A New Consensus for Prosperity, Opportunity, and a Healthy Environment for the Future,* chapter 6, "U.S. Population and Sustainability."

4   President's Council on Sustainable Development, *Toward a Sustainable America: Advancing Prosperity, Opportunity, and a Healthy Environment for the 21st Century,* iii. This goal was watered down from an earlier recommendation by the Council's Task Force on Population and Consumption: "Stabilize U.S. population *as early as possible in the next century*" (emphasis added). President's Council on Sustainable Development, *Population and Consumption Task Force Report,* chapter 4, "Goals and Policy Recommendations."

5   President's Council on Sustainable Development, *Population and Consumption Task Force Report,* Executive Summary.

6   US Commission on Immigration Reform, *U.S. Immigration Policy: Restoring Credibility,* i.

7   Andrew Sum, Paul Harrington, and Ishwar Khatiwada, "The Impact of New Immigrants on Young Native-Born Workers, 2000–2005," 6.

8   Neil Kotler, "The Statue of Liberty as Idea, Symbol, and Historical Presence," 6.

9   Ibid., 8.

10 Rudolph Vecoli, "The Lady and the Huddled Masses: The Statue of Liberty as a Symbol of Immigration," 41.

11 National Park Service, "The Statue of Liberty Exhibit," unpaginated.

12 As Laboulaye himself remarked, in a speech in 1876: "The statue is well named; she is truly Liberty . . . in one hand [she] holds the torch, —no, not the torch that sets afire, but . . . the candle-flame that enlightens. In her other, she holds the tablets of the Law. . . . This statue, symbol of liberty, tells us at one and the same time that Liberty lives only through Truth and Justice, Light and Law. This is the Liberty that we desire." Quoted in Christian Blanchet and Bertrand Dard, *Statue of Liberty: The First Hundred Years,* 44.

13 Aleksandra Kollontai, quoted in Vecoli, "The Lady and the Huddled Masses," 50–51.

BIBLIOGRAPHY

Alexander, Richard, and Richard Smith. "County-Level Estimates of Nitrogen and Phosphorus Fertilizer Use in the United States, 1945 to 1985." USGS report 90–130. Reston, VA: US Geological Survey, 1990.

American Academy of Pediatrics, Committee on Communications. "Policy Statement: Children, Adolescents, and Advertising." *Pediatrics* 118 (2006): 2563–69.

American Lung Association. "State of the Air 2012." Accessed March 4, 2013. http://www.stateoftheair.org.

Andreas, Carol. *Meatpackers and Beef Barons: Company Town in a Global Economy.* Boulder: University Press of Colorado, 1994.

Appiah, Kwame Anthony. *Experiments in Ethics.* Cambridge, MA: Harvard University Press, 2010.

Ariely, Dan. "Americans Want to Live in a Much More Equal Country (They Just Don't Realize It)." *Atlantic,* August 2, 2012.

Atkinson, Anthony, Thomas Piketty, and Emmanuel Saez. "Top Incomes in the Long Run of History." *Journal of Economic Literature* 49 (2011): 3–71.

Autor, David, Lawrence Katz, and Melissa Kearney. "Trends in U.S. Wage Inequality: Revising the Revisionists." *Review of Economics and Statistics* 90 (2008): 300–323.

Aydemir, Abdurrahman. "Immigrant Selection and Short-Term Labour Market Outcomes by Visa Category." Bonn, Germany: Forschungsinstitut zur Zukunft der Arbeit, 2010. Discussion paper 4966.

Aydemir, Abdurrahman, and George Borjas. "Cross-Country Variation in the Impact of International Migration: Canada, Mexico, and the United States." *Journal of the European Economic Association* 5 (2007): 663–708.

Barroso, Carmen. "Cairo: The Unfinished Revolution." In Laurie Mazur, editor, *A Pivotal Moment: Population, Justice and the Environmental Challenge,* 245–59. Washington, DC: Island Press, 2009.

Bartlett, Albert. "Reflections on Sustainability and Population Growth." In Philip Cafaro and Eileen Crist, editors, *Life on the Brink: Environmentalists Confront Overpopulation*, 29–40. Athens: University of Georgia Press, 2012.

Bartlett, Albert. "Thoughts on Immigration into the United States." Washington, DC: Negative Population Growth, 2007.

Beck, Roy. *The Case against Immigration: The Moral, Economic, Social, and Environmental Reasons for Reducing U.S. Immigration Back to Traditional Levels*. New York: W. W. Norton, 1996.

Beck, Roy, and Steven Camarota. "Elite vs. Public Opinion: An Examination of Divergent Views on Immigration." Washington, DC: Center for Immigration Studies, 2002.

Beck, Roy, Leon Kolankiewicz, and Steven Camarota. *Outsmarting Smart Growth: Population Growth, Immigration, and the Problem of Sprawl*. Washington, DC: Center for Immigration Studies, 2003.

Bertola, Giuseppe, and Andrea Ichino. "Wage Inequality and Unemployment: United States vs. Europe." *NBER Macroeconomics Annual* 10 (1995): 13–54.

Bish, Joe. "Toward a New Armada: A Globalist Argument for Stabilizing U.S. Population." In Philip Cafaro and Eileen Crist, editors, *Life on the Brink: Environmentalists Confront Overpopulation*. 189–201. Athens: University of Georgia Press, 2012.

Blanchet, Christian, and Bertrand Dard. *Statue of Liberty: The First Hundred Years*. New York: American Heritage Society, 1985.

Boden, T. A., G. Marland, and R. J. Andres. "Global, Regional, and National Fossil-Fuel CO_2 Emissions." Oak Ridge, TN: Carbon Dioxide Information Analysis Center, 2013.

Borjas, George. "The Economic Benefits from Immigration." *Journal of Economic Perspectives* 9 (1995): 3–22.

Borjas, George. *Heaven's Door: Immigration Policy and the American Economy*. Princeton: Princeton University Press, 1999.

Borjas, George. "Immigration and the American Worker: A Review of the Academic Literature." Washington, DC: Center for Immigration Studies, 2013.

Borjas, George. "Increasing the Supply of Labor through Immigration: Measuring the Impact on Native-Born Workers." Washington, DC: Center for Immigration Studies, 2004.

Borjas, George. "The Labor Demand Curve *Is* Downward Sloping: Reexamining the Impact of Immigration on the Labor Market." *Quarterly Journal of Economics* (2003): 1335–74.

Borjas, George. "The Labor Market Impact of High-Skill Immigration." Cambridge, MA: National Bureau of Economic Research, 2005. Working paper 11217.

Borjas, George, Jeffrey Grogger, and Gordon Hanson. "Immigration and African-American Employment Opportunities: The Response of Wages, Employment and Incarceration to Labor Supply Shocks." Cambridge, MA: National Bureau of Economic Research, 2007. NBER working paper 12518.

Borjas, George, Jeffrey Grogger, and Gordon Hanson. "Immigration and the Economic Status of African-American Men." *Economica* (2010) 77: 255–82.

Borjas, George, Jeffrey Grogger, and Gordon Hanson. "Substitution between Immigrants, Natives, and Skill Groups." Working paper, July 2011. Accessed April 2013. www.hks.harvard.edu/fs/gborjas/index.html.

Bouvier, Leon. "The Impact of Immigration on United States' Population Size: 1950–2050." Washington, DC: Negative Population Growth, 1998.

Briggs, Vernon. "The Economic Well-Being of Black Americans: The Overarching Influence of U.S. Immigration Policies." *Review of Black Political Economy* 31 (2003): 15–42.

Briggs, Vernon. "Illegal Immigration: The Impact on Wages and Employment of Black Workers." Washington, DC: Center for Immigration Studies, 2008. Testimony before US Commission on Civil Rights.

Briggs, Vernon. *Immigration Policy and the American Labor Force*. Baltimore: Johns Hopkins University Press, 1984.

Briggs, Vernon. *Mass Immigration and the National Interest: Policy Directions for the New Century*. Armonk, NY: M. E. Sharpe, 2003.

Broder, John. "Emissions Fell in 2009, Showing Impact of Recession." *New York Times*, February 16, 2011.

Brookens, Jenn. "Population Trends Here to Stay." *Fairmont (Minnesota) Sentinel*, February 27, 2013.

Brown, Donald. *American Heat: Ethical Problems with the United States' Response to Global Warming*. Lanham, MD: Rowman and Littlefield, 2002.

Brown, Donald, Nancy Tuana, Marilyn Averill, et al. *White Paper on the Ethical Dimensions of Climate Change*. State College, PA: Rock Island Ethics Institute, 2007.

Brown, Lester. *World on the Edge: How to Prevent Environmental and Economic Collapse*. New York: W. W. Norton, 2011.

Bureau of Labor Statistics. "Employment, Hours, and Earnings from the Current Employment Statistics Survey (National) SIC." Washington, DC: US Department of Labor. Data extracted December 2007.

Bureau of Labor Statistics. "International Comparisons of Hourly Compensation Costs in Manufacturing." BLS news release, March 8, 2011. Washington, DC: US Department of Labor.

Butler, Tom, and George Wuerthner, eds. *Energy: Overdevelopment and the Delusion of Endless Growth*. Santa Rosa, CA: Post-Carbon Institute and Watershed Media, 2012.

Cafaro, Philip. "Beyond Business as Usual: Alternative Wedges to Avoid Catastrophic Climate Change and Create Sustainable Societies." In Denis Arnold, editor, *The Ethics of Global Climate Change*, 192–215. Cambridge: Cambridge University Press, 2011.

Cafaro, Philip. "Climate Ethics & Population Policy." *WIREs Climate Change* 3 (2012): 45–61.

Cafaro, Philip. "Economic Consumption, Pleasure and the Good Life." *Journal of Social Philosophy* 32 (2001): 471–86.

Cafaro, Philip. "Economic Growth or the Flourishing of Life: The Ethical Choice Global Climate Change Puts to Humanity in the 21st Century." *Essays in Philosophy* 11 (2010): article 6.

Cafaro, Philip. "Patriotism as an Environmental Virtue." *Journal of Agricultural and Environmental Ethics* 23 (2010): 185–206.

Cafaro, Philip. "Reducing Consumption to Avert Catastrophic Global Climate Change: The Case of Aviation." *Natural Science* 5 (2013): 99–105.

Cafaro, Philip. "Wild Nature." In Allen Thompson and Stephen Gardiner, editors, *Oxford Handbook to Environmental Ethics*. Oxford: Oxford University Press, forthcoming.

Cafaro, Philip, and Eileen Crist, eds. *Life on the Brink: Environmentalists Confront Overpopulation*. Athens: University of Georgia Press, 2012.

Camarota, Steven. "Birth Rates among Immigrants in America: Comparing Fertility in the U.S. and Home Countries." Washington, DC: Center for Immigration Studies, 2005.

Camarota, Steven. "Births to Immigrants in America, 1970 to 2002." Washington, DC: Center for Immigration Studies, 2005.

Camarota, Steven. "Immigrants in the United States—2002: A Snapshot of America's Foreign-Born Population." Washington, DC: Center for Immigration Studies, 2002.

Camarota, Steven. "Immigration and Economic Stagnation: An Examination of Trends 2000 to 2010." Washington, DC: Center for Immigration Studies, 2010.

Camarota, Steven. "Immigration's Impact on American Workers." Washington, DC: Center for Immigration Studies, 2007. Testimony before House Judiciary Committee.

Camarota, Steven. "A Jobless Recovery? Immigrant Gains and Native Losses." Washington, DC: Center for Immigration Studies, 2004.

Camarota, Steven. "Projecting Immigration's Impact on the Size and Age Structure of the 21st Century American Population." Washington, DC: Center for Immigration Studies, 2012.

Camarota, Steven. "A Record-Setting Decade of Immigration: 2000–2010." Washington, DC: Center for Immigration Studies, 2011.

Camarota, Steven, and Karen Zeigler. "Are There Really Jobs Americans Won't Do? A Detailed Look at Immigrant and Native Employment across Occupations." Washington, DC: Center for Immigration Studies, 2013.

Camarota, Steven, and Karen Zeigler. "Immigrant Gains and Native Losses in the Job Market, 2000 to 2013." Washington, DC: Center for Immigration Studies, 2013.

Camarota, Steven, and Karen Zeigler. "Still No Evidence of a Jobs Shortage: Immigrant and Native Employment in the Fourth Quarter of 2013." Washington, DC: Center for Immigration Studies, 2013.

Carbon Dioxide Information Analysis Center. "National Fossil Fuel CO_2 Emissions—All Countries." US Department of Energy. Accessed August 9, 2007. http://cdiac.ornl.gov/trends/emis/tre_coun.htm.

Card, David. "How Immigration Affects U.S. Cities." London: University College, 2007. Centre for Research and Analysis of Migration (CREAM) discussion paper 11/07.

Card, David. "Immigrant Inflows, Native Outflows, and the Local Market Impacts of Higher Immigration." *Journal of Labor Economics* 19 (2001): 22–64.

Card, David. "Immigration and Inequality." *American Economic Review: Papers & Proceedings* 99 (2009): 1–21.

Card, David, and John DiNardo. "Skill-Biased Technological Change and Rising Wage Inequality: Some Problems and Puzzles." *Journal of Labor Economics* 20 (2002): 733–83.

Castañeda, Jorge. *Mañana Forever? Mexico and the Mexicans*. New York: Knopf, 2011.

Centers for Disease Control and Prevention. "Trends in Health Care Coverage and Insurance for 1968–2011." CDC website. Accessed April 4, 2013. www.cdc.gov/nchs/health_policy/trends_hc_1968_2011.htm.

Chapman, Robert. "Confessions of a Malthusian Restrictionist." *Ecological Economics* 59 (2006): 214–19.

Cincotta, Richard, and Larry Gorenflo, eds. *Human Population: Its Influences on Biological Diversity*. Dordrecht: Springer, 2011.

Clark, William. *The California Cauldron: Immigration and the Fortunes of Local Communities*. New York: Guilford Press, 1998.

Cleetus, Rachel, Stephen Clemmer, and David Friedman. *Climate 2030: A National Blueprint for a Clean Energy Economy*. Cambridge, MA: Union of Concerned Scientists, 2009.

Cohen, Joel. *How Many People Can the Earth Support?* New York: W. W. Norton, 1996.

Collier, Paul. *Exodus: How Migration Is Changing Our World*. New York: Oxford University Press, 2013.

Cook, Martin. "Immigration and Ethics." *Issues in Ethics* 7 (Spring 1996). Santa Clara, CA: Markkula Center for Applied Ethics, Santa Clara University.

Cottingham, John. "Partiality and the Virtues." In Roger Crisp, editor, *How Should One Live? Essays on the Virtues*, 57–76. Oxford: Oxford University Press, 1996.

Crist, Eileen, and Philip Cafaro. "Human Population Growth as if the Rest of Life Mattered." In Philip Cafaro and Eileen Crist, editors, *Life on the Brink: Environmentalists Confront Overpopulation*, 3–15. Athens: University of Georgia Press, 2012.

Cromer, Mark. "Hey Buddy, Can You Spare a Job?" Washington, DC: Progressives for Immigration Reform, 2011.

Czech, Brian. *Shoveling Fuel for a Runaway Train: Errant Economists, Shameful Spenders, and a Plan to Stop Them All*. Berkeley: University of California Press, 2002.

Czech, Brian, Paul R. Krausman, and Patrick K. Devers. "Economic Associations among Causes of Species Endangerment in the United States." *BioScience* 50 (2000): 593–601.

Daly, Herman. *Beyond Growth: The Economics of Sustainable Development*. Boston: Beacon Press, 1997.

Daly, Herman, and John Cobb Jr. *For the Common Good*. Boston: Beacon Press, 1989.

Despommier, Dickson. *The Vertical Farm: Feeding the World in the 21st Century*. New York: Picador, 2011.

Diener, Ed, Richard Lucas, and Christie Scollon. "Beyond the Hedonic Treadmill: Revising the Adaptation Theory of Well-Being." *American Psychologist* 61 (2006): 305–14.

Diener, Ed, W. Ng, J. Harter, and R. Arora. "Wealth and Happiness across the World: Material Prosperity Predicts Life Evaluation, Whereas Psychosocial Prosperity Predicts Positive Feeling." *Journal of Personality and Social Psychology* 99 (2010): 52–61.

Diener, Ed, and Martin Seligman. "Beyond Money: Toward an Economy of Well-Being." *Psychological Science in the Public Interest* 5 (2004): 1–31.

Dietz, Rob, and Dan O'Neill. *Enough Is Enough: Building a Sustainable Economy in a World of Finite Resources.* San Francisco: Berrett-Koehler Publishers, 2013.

Dietz, Simon, and W. Neil Adger. "Economic Growth, Biodiversity Loss and Conservation Effort." *Journal of Environmental Management* 68 (2003): 23–35.

DiNardo, James, Nicole Fortin, and Thomas Lemieux. "Labor Market Institutions and the Distribution of Wages, 1973–1992." *Econometrica* 64 (1996): 1001–44.

Dummett, Michael. "Immigration." *Res Publica* 10 (2004): 115–22.

Ehrenreich, Barbara. "Maid to Order: The Politics of Other Women's Work." *Harper's Magazine*, April 1, 2000.

Ehrlich, Paul. *The Population Bomb.* New York: Ballantine Books, 1968.

Farber, Henry. "Nonunion Wage Rates and the Threat of Unionization." *Industrial and Labor Relations Review* 58 (2005): 335–52.

Feere, John. "Birthright Citizenship in the United States: A Global Comparison." Washington, DC: Center for Immigration Studies, 2010.

Feere, John. "An Overview of E-Verify Policies at the State Level." Washington, DC: Center for Immigration Studies, 2012.

Feiss, Norbert, and Daniel Lederman. "Trade Note 18: Mexican Corn: The Effects of NAFTA." Washington, DC: World Bank, 2004.

Flesch, Aaron, Clinton Epps, James Cain, Matt Clark, Paul Krausman, and John Morgart. "Potential Effects of the United States–Mexico Border Fence on Wildlife." *Conservation Biology* 24 (2009): 171–81.

Fodha, Mouez, and Oussama Zaghdoud. "Economic Growth and Pollutant Emissions in Tunisia: An Empirical Analysis of the Environmental Kuznets Curve." *Energy Policy* 38 (2010): 1150–56.

Foreman, Dave. *Man Swarm and the Killing of Wildlife.* Durango, CO: Raven's Eye Press, 2011.

Fredrick, Shane, and George Loewenstein. "Hedonic Adaptation." In Daniel Kahneman, Ed Diener, and Norbert Schwarz, editors, *Well-Being: The Foundations of a Hedonic Psychology*, 302–29. New York: Russell Sage Foundation, 1999.

Friedman, Benjamin. "Brave New Capitalists' Paradise: The Jobs?" *New York Review of Books*, November 7, 2013.

Friedman, Benjamin. *The Moral Consequences of Economic Growth.* New York: Vintage Press, 2005.

Gambrel, Joshua, and Philip Cafaro. "The Virtue of Simplicity." *Journal of Agricultural and Environmental Ethics* 23 (2010): 85–108.

Gardiner, Stephen. *A Perfect Moral Storm: The Ethical Tragedy of Climate Change.* New York: Oxford University Press, 2011.

Gershuny, Jonathan. "National Utility: Measuring the Enjoyment of Activities." *European Sociological Review* 28 (2012).

Global Footprint Network. "National Footprint Accounts." 2010 ed. Accessed December 26, 2013. www.footprintnetwork.org.

Gore, Al. "Moving beyond Kyoto." *New York Times*, July 1, 2007.

Graham, Otis. *Unguarded Gates: A History of America's Immigration Crisis*. Lanham, MD: Rowman and Littlefield, 2004.

Grant, Lindsey. "The Great Silence: U.S. Population Policy." Washington, DC: Negative Population Growth, 2010.

Greenspan, Alan. "Testimony of Dr. Alan Greenspan." Subcommittee on Immigration, Refugees, and Border Security. US Senate Judiciary Committee. Washington, DC: April 30, 2009.

Greenstone, Michael, and Adam Looney. "The Uncomfortable Truth about American Wages." *New York Times* online Economix blog, October 22, 2012.

Hardin, Garret. *Living within Limits: Ecology, Economics, and Population Taboos*. Cambridge: Cambridge University Press, 1993.

He, Jie, and Patrick Richard. "Environmental Kuznets Curve for CO_2 in Canada." *Ecological Economics* 69 (2010): 1083–93.

Heinberg, Richard. *The End of Growth: Adapting to Our New Economic Reality*. Gabriola Island, Canada: New Society, 2011.

Hollmann, Frederick, Tammany Mulder, and Jeffrey Kallan, "Methodology and Assumptions for the Population Projections of the United States: 1999 to 2100." Population Division Working Paper 38. Washington, DC: US Census Bureau, 2000.

"Immigration Overhaul Would Benefit Big States the Most." *Wall Street Journal*, July 16, 2013.

"An Immigration Raid Aids Blacks for a Time." *Pittsburgh Post-Gazette*, January 17, 2007.

"Immigration Raids May Affect Meat Prices." *Washington Post*, December 15, 2006.

"Immigration Wage Debate Rages: Pay Stagnates in Sectors Full of Foreign-Born Workers." *Rocky Mountain News*, August 26, 2006.

"The Incredible Shrinking Country," *Economist*, March 25, 2014.

"In Praise of Huddled Masses." Editorial. *Wall Street Journal*, July 3, 1984.

Intergovernmental Panel on Climate Change. *Climate Change 2007: Mitigation Report*. Geneva: IPCC, 2007.

Intergovernmental Panel on Climate Change. *Climate Change 2007: Synthesis Report*. Geneva: IPCC, 2007.

Intergovernmental Panel on Climate Change. *Climate Change 2013: The Physical Science Basis*. Geneva: IPCC, 2013.

Jacoby, Tamar. "Immigration Nation." *Foreign Affairs* (November/December 2006).

Jones, Jeffrey. "Americans More Positive about Immigration: Sixty-Six Percent Say It's a Good Thing for the U.S., Highest since 2006." Gallup Poll. June 2012. www.gallup.com/poll/155210/americans-positive-immigration.aspx.

Jones, Jeffrey. "More Americans Favor than Oppose Arizona Immigration Law: Among Those Who Have Heard of Law, 51% Favor and 39% Oppose It." Gallup Poll. April 2010. http://www.gallup.com/poll/127598/Americans-Favor-Oppose-Arizona-Immigration-Law.aspx.

Kammer, Jerry. "The 2006 Swift Raids: Assessing the Impact of Immigration Enforcement Actions at Six Facilities." Washington, DC: Center for Immigration Studies, 2009.

Kammer, Jerry. "All the News that Fits: Ideologically Skewed Coverage of Immigration at the *New York Times*." Washington, DC: Center for Immigration Studies, 2013.

Kammer, Jerry. "The Carnegie Corporation and Immigration: How a Noble Vision Lost Its Way." Washington, DC: Center for Immigration Studies, 2011.

Kammer, Jerry. "Strategic Negligence: How the Sierra Club's Distortions on Border and Immigration Policy Are Undermining Its Environmental Legacy." Washington, DC: Center for Immigration Studies, 2009.

Kammer, Jerry. "Sulzberger's Voice: How Arthur Sulzberger Radicalized the *New York Times* Editorial Page on Immigration." Washington, DC: Center for Immigration Studies, 2013.

Kasser, Tim. *The High Price of Materialism*. Cambridge, MA: MIT Press, 2003.

Kasser, Tim, and Allen Kanner, eds. *Psychology and Consumer Culture: The Struggle for a Good Life in a Materialistic World*. Washington, DC: American Psychological Association, 2004.

Kasser, Tim, Richard Ryan, Charles Couchman, and Kennon Sheldon. "Materialistic Values: Their Causes and Consequences." In Tim Kasser and Allen Kanner, editors, *Psychology and Consumer Culture: The Struggle for a Good Life in a Materialistic World*, 11–28. Washington, DC: American Psychological Association, 2004.

Kaufman, Stuart, ed. *The Samuel Gompers Papers*. Urbana: University of Illinois Press, 1986.

Kay, Steven. "The Nature of Turnover: Packers Attempt to Reverse a Financial Drain." *Meat & Poultry* 43 (1997): 30–34.

Kelton, Steve. "Too Many New Americans: Why NEPA Should Be Applied to Immigration Policy." *Vermont Journal of Environmental Law* 6 (2005).

Kennickell, Arthur. "Ponds and Streams: Wealth and Income in the U.S., 1989 to 2007." FEDS Working Paper 2009-13. Washington, DC: Federal Reserve Board, 2009.

Kershnar, Stephen. "There Is No Right to Immigrate to the United States." *Public Affairs Quarterly* 14 (2000): 141–58.

Kolankiewicz, Leon. "From Big to Bigger: How Mass Immigration and Population Growth Have Exacerbated America's Ecological Footprint." Washington, DC: Progressives for Immigration Reform, 2010.

Kolankiewicz, Leon, and Roy Beck. "Forsaking Fundamentals: The Environmental Establishment Abandons U.S. Population Stabilization." Washington, DC: Center for Immigration Studies, 2001.

Kolankiewicz, Leon, and Steven Camarota. "Immigration to the United States and World-Wide Greenhouse Gas Emissions." Washington, DC: Center for Immigration Studies, 2008.

Kotler, Neil. "The Statue of Liberty as Idea, Symbol, and Historical Presence." In Wilton Dillon and Neil Kotler, editors, *The Statue of Liberty Revisited*. Washington, DC: Smithsonian Institution, 1994.

Krebs, A. V. *Heading toward the Last Roundup: The Big Three's Prime Cut*. Washington, DC: Corporate Agribusiness Project, 1990.

Krikorian, Mark. *The New Case against Immigration: Both Illegal and Legal.* New York: Penguin, 2008.

Krugman, Paul. *The Conscience of a Liberal.* New York: W. W. Norton, 2007.

Krugman, Paul. *The Great Unraveling: Losing Our Way in the New Century.* New York: W. W. Norton, 2004.

Kukathas, Chandran. "Immigration." In Hugh LaFollette, editor, *The Oxford Handbook of Practical Ethics.* Oxford: Oxford University Press, 2003.

"Landscaping Services." IbisWorld industry report. Accessed January 2009. www .ibisworld.com.

Lane, Robert. *The Loss of Happiness in Market Democracies.* New Haven: Yale University Press, 2001.

Lane, Robert. *The Market Experience.* Cambridge: Cambridge University Press, 1991.

Leopold, Aldo. "A Criticism of the Booster Spirit." In *The River of the Mother of God and Other Essays.* Madison: University of Wisconsin Press, 1991.

Leopold, Aldo. *A Sand County Almanac.* New York: Oxford University Press, 1949.

"Liberalism Requires Immigration Controls." Posted at *The Philosopher's Beard.* http:// www.philosophersbeard.org/2011/08/liberalism-requires-immigration.html.

Llorente, Elizabeth. "Struggling with a Population Decline, Baltimore Pins Its Hopes on Immigrants." *Fox News Latino* (online), March 27, 2013.

Luers, Amy, Michael Mastrandrea, Katharine Hayhoe, and Peter Frumhoff. *How to Avoid Dangerous Climate Change: A Target for U.S. Emissions Reductions.* Cambridge, MA: Union of Concerned Scientists, 2007.

Lytwak, Edward. "A Tale of Two Futures: Changing Shares of U.S. Population Growth." Washington, DC: Negative Population Growth, 1999.

Macedo, Stephen. "The Moral Dilemma of U.S. Immigration Policy: Open Borders vs. Social Justice?" In Carol Swain, editor, *Debating Immigration,* 63–82. Cambridge: Cambridge University Press, 2007.

Malloy, Robert. "Cast Down Your Bucket Where You Are: Black Americans on Immigration." Washington, DC: Center for Immigration Studies, 1996.

Marsh, John. *Class Dismissed: Why We Cannot Teach or Learn Our Way Out of Inequality.* New York: Monthly Review, 2011.

McCloskey, Deirdre. *The Bourgeois Virtues: Ethics for an Age of Commerce.* Chicago: University of Chicago Press, 2006.

McKee, Jeffrey. *Sparing Nature: The Conflict between Human Population Growth and Earth's Biodiversity.* New Brunswick, NJ: Rutgers University Press, 2003.

McKibben, Bill. *Deep Economy: The Wealth of Communities and the Durable Future.* New York: Henry Holt, 2007.

Miller, Celia, and Cynthia Green. "A U.S. Population Policy: ZPG's Recommendations." Zero Population Growth policy paper. 1976.

Miller, David. *On Nationality.* New York: Oxford University Press, 1995.

Miller, David. *Principles of Social Justice.* Cambridge, MA: Harvard University Press, 1999.

Mills, Julianne, and Thomas Waite. "Economic Prosperity, Biodiversity Conservation, and the Environmental Kuznets Curve." *Ecological Economics* 68 (2009): 2087–95.

Mink, Gwendolyn. *Old Labor and New Immigrants in American Political Development: Union, Party, and State, 1875–1920.* Ithaca: Cornell University Press, 1990.

Mochon, Daniel, Michael Norton, and Dan Ariely. "Getting Off the Hedonic Treadmill, One Step at a Time: The Impact of Regular Religious Practice and Exercise
on Well-Being." *Journal of Economic Psychology* 29 (2008): 632–42.

Moore, Kathleen Dean, and Michael Nelson, eds. *Moral Ground: Ethical Action for a
Planet in Peril*. San Antonio, TX: Trinity University Press, 2010.

Morales, Lyman. "Americans' Immigration Concerns Linger: Nearly Two-Thirds Are
Dissatisfied with the Current Levels of Immigration." Gallup Poll. January 2012.
www.gallup.com/poll/152072/Americans-Immigration-Concerns-Linger.aspx.

Nathanson, Stephen. "In Defense of Moderate Patriotism." *Ethics* 99 (1989): 535–52.

National Park Service. "The Statue of Liberty Exhibit." Washington, DC: US Government Printing Office, 1988. GPO: 1988-506-174.

National Research Council. *Urban Pest Management: A Report*. Washington, DC:
National Academy of Sciences, 1980.

Natural Resources Conservation Service. *National Resources Inventory 2001, Urbanization and Development of Rural Land*. Washington, DC: US Department of Agriculture, 2001.

Noah, Timothy. *The Great Divergence: America's Growing Inequality Crisis and What
We Can Do about It*. New York: Bloomsbury Press, 2012.

North, David. "Motivation for Hiring Alien Workers? Hint: It's Not a Labor Shortage."
Washington, DC: Center for Immigration Studies, 2013.

Norton, Michael, and Dan Ariely. "Building a Better America—One Wealth Quintile
at a Time." *Perspectives on Psychological Science* 6 (2011): 9–12.

Nussbaum, Martha. *For Love of Country: Debating the Limits of Patriotism*. Boston:
Beacon Press, 1996.

Nussbaum, Martha. *Frontiers of Justice: Disability, Nationality, Species Membership*.
Cambridge, MA: Harvard University Press, 2006.

Nussbaum, Martha. *The Therapy of Desire*. Princeton: Princeton University Press,
1994.

Office of Immigration Statistics. "Annual Flow Report, U.S. Legal Permanent Residents: 2011." Washington, DC: Department of Homeland Security, 2012.

O'Neill, Dan, Rob Dietz, and Nigel Jones, eds. *Enough Is Enough: Ideas for a Sustainable Economy in a World of Finite Resources: The Report of the Steady State Economy Conference*. Arlington, VA: Center for the Advancement of the Steady State
Economy, 2010.

Ortman, Jennifer, and Christine Guarneri. "United States Population Projections:
2000 to 2050." Washington, DC: US Census Bureau, 2009.

Ottaviano, Gianmarco, and Giovanni Peri. "Immigration and National Wages: Clarifying the Theory and the Empirics." Cambridge, MA: National Bureau of Economic Research, 2008. NBER working paper 14188.

Ottaviano, Gianmarco, and Giovanni Peri. "Rethinking the Effect of Immigration on
Wages." *Journal of the European Economic Association* 10 (2012): 152–97.

Palmer, Tim. "Beyond Futility." In Philip Cafaro and Eileen Crist, editors, *Life on the
Brink: Environmentalists Confront Overpopulation*, 98–107. Athens: University of
Georgia Press, 2012.

Parker, Kathleene. "The Day of Seven Billion and the World's Most Overpopulated
Nation." Washington, DC: Progressives for Immigration Reform, 2011.

Parker, Kathleene. "Population, Immigration, and the Drying of the American South-west." Washington, DC: Center for Immigration Studies, 2010.

Passel, Jeffrey, and D'Vera Cohn. *U.S. Population Projections: 2005–2050*. Washington, DC: Pew Research Center, 2008.

Passel, Jeffrey, and Paul Taylor. "Unauthorized Immigrants and Their U.S.-Born Children." Washington, DC: Pew Hispanic Center, 2010.

Patten, Eileen. "Statistical Portrait of the Foreign-Born Population in the United States, 2010." Washington, DC: Pew Hispanic Research Center, 2012.

Paul, Ellen Frankel, Fred Miller, and Jeffrey Paul, eds. *Self-Interest*. Cambridge: Cambridge University Press, 1997.

Pear, Robert. "Percentage of Americans Lacking Health Coverage Falls Again." *New York Times*, September 17, 2013.

Peri, Giovanni. "Immigration, Labor Markets, and Productivity." *Cato Journal* 32 (2012): 35–53.

Peterson, Lindsay, and Chris Echegaray. "Immigrants Would Leave Big Hole." *Tampa Tribune*, April 27, 2006.

Pevnick, Ryan, Philip Cafaro, and Mathias Risse. "An Exchange: The Morality of Immigration." *Ethics & International Affairs* 22 (2008): 241–59.

Piketty, Thomas, and Emmanuel Saez. "How Progressive is the U.S. Federal Tax System? A Historical and International Perspective." *Journal of Economic Perspectives* 21 (2007): 3–24.

Piketty, Thomas, and Emmanuel Saez. "Income Inequality in the United States, 1913–1998." *Quarterly Journal of Economics* 118 (2003): 1–39.

Pimentel, David, and Marcia Pimentel. "Land, Energy and Water: The Constraints Governing Ideal U.S. Population Size." Washington, DC: Negative Population Growth, 1990.

Podobnik, Boris, Jia Shao, Djuro Njavro, Plamen Ivanov, and H. E. Stanley. "Influence of Corruption on Economic Growth Rate and Foreign Investment." *European Physical Journal B* 63 (2008): 547–50.

Polling Company. "The Public's View of Immigration: A Comprehensive Survey and Analysis." Washington, DC: Center for Immigration Studies, 2006.

Population Reference Bureau. "2011 World Population Data Sheet: The World at 7 Billion." Washington, DC: PRB, 2011.

Population Reference Bureau. "2012 World Population Data Sheet." Washington, DC: PRB, 2012.

President's Council on Sustainable Development. *Population and Consumption Task Force Report*. Washington, DC: Government Printing Office, 1996.

President's Council on Sustainable Development. *Sustainable America: A New Consensus for Prosperity, Opportunity, and a Healthy Environment for the Future*. Washington, DC: Government Printing Office, 1996.

President's Council on Sustainable Development. *Toward a Sustainable America: Advancing Prosperity, Opportunity, and a Healthy Environment for the 21st Century*. Washington, DC: Government Printing Office, 1999.

Rachleff, Peter. *Hard-Pressed in the Heartland: The Hormel Strike and the Future of the Labor Movement*. Cambridge, MA: South End Press, 1992.

Rawls, John. *Justice as Fairness: A Restatement*. Cambridge, MA: Harvard University Press, 2001.

Rawls, John. *A Theory of Justice*. Cambridge, MA: Harvard University Press, 1971.

Reid, Walter, Harold Mooney, Angela Cropper, et al. *The Millennium Ecosystem Assessment: Ecosystems and Human Well-Being: Synthesis*. Washington, DC: Island, 2005.

Richards, R. P., and D. B. Baker. "Trends in Water Quality in LEASEQ Rivers and Streams (Northwestern Ohio), 1975–1995." *Journal of Environmental Quality* 31 (2002): 90–96.

Rifkin, Jeremy. *The European Dream: How Europe's Vision of the Future Is Quietly Eclipsing the American Dream*. New York: Tarcher/Penguin, 2004.

Ring, Ray. "The New West's Service Economy." *High Country News*, April 17, 1995.

Risse, Mathias. "On the Morality of Immigration." *Ethics & International Affairs* 22 (2008): 25–33.

Ritter, Bill. *Colorado Climate Action Plan: A Strategy to Address Global Warming*. Denver: Governor's Energy Office, 2007.

Roach, Brian. "Progressive and Regressive Taxation in the United States: Who's Really Paying (and Not Paying) Their Fair Share?" Medford, MA: Global Development and Environment Institute, 2003. Working Paper no. 03–10.

Rolston, Holmes, III. *Conserving Natural Value*. New York: Columbia University Press, 1994.

Rolston, Holmes, III. "Duties to Endangered Species." *BioScience* 35 (1985): 718–26.

Rolston, Holmes, III. "Values in Nature." *Environmental Ethics* 3 (1981): 113–28.

Saad, Lydia. "Americans Value Both Aspects of Immigration Reform: Strengthening the Border and Dealing with Illegals Already Here Both Have Appeal." Gallup Poll. May 2010. http://www.gallup.com/poll/127649/Americans-Value-Aspects-Immigration-Reform.aspx.

Samuelson, Paul. *Economics: An Introductory Analysis*. 6th ed. New York: McGraw Hill, 1964.

Samuelson, Paul. "Importing Poverty." *Washington Post*, September 5, 2007.

Schiller, Bradley. *The Macro Economy Today*. 12th ed. New York: McGraw-Hill, 2009.

Schlosser, Eric. *Fast Food Nation: The Dark Side of the All-American Meal*. New York: Harper Perennial, 2001.

Schmidtz, David. *Elements of Justice*. Cambridge: Cambridge University Press, 2006.

Schor, Juliet. *The Overworked American: The Unexpected Decline of Leisure*. Boston: Basic Books, 1993.

Schuck, Peter. "The Disconnect between Public Attitudes and Policy Outcomes in Immigration." In Carol Swain, editor, *Debating Immigration*, 17–31. New York: Cambridge University Press, 2007.

Schumacher, E. F. *Small Is Beautiful: A Study of Economics as if People Mattered*. London: Blond and Briggs, 1973.

Scott, Daryl. "Immigrant Indigestion: A. Philip Randolph: Radical and Restrictionist." Washington, DC: Center for Immigration Studies, 1999.

Secretariat of the Convention on Biological Diversity. *Global Biodiversity Outlook 3*. Montreal: United Nations Environment Programme, 2010.

Secretary-General OECD. *Growing Unequal? Income Distribution and Poverty in*

OECD Countries. Paris: Organization for Economic Co-operation and Development, 2008.

Segal, Jerome. *Graceful Simplicity: The Philosophy and Politics of the Alternative American Dream*. Berkeley: University of California Press, 2003.

Sen, Amartya. *Development as Freedom*. Oxford: Oxford University Press, 1999.

Sen, Amartya. "Women's Empowerment and Human Rights: The Challenge to Policy." In F. Graham-Smith, editor, *Population: The Complex Reality: A Report of the Population Summit of the World's Scientific Academies*. London: Royal Society, 1994.

"Serving U.S. Parishes, Fathers without Borders." *New York Times*, December 28, 2008.

Seuc, Tyler. "The Real Unemployment." Washington, DC: Progressives for Immigration Reform, 2011.

Shearer, Lee. "Bear Creek a Boon So Far, But Will It Be Enough?" *Athens Banner-Herald*, September 22, 2002.

Shulman, Steven, ed. *The Impact of Immigration on African Americans*. Piscataway, NJ: Transaction, 2004.

Sierra Club Board of Directors. "Sierra Club Supports Path to Citizenship for Undocumented Immigrants." Press release. April 25, 2013. Washington, DC.

Sierra Club Board of Directors. "U.S. Population Policy and Immigration." Adopted May 6–7, 1978.

"Sierra Club Population Report." Testimony before the US Select Committee on Immigration and Refugee Reform (the Hesburgh Committee). Washington, DC: Spring, 1989.

Singer, Peter. *One World: The Ethics of Globalization*. New Haven: Yale University Press, 2002.

Solberg, Emily, Edward Diener, and Michael Robinson. "Why Are Materialists Less Satisfied?" In Tim Kasser and Allen Kanner, editors, *Psychology and Consumer Culture: The Struggle for a Good Life in a Materialistic World*, 29–48. American Psychological Association, 2004.

South Coast Air Quality Management District. "Historic Ozone Air Quality Trends." Accessed March 4, 2013. http://www.aqmd.gov/smog/o3trend.html.

Speth, Gustave. *The Bridge at the Edge of the World: Capitalism, the Environment, and Crossing from Crisis to Sustainability*. New Haven: Yale University Press, 2009.

Staples, Winthrop III. "Population Growth Is a Cause of Many Projects Requiring Environmental Impact Statements." Website for US Immigration Policy Environmental Impact Statement. Accessed April 17, 2014. http://www.immigrationeis.org/eis-documents/population-growth-stated-cause.

Staples, Winthrop, III, and Philip Cafaro. "For a Species Right to Exist." In Philip Cafaro and Eileen Crist, editors, *Life on the Brink: Environmentalists Confront Overpopulation*, 283–300. Athens: University of Georgia Press, 2012.

Stevenson, Betsey, and Justin Wolfers. "Economic Growth and Subjective Well-Being: Reassessing the Easterlin Paradox." Washington, DC: Brookings Institution, 2008.

Stiglitz, Joseph, Amartya Sen, and Jean-Paul Fitoussi. *Report by the Commission on the Measurement of Economic Performance and Social Progress.* Paris: Republique Francaise, 2009.

Stromquist, Shelton, and Marvin Bergman, eds. *Unionizing the Jungles: Labor and Community in the Twentieth-Century Meat-Packing Industry.* Iowa City: University of Iowa Press, 1997.

Sum, Andrew, Paul Harrington, and Ishwar Khatiwada. "The Impact of New Immigrants on Young Native-Born Workers, 2000–2005." Washington, DC: Center for Immigration Studies, 2006.

Swain, Carol. "The Congressional Black Caucus and the Impact of Immigration on African American Unemployment." In Carol Swain, editor, *Debating Immigration,* 175–88. Cambridge: Cambridge University Press, 2007.

Tarnoff, Curt, and Larry Nowels. "Foreign Aid: An Introductory Overview of U.S. Programs and Policy." Washington, DC: Congressional Research Service, 2005.

Taylor, Paul, Cary Funk, and Peyton Craighill. "Are We Happy Yet?" Washington, DC: Pew Research Center, 2006.

Thiess, Rebecca. "The Future of Work: Trends and Challenges for Low-Wage Workers." Washington, DC: Economic Policy Institute, 2012. EPI Briefing Paper no. 341.

Thoreau, Henry. *Journal.* New York: Dover Press, 1962. Originally published Boston: Houghton Mifflin, 1906.

Thoreau, Henry. *Walden.* Princeton: Princeton University Press, 1971. Originally published Boston: Ticknor and Fields, 1854.

Tordella, Stephen, Steven Camarota, Tom Godfrey, and Nancy Rosene. "Evaluating the Role of Immigration in U.S. Population Projections." Unpublished essay. Washington, DC: Center for Immigration Studies, 2012.

United Nations Department of Economic and Social Affairs, Population Division. "World Population Prospects, the 2010 Revisions." Country Profiles. Accessed March 6, 2013. http://esa.un.org/unpd/wpp/index.htm.

United Nations Population Fund. *State of World Population 2010: From Crisis and Conflict to Renewal: Generations of Change.* New York: UNFPA, 2010.

United Nations Population Fund. *State of World Population 2012: By Choice, Not by Chance: Family Planning, Human Rights and Development.* New York: UNFPA, 2012.

US Census Bureau. "2008 National Population Projections." www.census.gov.

US Census Bureau. "Annual Projections of the Total Resident Population as of July 1: Middle, Lowest, Highest, and Zero International Migration Series, 1999 to 2100." Washington, DC: USCB, 2000.

US Census Bureau. "Country Summaries." International database. Accessed March 15, 2013. www.census.gov.

US Census Bureau. "Current Population Survey, Annual Social and Economic Supplements." Accessed January 2009. www.census.gov.

US Census Bureau. "Midyear Population and Density." International database. Accessed November 2, 2012. www.census.gov.

US Census Bureau. *Statistical Abstract of the United States: 2003.* Washington, DC: USCB, 2003.

US Central Intelligence Agency (CIA). *World Factbook.* 2011 ed. https://www.cia.gov/library/publications/the-world-factbook/.

US Citizenship and Immigration Services. "What Is E-Verify?" Accessed November 12, 2012. www.uscis.gov.

US Commission on Immigration Reform. *Becoming an American: Immigration and Immigrant Policy.* Washington, DC: Government Printing Office, 1997.

US Commission on Immigration Reform. *Legal Immigration: Setting Priorities.* Washington, DC: Government Printing Office, 1995.

US Commission on Immigration Reform. *U.S. Immigration Policy: Restoring Credibility.* Washington, DC: Government Printing Office, 1994.

US Congressional Budget Office. "Trends in the Distribution of Household Income between 1979 and 2007." Washington, DC: Congress of the United States, 2011.

US Department of Commerce, Bureau of Economic Analysis. "National Economic Accounts." Accessed May 2008. http://www.bea.gov/national/nipaweb/.

US Department of Homeland Security. *Yearbook of Immigration Statistics: 2011.* Washington, DC: USDHS, 2012.

US Department of State. "2008 Diversity Visa Lottery Registrations." Office of the Spokesman. Press release. December 15, 2006.

US Energy Information Administration. "Energy Sources Have Changed throughout the History of the United States." Today in Energy website, July 3, 2013. Accessed August 2013. http://www.eia.gov.

US Energy Information Administration. "International Energy Outlook 2009." Washington, DC: Department of Energy, 2009.

US Environmental Protection Agency. "Air Quality Trends." Accessed March 4, 2013. http://www.epa.gov/airtrends/aqtrends.html.

US Environmental Protection Agency. *Draft Inventory of U.S. Greenhouse Gas Emissions and Sinks: 1990–2011.* Washington, DC: 2013.

US Environmental Protection Agency. *Our Nation's Air: Status and Trends through 2010.* Research Triangle Park, NC: Office of Air Quality Planning and Standards, 2012. EPA-454/R-12-001.

US Environmental Protection Agency. *Wadeable Streams Assessment: A Collaborative Assessment of the Nation's Streams.* Washington, DC: EPA, 2006. EPA841-B-06-002.

"U.S. Fight against E.U. Airline Emissions Plan Heats Up." *New York Times,* August 6, 2012.

US Fish and Wildlife Service. "Summary of Listed Species, Listed Populations and Recovery Plans." Endangered Species Program website. Accessed November 2012. www.fws.gov.

US Geological Survey. "National Water-Quality Assessment (NAWQA) Program." Accessed March 5, 2013. http://water.usgs.gov/nawqa/about.html.

US Office of Immigration Statistics. *Annual Flow Report, U.S. Legal Permanent Residents: 2011.* Washington, DC: US Department of Homeland Security, 2012.

Van der Zwaan, Bob, and Arthur Petersen, eds. *Sharing the Planet: Population—Consumption—Species: Science and Ethics for a Sustainable and Equitable World.* Delft, Netherlands: Eburon Academic Publishers, 2003.

Vecoli, Rudolph. "The Lady and the Huddled Masses: The Statue of Liberty as a Symbol of Immigration." In Wilton Dillon and Neil Kotler, editors, *The Statue of Liberty Revisited*. Washington, DC: Smithsonian Institution, 1994.

Velasquez, Manuel. "Immigration: Is Exclusion Just?" *Issues in Ethics* 7 (Spring 1996). Markkula Center for Applied Ethics, Santa Clara University.

Victor, Peter. *Managing without Growth: Slower by Design, Not Disaster*. Cheltenham: Edward Elgar, 2008.

Wadhwa, Vivek, Anna Lee Saxenian, Ben Rissing, and Gary Gereffi. "Skilled Immigration and Economic Growth." *Applied Research in Economic Development* 5 (2008): 6–14.

Walzer, Michael. "Spheres of Affection." In Martha Nussbaum, editor, *For Love of Country: Debating the Limits of Patriotism*. Boston: Beacon Press, 1996.

Walzer, Michael. *Spheres of Justice: A Defense of Pluralism and Equality*. New York: Basic Books, 1983.

Waterman, Alan. "On the Importance of Distinguishing Hedonia and Eudaimonia When Contemplating the Hedonic Treadmill." *American Psychologist* 62 (2007): 612–13.

Watson, Robert, A. H. Zakri, Salvatore Alrico, et al. *The Millennium Ecosystem Assessment: Living beyond Our Means: Natural Assets and Human Well-Being: Statement from the Board*. Washington, DC: World Resources Institute, 2005.

Wattenberg, Ben. *The Birth Dearth*. New York: Pharos Books, 1987.

Wernick, Iddo, Robert Herman, Shekhar Govind, and Jesse Ausubel. "Materialization and Dematerialization: Measures and Trends." *Daedalus* 125 (1996): 171–98.

Western, Bruce, and Jake Rosenfeld. "Unions, Norms, and the Rise in U.S. Wage Inequality." *American Sociological Review* 76 (2011): 513.

"What Is GDP and Why Is It So Important?" Investopedia website. Posted February 26, 2009. www.investopedia.com.

White, Marceline, Carlos Salas, and Sarah Gammage. *Trade Impact Review: Mexico Case Study—NAFTA and the FTTA: A Gender Analysis of Employment and Poverty Impacts in Agriculture*. Washington, DC: Women's Edge Coalition, 2003.

White, Stuart. *The Civic Minimum: On the Rights and Obligations of Economic Citizenship*. New York: Oxford University Press, 2003.

Wilcove, D. S., D. Rothstein, J. Dubow, A. Phillips, and E. Losos. "Quantifying Threats to Imperiled Species in the United States: Assessing the Relative Importance of Habitat Destruction, Alien Species, Pollution, Overexploitation, and Disease." *BioScience* 48 (1998): 607–15.

Wire, Thomas. *Fewer Emitters, Lower Emissions, Less Cost: Reducing Future Carbon Emissions by Investing in Family Planning: A Cost/Benefit Analysis*. London: London School of Economics, 2009.

World Commission on Environment and Development. *Our Common Future*. Oxford: Oxford University Press, 1987.

Yellen, Janet. "Economic Inequality in the United States." Federal Reserve Bank of San Francisco Economic Letter, December 1, 2006 (no. 2006-33-34).

INDEX